JOHN SUMMERS

The Untold Story of Corruption, Systemic Racism and Evil at Bell Baker LLP

Peter Tremblay, ed.

Agora Books™
Ottawa, Canada

John Summers: The Untold Story of Corruption, Systemic Racism and Evil at Bell Baker Llp

© 2020 by Peter Tremblay

All Rights Reserved. No part of this book may be reproduced, stored in a retrieval system, or transmitted in any form or by any means, electronic or mechanical, including photocopying, recording, or otherwise without the expressed written consent of The Agora Cosmopolitan.

Care has been taken to trace ownership / source of any academic or other reference materials contained in this text. The publisher will gratefully accept any information that will enable it to rectify any reference or credit in subsequent edition(s), of any incorrect or omitted reference or credit.

Agora Books
P.O. Box 24191
300 Eagleson Road
Kanata, Ontario K2M 2C3

Agora Books is a self-publishing agency for authors that was launched by The Agora Cosmopolitan which is a registered not-for-profit corporation.

ISBN 978-1-927538-63-0

Printed in Canada

Contents

Preface 5
1. The Societal Context 11
2. Rogues in our Legal System 15
3. The Human Sacrifice Ritual of an Evil Cabal? 25
4. A Lawyer's Conspirators 33
5. Satan's Allies against Motherhood? 39
6. The Hypocrite 43
7. The Devil's Accomplice 45
8. The Smiling Demon 47
9. The Psychopath 49
10. The Paranormal and Extra-Dimensional 57
11. The Treacherous Liar 63
12. The Attack Against Motherhood 67
13. The Perpetuator of Domestic Abuse and Terror 71
14. Non-Humans in Our Midst? 73
15. The False Affidavit 77
16. Contempt for Human Decency 79
17. The Twisted Ego 83
18. No Rights for Disabled People 87
19. The Abomination: Crimes Against Humanity 89
Epilogue 93
Appendix. Supreme Court of Canada: File Number SCC 38391 . . 95

Preface

For every high-profile case involving brutality and systemic racism that gets aired on television and other "mainstream" mass media outlets, there are countless other cases that either are missed or are the subject of cover-ups by the ultra-insiders who control these outlets. *John Summers: The Untold Story of Corruption, Systemic Racism and Evil at Bell Baker LLP* explores one such case repressed by the mass media. This particular case provides insight into the kinds of racist and oppressive activities that take place in the Canadian legal system away from the prying eyes of Canadians, who observe only a tiny fraction of such activities that the ultra-insiders choose to show via their media outlets. This book reveals the evil machinations of John Summers, who is part of a deeply embedded network of apparently corrupt operatives. These apparently corrupt operatives united in their efforts to destroy a black woman who became disabled as a result of the activities of an abusive husband that they banded together to protect.

Court archives will show that John Summers was the lawyer of "official" record acting on behalf of Mr. Horace Carby-Samuels, who began to actively engage in domestic violence starting in

January 2013. The problem with this "official" record, though, is that Mr. Horace Carby-Samuels can in no way afford such a lawyer; it has been revealed John Summers demands a payment of $300 per hour. John Summers was, in actual fact, working for a third party that Mr. Summers and the corrupt judges that he colluded with in the Ontario legal system sought to conceal. Effectively, John Summers was a paid mercenary acting on behalf of an anonymous third party. This third party apparently took a vested interest in both destroying the life of Dezrin Carby-Samuels by depriving her of access to her son, who sought to defend her rights as others deserted her, and a bizarre experiment that turned her husband into a psychopath who perpetrated grotesque abuses of his wife.

It is quite obvious that John Summers was hired by an undisclosed and sadistic third party who apparently sought to perpetuate and empower the ability of Mr. Carby-Samuels to abuse Dezrin, his wife.

Raymond Carby-Samuels, who is Dezrin's son, intervened to uncover and document to the court John Summers' pattern of unlawful activities, which included aiding and abetting the depriving of Dezrin Carby-Samuels of the necessities of life, and Mr. Summers' collusion with a clique of three particularly corrupt judges at the Ontario Superior Court of Justice in Ottawa. Justice Beaudoin, who is an administrative judge there, had consented to a motion to remove one of the corrupt judges who had been actively working with Mr. Summers to perpetuate the abuse of Dezrin Carby-Samuels. The name of that corrupt judge is Sylvia Corthorn.

When confronted with a motion that promised to remove Sylvia Corthorn from engaging in an apparent unlawful conspiracy and collusion with John Summers, Corthorn then colluded with John Summers to support a motion to declare Raymond Carby-Samuels a "vexatious litigant."

John Summers was not able to obtain the endorsement of this motion by Horace Carby-Samuels, his alleged client. But this was no problem for John Summers, who simply cooked up a motion illegally endorsed by his own secretary and then got the corrupt Sylvia Corthorn to endorse it.

Raymond Carby-Samuels was illegally declared a "vexatious litigant" for simply seeking to see his mother and to protect her from ongoing domestic violence, and after, Raymond Carby-Samuels had in fact won a default judgement in February 2016 issued by Justice Patrick Smith before the illegal intervention of John Summers in March 2016. Raymond pursued an appeal with the Ontario Courts of Appeal, whose judges acted in league with a corrupt clique of three judges at the Ottawa Superior. Their names are McNamara, J., Roger, J. and Corthorn, J.

But it was apparent from court proceedings that the Court of Appeal judges simply ignored a well-documented court filing that court clerks said was better prepared than many lawyers. This was apparent when they didn't even bother listening to what John Summers had to present at the Ontario Court of Appeal, while also cutting off Raymond Carby-Samuels from making a full presentation of his appeal to the court. The Ontario Court of Appeal was a veritable kangaroo court.

This case was then further appealed to the Supreme Court of Canada (Appendix), but out of the media spotlight, the Supreme Court of Canada refused to consider Raymond's last-ditch efforts to save his disabled mother from destruction and death under the hands of abuse and isolation that John Summers and his handlers sought to enforce.

All calls by judges outside the cabal of judges under John Summers' control to get an independent verification of the well-being and desire of Dezrin Carby-Samuels to seek safe refuge from abuse were completely thwarted by the unlawful activities that this book documents in the context of an apparent fifth column of judges.

This book is a journalistic chronicle detailing the machinations of John Summers. It was written to document and contribute to efforts for legal reform to create the equivalent of a "hypocratic oath" for lawyers and judges in Canada to ensure that members of the legal and judicial profession who engage in activities that are against the protection of life may be subject to disbarment from the legal profession, as John Summers and his judicial operatives ought to be for their role in the destruction of Dezrin Carby-Samuels.

The series of strange activities surrounding John Summers suggests that he is no normal lawyer but rather an apparent demonic face of the evil responsible for systemic racism and other such oppression that is worsening in our world. What normal lawyer could exert such apparent control to direct judges into perpetuating such an orchestrated evil against a disabled, abused, and elderly black woman who was a retired registered nurse who was a model citizen throughout her life?

This book includes lucid articles originally prepared over the nearly four-year period chronicling that John Summers acted without empathy as a mercenary to extinguish the life of Dezrin Carby-Samuels.

Accompanying this book is the full Leave of Motion to Appeal that was used by the plaintiff to make a final effort to save Dezrin Carby-Samuels from demise. The motion had passed very stringent Supreme Court of Canada administrative packaging standards, but thanks to the bizarre string of corruption that John Summers was able to orchestrate against a disabled elderly black woman and her son, this final appeal was completely ignored by Supreme Court judges who lacked any visible minority representation among them.

CHAPTER 1

THE SOCIETAL CONTEXT

Marginalization: A legal system which doesn't respect the spirit of *Canada's Charter of Rights and Freedoms*

MARGINALIZED GROUPS WHICH OUR *CANADIAN Charter of Rights and Freedoms* seeks to support are being needlessly perpetuated by an archaic and regressive legal system. The Charter's promise in its 1982 constitutional enactment of a forward-thinking egalitarian, cosmopolitan community and 'Just Society' is being held back. A neo-colonial system of law which was well entrenched in Canadian society from the nineteenth century has promoted an elite structure of power which actively seeks to frustrate marginalized Canadians through judges who prevail over the justice system; lawyers; and the police. It has become self-evident that many judges, lawyers and the police in their behavioural norms view the Charter as a threat to their "authority". This authority has brought with it both economic and political power in association with maintaining corporate power, which is largely under the patriarchal control of wealthy white males. It is apparent that affluent white males whose wealth has been accrued from legal infringements like those which stole the lands of First Nations and have denied women opportunities have sought to maintain legally oppressive control through an organized "Fifth Column" of judges, lawyers, and police who preside over a culture of law inimical to Charter rights. In order for the "Charter's promise" for a rejuvenated context of "equal rights for all" among rights and freedoms to be fulfilled, Canada's entire legal system must be rejuvenated to promote empathy and accessibility for all regardless of economic or other status.

In order for our legal system and its outcomes through litigation and other means to reflect the Charter's values, the system must begin to fully embrace accessibility. Through Section 24(1) of the Charter, Canadians are empowered with having the right to affirm their rights and freedoms through courts of law. But individuals from marginalized communities cannot effectively seek to "de-marginalize" themselves when police, lawyers, and judges operate within a culture in which the active pursuit of justice is reserved for those who have the wealth to hire the expensive lawyers needed to interpret laws and to navigate a legal system the average Canadian can barely, if at all, comprehend.

The *Canada Health Act*, inspired by Tommy Douglas, who sought to "de-marginalize" Canadians in matters of healthcare, provides a constructive basis to progressively move our legal system to "de-marginalize" Canadians from legal oppression. Through a *Canada Health Act*-inspired context, Canadians who face ongoing infringements to their Charter rights would be able to access universal legal assistance in a way that corresponds to the manner by which Canadians currently obtain medical assistance. Once Canadians have been empowered through universal access to lawyers, who are in turn sensitized to the vital importance of serving all Canadians in a manner which promotes equality and justice for all, the lawyers promoted to positions as judges will have been socialized to embrace a progressive system of constitutional governance, which will help to transform policing. A new culture of lawyers who embrace universality would help to support a rejuvenated legal culture in replacing the current neo-colonial system of patriarchal laws with a legal system based in the same down-to-earth language that inspired the writing of our Charter toward a de-marginalized society.

CHAPTER 2

Rogues in our Legal System

Our *Canadian Charter of Rights and Freedoms* has truly become a substantive reflection of the legal ideals held by a broadening majority of Canadians. This observation is based upon statistical data from national firms that claim to have a very small margin of error. It would therefore perhaps be considered unfortunate by this broadening majority that the *Canadian Charter of Rights and Freedoms'* apparent promise of an egalitarian society in matters of civil rights appears to be stifled by a perpetuating context of marginalization. Indeed, it appears that marginalization is increasingly becoming a fact of life for many Canadians despite the equalizing effect that the Charter is supposed to have.

The aim of this book is part is to help illuminate the apparent presence of a system of legal actors who seek to reinforce oppressive patriarchal norms in our society, which manifests in marginalization. This system of socio-legal thought ossifies and stifles Canada's entire system and the administration of justice in a manner which is incongruent with the Charter's intent of creating the "Just Society" envisioned by former Prime Minister Pierre Elliot Trudeau.

When Canadians picture a judge in our Canadian system of justice, they likely envision a highly noble character like Frank Iacobucci, CC QC, who was a *puisne justice* of the Supreme Court of Canada from 1991 to 2004 when he retired from the bench, and a staunch defender of human rights and supporter of the Charter. However, we would be forgetting our colonial past, which produced a system of law and administration of justice founded in that colonial past, with actors who preside over that system and seek to maintain it. It is this system and culture which is responsible for marginalization.

There are two discernible schools of legal thought, which creates confusion between the way in which the system is supposed to operate and the way the system appears to operate most of the time. The school of legal thought that inspired the creation of the Charter could be best described as "egalitarianism," which regards equity as a central basis to guide desirable legal outcomes in relation to the operation of justice. However, the second and perhaps most dominant school of legal thought is held by what can be best referred to as the "apologists"; it is this school of thought which Leo Strauss sought to convey and galvanize through his books, teachings and movement.

This book will therefore seek to inspire an exploration of the apparent intellectual prism which shapes the enforcement of oppression and marginalization. The three principle actors of this system are judges, lawyers and the police. The apologists' intellectual prism shapes these actors' apparent worldview, which was articulated by Leo Strauss, who wrote books in law and philosophy. Former U.S. Supreme Court Justice Clarence Thomas was one of Leo Strauss's former students. However, Leo Strauss's socio-legal thought permeates the thinking of principal actors in The Establishment in general, and in the legal system specifically, who seek to resist values which they view as being threatened by legal values of equity and social justice.

Both the egalitarians and the apologists believe in the idea of democracy, but their views on the roles of law and democracy are in opposition to one another. Egalitarians who are inspired by the Charter embrace the diversity and pluralism of Canada and look to the Charter as a constitutional mechanism for supporting inclusion and fulfilling governance in a participatory democracy. In contrast, the apologists embrace what they view to be the proper original construct of democracy in early Greece, which limited the exercise of governance to the most wise, learned and wealthy men of society. In the apologist view, "elites" have an inherent "natural right" to exercise authority. Apologists championed by Leo Strauss and Murray Rothbard despised the "liberal" idea of democracy as a dangerous idea which would create a tyranny run by unruly masses.

In 1935, having written the book *Philosophy and Law: Contributions to the Understanding of Maimonides and His Predecessors*, Leo Strauss went onto write in *Liberalism Ancient and Modern* (1968), in which he says:

> It was once said that democracy is the regime that stands or falls by virtue: a democracy is a regime in which all or most adults are men of virtue, and since virtue seems to require wisdom, a regime in which all or most adults are virtuous and wise, or the society in which all or most adults have developed their reason to a high degree, or the rational society. *Democracy, in a word, is meant to*

> be an aristocracy which has broadened into a universal aristocracy. ... There exists a whole science—the science which I among thousands of others profess to teach... —which so to speak has no other theme than the contrast between the original conception of democracy, or what one may call the ideal of democracy, and democracy as it is. (pp. 4–5)

The apologists don't regard the Charter as "substantive law" which should inherently moderate their exercise of power. Rather, apologists view the Charter to be a myth that is useful for pacifying the masses so that they feel good about themselves while the exercise of patriarchal legal power continues to operate on behalf of the natural rights of its rules, as it always has. In *Natural Right and History* (1953) Leo Strauss further characterizes marginalization as natural; he claims that people of relative superiority naturally form the upper strata of society that those people who are marginalized are in such a position as a result of having inferior qualities that relegate them to a lower strata, and that the legal system should not interfere with such societal differentiation.

> The character, or tone, of a society depends on what the society regards as the most respectable or most worthy of admiration. But by regarding certain habits or attitudes as most respectable, a society admits the superiority, the superior dignity, of those human beings who most perfectly embody the habits or attitudes in question. That is to say, every society regards a specific human type (or a specific mixture of human types) as authoritative. When the authoritative type is the common man, everything has to justify itself before the tribunal

of the common man; everything which cannot be justified before that tribunal becomes, at best, merely tolerated, if not despised or suspect. And even those who do not recognize that tribunal are, willy-nilly, moulded by its verdicts. (p. 137)

In rejecting the Charter, the silent rallying cry of the apologist thought which dominates legal governance in Canada is the old British North American Act phrase "Peace, Order and Good Government."

The legal theorizing of Murray Rothbard is evident in the manner in which the prevailing actors in our legal system seem to have such a hypocritical and lethargic response when dealing with inequity and injustice in relation to the Charter's desire to advance equality. In Rothbard's book *Egalitarianism as a Revolt Against Nature* (1974), he elaborates that "almost everyone assumes that equality is a 'good thing." Rothbard goes on to pose the question, "Why assume that equality is desirable?"

Rothbard argues in support of a "correct ethics" in accord with nature, which ought to pivot on the "survival of the fittest," and that efforts to affirm "equality" as central to justice, as the Charter seeks to support, are inherently "un-natural" and would only lead to "tyranny" by "undisciplined masses" who lack the wisdom and overall superiority of the upper strata. Leo Strauss echoed this theme in his book *On Tyranny* (1963), which further provides a socio-legal analytical framework for understanding the apparent organized perpetuation of conditions for marginalization alongside legal inequity. The apologists out of the media spotlight would further argue, as Leo Strauss had, that the creation of myths is a useful device to unify the masses under the control of its rulers who preside over the legal system and, as a result, the "*modus operandi*" of the legal system should not be bound by the Charter as it is by and large a useful instrument of propaganda.

Rothbard broadens his criticisms of equality in *Freedom, Inequality, Primitivism and the Division of Labor* (1970). In this further expansion of the apologist plane of socio-legal consciousness, he asserts that not only do biology and history make human beings inherently different from one another, but that civilization depends on these differences. To the apologist, marginalization should not be eradicated under the "equality rubric" of the Charter's "public myth making," but rather, should be embraced as part of "the natural order of things" in a "Great Society." The marginalization of First Nations and individuals in "so-called" oppressed communities are simply the outcomes of "God's Will" that manifests in human civilization. In America, such an embracing of "God's Will" is expressed in that nation's national motto, "In God We Trust," and such a belief is similarly vaunted in Canada.

Today in Canadian society, the apparent legal enforcement of marginalization has empowered the ability of the "haves" to oppress and worsen the conditions of the "have nots" against the spirit of the Charter. When Canadians believe their protected rights and freedoms are being infringed, they are supposed to able to rely on re-asserting those rights through Section 24(1) of the *Canadian Charter of Rights and Freedoms*. This section empowers all Canadians to be able to apply to a court of competent jurisdiction to obtain the protection of those rights and freedoms, which the court is supposed to defend without prejudice.

Indeed, our Charter is only as strong as the extent to which Canadians can easily enforce their rights free of systemic barriers. However, the author has studied the inner workings of the Ontario court system for more than three years, and finds it apparent that marginalized Canadians face three distinct barriers that have been designed to prevent "have nots," or more specifically, legally disenfranchised individuals, from challenging the elites who hold positions as the lawyers and judges that preside over the justice system in general and specifically the administration of justice.

Barrier number one is that the lawyers who preside over the system have created a culture that demands financial compensation, which limits the use of lawyers to the most financially affluent Canadians. Barrier number two is that the system dissuades the average Canadian from being able to easily represent themselves in court without a lawyer by creating a system of language and formality including court procedures which elude the comprehension of most Canadians. However, the third barrier, which is unknown to most Canadians because of the difficulty marginalized Canadians have in successfully getting around barriers number one and two is that judges in the Canadian system who cling to a Straussian socio-legal view will be predisposed to totally ignore a challenge by a marginalized Canadian to the legal Establishment, irrespective of any evidence or soundness of presentation which that Canadian may present.

It is this third barrier, which has shown itself in cases of racism, sexism, and other discriminations that have subverted the equitable rendering of judicial decisions, which reveals a Straussian prism behind a perpetuated context of marginalization faced by First Nations, visible minorities, women, homeless, the working poor, the sick, the disabled, many seniors, and other disenfranchised Canadians.

The Canadian court system presents a context in which judges who would be inclined to defend Charter rights in the spirit of

Supreme Court Justice Frank Iacobucci, when out of the spotlight of a case that has garnered mass media attention, face pressure from the patriarchal system to thwart any challenge brought to it by a self-represented marginalized Canadian who has managed to evade the "natural barriers" of lack of financial wherewithal and a legal education on the court system which have been designed to keep marginalized Canadians "in their place".

The judges are appointed from lawyers, who, in turn, are from a profession known for often supporting and helping to prosecute in favour of the property and other interests of the most wealthy Canadians against marginalized individuals who have been disenfranchised by the prevailing legal system, and the police are the "front lines" of the perpetuation of marginalization on behalf of the Establishment. Together, through a "Straussian" prism and neo-colonial system and administration of justice, these actors work as a "fifth column" against the ability of Canadians to constructively use the Charter to "de-marginalize" themselves.

Arguably, the Charter is an insufficient constitutional enactment to empower all Canadians who seek to defend their rights and freedoms from infringements. For the Charter to be able to "do its job," the prevailing Canadian legal system and administration of justice would firstly need to affirm universal access to lawyers in a regulated system analogous to the Canada Health Act, which supports universal access by Canadians to doctors and healthcare. Secondly, even if Canadians are empowered with universal access to lawyers, it would be vital for the entire system of laws to be rewritten in a manner inspired by the down-to-earth language of the Charter and the formality of the court system and police authority to reflect that of public service to all Canadians based upon the values of the Charter and not based on the context of patriarchy which presently dominates our legal system.

The apologists would argue away from the media spotlight that the central role of the justice system is not to support equitable outcomes like those also envisioned by Section 96 of the *Ontario Courts of Justice Act*. Rather, the apologists would argue that the central role of justice is simply to defend "the system" and that "equality" ought to be regarded as no more than an accidental by-product of the system, which may have been simply created to provide a theatrical illusion that the system supports equality.

Some may consider the apologist school of socio-legal thought to be cynical. But the apologists would regard themselves as true "realists" who appreciate the role of law in a capitalist system such as Canada's, and recognize marginalization as a necessary part of the system—after all, for society to work, not everyone can be equally legally empowered.

The role of law in the "realist" and also "pragmatic" thinking of the apologists is therefore to view actors who prevail over the legal system as entrusted "managers" of "natural inequities" who are there to maintain "Peace, Order and Good Government," as expressed in the former *British North America Act, 1867*. The role of the prevailing actors of the legal system in apologist thinking is not to push our system to the brink of a "tyranny of the masses" by an unending march to equity, but rather to promote equitable outcomes in selected court decisions and other legal matters that can be used to promote the "myth of equality."

While the Charter envisions judges as impartial purveyors of the system, by acknowledging the existence of the apologists, the author furthermore proposes to present a rejuvenated perspective of judges as "astute political actors." In the spotlight of high-profile cases such as gay marriage, which has garnered sufficient media attention and public support, judges would be wise to support these rights in order to legitimate the court as standing up for legal equity and affirming the values of the Charter. However, these same judges, outside the media spotlight, are free to engage in ignoring any litigant who, in coming from a marginalized community, is without the money to pay the price demanded by lawyers in the commodification of civil rights that apologists seek to maintain.

Thus, while egalitarians envision judges as the impartial purveyors of the system supported by the *Canadian Charter of Rights and Freedoms*, the apologists view judges as being astute political actors who decide on cases in matters of equality based upon how much media attention there may be in any particular case they preside over.

CHAPTER 3

THE HUMAN SACRIFICE RITUAL OF AN EVIL CABAL?

I'm about to tell you something so unbelievable but true.

FOR OVER THREE YEARS NOW, it appears that a group of judges at the Ontario Superior Court of Justice in Ottawa who are are all alumni of the University of Ottawa, Faculty of Law have been coordinating an apparent human sacrifice conspiracy against an Ottawa woman named Dezrin Carby-Samuels who has been severely disabled as a result of the activities of these judges.

In a nutshell, "human sacrifice" is a reputed activity of "non-human entities" who have coordinated and then reinforce the promotion of certain people into positions of power provided that they show their "loyalty" to the non-human entities when called-upon. The most vulnerable members of our society are targeted for "human sacrifice". The most heinous, barbaric acts of cruelty, torture, and destruction, are a part of a "human sacrifice" ritual.

The alleged practice has taken place since the earliest and most tyrannical societies came into existence on our planet Earth. In these societies, power-seeking elites and demonic aliens elites sought to worship demonic aliens as their God or gods that often brought technology that would then be used to support military oppression and torture.

Unfortunately, Dezrin Carby-Samuels, like so many vulnerable people on our planet is being targeted by non-human beings which can appear as "people". But these "people" are in no way human.

Dr. Michael Salla referred to such entities as 'shape-shifters'. David Icke has further described such entities to be reptilian that operate from a different dimension that reaches into ours.

Such victims like Dezrin include children who go missing as targets of alien abduction (or become victims of pedophile rings) to homeless people on the street who from time to time appear to be been chosen by the non-human handlers as targets of apparent human sacrifice rituals.

My name is Jesse, and I'm an investigative journalist. Since 2015 I have watched the bizarre activities at the Ottawa courthouse at 161 Elgin Street.

I have also investigated activities by non-human entities which include alien abductions. But I never expected that my investigation about Dezrin's plight would take me to apparent non-human interference at the Ottawa courthouse through judges working in tandem with Ottawa lawyers John E. Summers and Jeremy Wright of the City of Ottawa.

Jeremy Wright is an apparent ringleader of the University of Ottawa psychopaths, somehow recruited to perpetuate demonic torture against Dezrin.

Jeremy Wright in his official capacity works to defend Bordeleau's ragtag gang of dirty cops who sought to block Raymond from getting help for his Mom for more than three years.

In one instance, when a Small Claims Court judge was just about to enable Raymond to see his Mom, Mr. Wright gave some weird "wink" at a Judge sending him into an immediate panic leading him to immediately reverse his inclination to assist Raymond in helping his Mom. Mr. Wright is a highly secretive lawyer embedded into the City of Ottawa as an apparent handler for a University of Ottawa "rogue group".

It's notable that while one set of judges at the Ottawa courthouse would seek to liberate Dezrin Carby-Samuels, from profound abuse and torture that she has been experiencing at the hand of her husband, the "rogue group" would seek to perpetuate it.

The rogue group is made up of all members of the University of Ottawa alumni community. This group was reinforced by an apparent dirty cop named Detective Robert Griffin and a lawyer named John E. Summers, who is the alleged lawyer for Dezrin's husband against Dezrin's son.

The funny thing is that Dezrin's husband can in no way afford Mr. Summers. When Raymond asked Mr. Summers, who he actually works for and pays his bills, he refused to say.

There is zero chance that Dezrin's retired husband who struggles to pay his bills could afford the legal services of John Summers who has been practicing law since 1999 and worked to perpetuate her abuse for more than three years at a pay rate of more than $300 per hour.

We, therefore, have 100% conclusive evidence that someone or more likely a "group" without any empathy for the plight of Dezrin in conditions of abuse, is paying a University of Ottawa trained lawyer who is getting the support of judges and others *ALL* directly affiliated with the University of Ottawa.

I don't believe in such coincidences.

But every time Dezrin was about to be liberated, another set of judges who simply ignore all the evidence and case law that Raymond presented.

Finally, one Judge named Sylvia Corthon, decided that she was going to "seize" the case, and declared not only Summary Judgement against Raymond, but also declared him to be a Vexatious Litigant.

It became apparent that Sylvia Corthorn had "seized the case" to prevent another judge who is not a member of an apparent University of Ottawa demon worshiping group from trying to again help Dezrin.

You see, Raymond, who is Dezrin's son, has sought to liberate his Mother from abuse as any loving and responsible son would want to do.

One of my favourite shows is Murdoch Mysteries like so many other Canadians. One of my favourite parts of Murdoch Mysteries is when Detective Murdoch connects criminal suspects by tying a common association with each other using a blackboard in his constabulary office.

Thinking of the Detective Murdoch character I decided that I was going to try the same technique to figure out an apparent bizarre pattern taking place against Dezrin Carby-Samuels.

However, I didn't expect to find anything though this exercise. But to my amazement, I did.

All three Judges at the Ottawa courthouse that have worked with Ottawa lawyer John E. Summers to perpetuate abuses against Dezrin are all University of Ottawa alumni.

These judges are Pierre Roger, Justice Sylvia Corthorn and Regional Senior Justice James MacNamara.

None of the three judges at the Ottawa courthouse who had sought to act fairly and support the liberation of Dezrin are connected with the University of Ottawa.

The judges who acted to spare Dezrin are Justice Patrick Smith, Justice Callum MacLoed and Justice Robert Beaudoin.

The apparent backdoor coordination of judicial activities with John Summers that violate principles of impartiality and ethics in this matter is apparent.

There's a very distinct pattern of psychopath behaviours by three judges at the Ottawa courthouse with shared ties to the University of Ottawa that is extremely distinct from the behaviours of judges who aren't connected with the University of Ottawa.

Coincidence? I think not.

I then took my "theory" that there's "fifth" column of Judges who are seeking to subvert civil and human rights in resistance to the Canadian *Charter of Rights and Freedoms* to different Faculties of Law across Canada to get their reaction. Only the University of Ottawa, Faculty of Law members were hostile to the notion. It was almost as if they were hypersensitive based upon their complicit behaviour.

Could the University of Ottawa be the home of other psychopathic activities in Canadian society which go above and beyond activities which sought to torture and destroy Dezrin Carby-Samuels?

Are we witnessing a human sacrifice ritual that has sought to seize and perpetuate Dezrin's abuse?

Is Dezrin, one of the possibly many people who have been subjugated to abuse in Ottawa, as a result of a "human sacrifice ritual"?

And guess where John E. Summers attended law school? You would be right if you said the University of Ottawa.

I then became more intrigued. I then looked up Ottawa's Chief of Police Charles Bordeleau's background whose Office supported the dirty cop that forcibly separated Raymond from his Mother.

Once again we have a perfect match. Bordeleau also graduated from the University of Ottawa and received an award from the Telfer School of Management.

After Bordeleau's dirty cop orchestrated Raymond's forcible separation from his Mother, who has suffered from profound domestic abuse, Dezrin lost the ability to walk, talk or write.

After months of unlawfully being prevented from seeing his Mother, Raymond filed an Emergency Motion at the Ottawa courthouse on December 2015.

Raymond appeared before the University of Ottawa, Faculty of Law graduate Justice Pierre Roger.

At first, Justice Roger was going to grant Raymond's requests, seeing as he began to say "no harm in it".

But that's when things began to get bizarre. Someone from the judge's chambers interrupted Judge Roger's deliberation.

When Justice Roger came out of this "meeting" he was a different person, declaring the matter "personal to him" and that he would say "no" to Raymond seeing his Mom and checking on her well-being.

Raymond persevered and eventually got a Default Judgement from Justice Patrick Smith, who has no affiliation with the University of Ottawa.

Justice Patrick Smith, who is a member of the Lakehead University community, granted Raymond's requests through an order dated 11 February 2016.

But shortly after, John E. Summers, who was a top graduate of the University of Ottawa entered the picture. He began to manufacture and support countless obvious lies to justify continued forcible separation.

Raymond and his Mother last saw each other on 12 June 2016.

John E. Summers' lies are easily transparent to any fair-minded judge. So, John E. Summers needed "help" if he was going to perpetuate Dezrin's abuse.

John E. Summers got that help when he and Raymond appeared in front of Regional Senior Justice James MacNamara, who threw out Justice Patrick Smith's Order to enable Raymond and his Mother to see each other, daily, so Raymond could ensure his Mother's care as she has wanted.

Raymond tried to appeal that decision. But that appeal was then intercepted by an angry Justice Roger, who declared his interception to be a "coincidence".

I don't believe in such coincidences. It was quite improper for Roger to 'coincidentally' get the file. He should have recused himself. But, instead, Justice Roger "fined" Raymond $1500 for his Appeal.

When the matter was referred to Justice Callum Macloed, he was quite concerned about Dezrin's well being and directed John E. Summers on 24 March 2017 to obtain independent verification to ensure Dezrin has not been held a prisoner against her wishes. On our "Murdoch blackboard," Justice Macloed is a graduate of Queens in Kingston, Ontario with no U of O affiliations.

John E. Summers then sought to get the matter thrown out of Court. But his request was blocked by Justice Robert Beaudoin whose ties are with the University of Windsor Faculty of Law.

Then all of a sudden after this decision by Justice Beaudoin, the matter was then "seized" by Justice Sylvia Corthorn who like John E. Summers, Justice Roger, Regional Justice McNamara and Ottawa Police Chief Charles Bordeleau are all University of Ottawa alumni.

Justice Sylvia Corthorn not only ignored all evidence and case law presented by Raymond but also ignored any support for Raymond articulated by the non-University of Ottawa Judges.

When Justice Beaudoin recognized her apparent judicial misconduct, by granting Raymond's request, that Justice Corthorn be recused from the trial, Justice Corthorn simply sped up her final rulings which were directed at preventing Raymond from his efforts to rescue his Mother from the "Hell on Earth" that she has lived for more than three years thanks to an apparent "University of Ottawa mafia" which has sought to perpetuate the abuse and torture of Dezrin Carby-Samuels.

CHAPTER 4

A Lawyer's Conspirators

Canadian judges, by and large, are champions of affirming the due process of law.

However, the letter below written to the Ontario Judicial Council suggests that there are judges who are less than ethical in their conduct. In Ontario, two particular Justices have been responsible for breaching all sorts of judicial guidelines as a result of having been unduly influenced by the efforts of John Summers who has sought to manipulate the judicial system.

As a result of the activities of these Justices, an elderly woman has been subjected to years of abuse and neglect by her husband who sought to keep her son away from championing the rights of his Mother. Evidence points to an apparent illicit relationship between these two Justices and the abusive husband, which have resulted in the Mother who has not seen her son in over one year (as of this chronicle) no longer being able to walk, talk or write.

Ontario Superior COURT FILE NO: 15-66772

Open Letter

The Ontario Judicial Council
P. O. Box 914,
Adelaide Street Postal Station,
31 Adelaide Street East,
Toronto, Ontario M5C 2K3

September 12, 2016

Criminal Misconduct–Justice P. E. Roger and The Hon. James McNamara

Dear Ontario Judicial Council,

It has been my experience that the great majority of judges in Ontario are steadfastly committed to the principles of balance, fairness, impartiality, ethics and the due process of law, even when judgments have not been in my favour. I have also observed Court administrative staff emulating the professional tone set by these judges.

However, bribery and collusion can affect the integrity of justice.

Justice P. E. Roger and The Hon. James McNamara, have been accepting "tribute" in exchange for favourable justice.

Does the Ontario Judicial Council support the practice of Judges meeting with a litigant in a case to then coordinate favourable justice for that litigant?

The Defendant was worried about possibly losing the Motion for Leave to Appeal to another Judge whom they could not unduly influence.

They then appealed to Justice P. E. Roger, who looked for, and seized control of the Plaintiff's Motion for Leave to Appeal in violation of 12.06 of the *Rules of Civil Procedure* and the following principles established by the Ontario Judicial Council.

3.1 Judges should maintain their conduct at a level that will ensure the public's trust and confidence.

3.2 Judges must avoid any conflict of interest, or the appearance of any conflict of interest, in the performance of their judicial duties

In the Eastern Division of the Superior Court of Justice, certain lawyers are also aware of The Hon. James McNamara's reported support for what is referred to as "donations".

"Donations" is also a word used by high-end escorts to avoid the legal jeopardy of clients paying for sex which is illegal. By making a "donation" prostitution laws can be circumvented. When a Judge correspondingly asks for a "donation" he or she seeks to circumvent the laws of s 119 of the *Criminal Code of Canada* against bribery and collusion.

Bribery of judicial officers, etc.–Criminal Code (R.S.C., 1985, c. C-46)

- 119 (1) Everyone is guilty of an indictable offense and liable to imprisonment for a term not exceeding fourteen years who:

  ▸ (a) being the holder of a judicial office, or being a member of Parliament or of the legislature of a province, directly or indirectly, corruptly accepts, obtains, agrees to accept or attempts to obtain, for themselves or another person, any money, valuable consideration, office, place or employment in respect of anything done or omitted or to be done or omitted by them in their official capacity, or

  ▸ (b) directly or indirectly, corruptly gives or offers to a person mentioned in paragraph (a), or to anyone for the benefit of that person, any money, valuable consideration, office, place or employment in respect of anything done or omitted or to be done or omitted by that person in their official capacity.

In Justice P. E. Roger's Endorsement dated 2016-09-07, he declared that he got the file for the Motion for Leave to Appeal as a "coincidence" – but it *was no coincidence*. Indeed, Justice Roger had specifically communicated to the Plaintiff in a very bellicose/hostile tone back in Fall 2015 that he regarded the matter as "personal". This admission violates his Oath of Office and Ontario Judicial Council guidelines.

His so-called "Endorsement" which levied $1500.00 against the Plaintiff seeking to see his own sick and disabled Mother is little more than a polemic that seeks to take vengeance against the Plaintiff for having received Justice Patrick Smith's Order that went against Justice P. E. Roger's commitment to his "handlers". In so doing, Justice Roger disregarded not only *s. 96* of the *Courts of Justice Act*, but Canadian laws which affirm the blocking of visitation access as constituting elder-abuse by the Defendant.

Justice P. E. Roger violated the integrity of the Superior Court of Justice for his self-aggrandizement and with the blessings of his accomplice The Hon. James McNamara. In the process, both these two Justices ignored all evidence and supporting documents by the Plaintiff in the execution of collusion and conspiracy.

Both these Justices have degraded the Superior Court of Justice to a corrupted *modus operandi* often found in the "Third World".

That is to say, a "Kangaroo Court".

It's apparent that Justice P. E. Roger and The Hon. James McNamara, have betrayed the high standards set forth by other justices of the Superior Court of Justice; and are acting as "operatives" of the Defendant. Justice P. E. Roger and The Hon. James McNamara, have committed *prima facie* criminal acts that require immediate investigation.

Justice P. E. Roger and The Hon. James McNamara subverted the honourable decision rendered by Justice Patrick Smith on 11 February 2016 that enabled and empowered the Plaintiff to see his Mom daily, as a result of Justice P. E. Roger and The Hon. James McNamara, having an illicit relationship with the manipulative Defendant.

Lacking a substantive Defence against the Plaintiff not being able to see his Mom who has been subjugated to abuse and neglect by the Defendant, criminal conspiracy became the only strategy to maintain the unlawful blocking of visitation access against the Plaintiff seeing his sick and physically disabled Mom who has sought to see her son.

Thanks for your consideration.

Regards,

HRC-S II

CHAPTER 5

Satan's Allies against Motherhood?

WHEN A JUDGE CHARGES $1500.00 against a son for seeking to care for his own sick and elderly Mom, you might wonder if our world is going upside down. But this is exactly what Justice P. E. Roger did. The son had complained to his father for having abused and neglected his Mother was then evicted from his parent's home against his Mother's wishes. The father has blocked the son from seeing his Mother since 12 June 2015. The son was then forced to sue his father for his blocking of access when he found out that his mother has lost the ability to walk, talk and write under his continued abuse and neglect, forcibly away from the protection of her son.

Justice P. E. Roger tried to arbitrarily throw out his Motions to see his Mom in fall 2015. However, the Plaintiff was able to get an Endorsement from Justice Patrick Smith to see his Mother on 11 February 2016. An undisclosed Third Party then foisted a lawyer to act as the agent of the psychopathic-behaving father in future court proceedings. Senior Justice McNamara quashed Justice

Patrick Smith's Order and when Raymond sought to appeal that quashing Justice Roger was further contacted to re-affirm the quashing to complete the conspiracy. This was a violation of 12.06 of the *Ontario Rules of Civil Procedure*.

Both Senior Justice J. MacNamara and Justice P. E. Roger lack the empathy that's associated with who we are as humans.

The letter below further details apparent judicial collusion and conspiracy to subvert not only the *Rules of Civil Procedure* but also the *Criminal Code of Canada*, the *Ontario Courts of Justice Act* and the guidelines of the Ontario Judicial Council. To make matters worse, the nefarious subversion of judicial ethics also had an apparent accomplice — the regional justice of the Eastern Division of the Superior Court of Justice.

Ontario Superior COURT FILE NO: 15-66772

Open Letter 1

The Ontario Judicial Council
P. O. Box 914,
Adelaide Street Postal Station,
31 Adelaide Street East,
Toronto, Ontario M5C 2K3

September 13, 2016

Dear Ontario Judicial Council,

Further to my faxed letter dated 12 September 2016, I respectfully request that the Ontario

Judicial Council obtain copies of the entire FILE NO: 15-66772–including a court transcript that the Plaintiff provided, to aid in your investigation.

An independent review of files submitted by the Plaintiff and the Defendant will corroborate the mishandling of this case as a result of the illicit relationship of Justice P. E. Roger and The Hon. James McNamara in relationship to the Defendant.

A 100% of the Plaintiff's evidence and Book of Authorities was ignored by Justice P. E. Roger and The Hon. James McNamara, as if the Plaintiff was "invisible", corroborating judicial prejudice. In contrast, the Defendant with the collusion of Justice P. E. Roger and The Hon. James McNamara was able to get Endorsements with a skeletal presentation without any independently verifiable evidence.

Furthermore, both Justice P. E. Roger and The Hon. James McNamara among other things accepted the truthfulness of Affidavits by the Defendant which declared that the Plaintiff "suffers from mental illness" – a complete fabrication.

Other evidence such as handwritten notes from the Plaintiff's Mom, Dezrin Carby-Samuels which stipulated "Dad Abuses Me" was also ignored in the haste of Justice P. E. Roger and The Hon. James McNamara to exonerate the Defendant.

In so doing, Justice P. E. Roger and The Hon. James McNamara subjected the Plaintiff not only to civil rights abuses, but also the Plaintiff's Mom to blocked visitation access which constitute elder abuse across Canadian jurisdictions and forcible confinement in breach of the *Criminal Code of Canada* for more than one year at the hands of the Defendant, Horace Carby-Samuels as a result of judicial prejudice and collusion.

The Defendant was not required to prove or substantiate anything, including allegations of "harassment" and "mental illness". The Plaintiff's evidence that the Defendant has used such allegations in Federal Court, which were thrown out by the presiding Judge was, once again, ignored, as ALL other evidence presented by the Plaintiff.

Justice P. E. Roger and The Hon. James McNamara over-turned the Order rendered by The Hon. Justice Patrick Smith on 11 February 2016 through collusion and criminal conspiracy. When Justice Patrick Smith was supposed to preside over the Plaintiff's Motion of Contempt, it is apparent after having correspondence with his secretary that he was taken off the subsequent Motion of Contempt as a result of orchestration.

Justice P. E. Roger's most recent Endorsement presented in my letter dated 12 September 2016 which subverted the *Rules of Civil Procedure*, the *Ontario Courts of Justice Act* and the principles of the Judicial Council further exposes the misconduct of Justice P. E. Roger and The Hon. James McNamara in the Eastern Division of the Ontario Superior Court of Justice.

Thanks for your consideration.

Regards,

HRC-S II

CHAPTER 6

The Hypocrite

John Summers calls himself a "Family Lawyer". But at least in one case, Mr. Summers can be described as a Family Destroyer.

The lawyer had told so many lies in Court designed to perpetuate the misery of Dezrin Carby-Samuels that it's a wonder how this man can sleep at night?

After more than three years of dealing with Mr. Summers lies and the Kangaroo Court he orchestrated with his conspirators on the Judicial Bench who all graduated from Summers' alma mater which is the University of Ottawa, Faculty of Law, Raymond has now skilfully navigated his legal plight to the Supreme Court of Canada.

Raymond has applied to the Supreme Court of Canada to seek a 'Leave to Appeal' in what would promise to be a landmark case against the control of our legal system in the hands of lying lawyers like John Summers, who seek to manipulate the courts with at times the willing support of certain judges who lack integrity.

John E. Summers appears to have sought to perpetuate the abuse of Dezrin Carby-Samuels by her husband and a dirty Ottawa Police Detective named Robert Griffin Jr. and Mr. Summers had done so with the apparent collaboration of the University of Ottawa fellow graduates Justice Pierre Roger, Regional Senior Justice James McNamara and Justice Sylvia Corthorn.

Isn't it time to put an end to the efforts of the cliques within our legal system that have sought to manipulate at the expense of the rule of law and human lives?

CHAPTER 7

THE DEVIL'S ACCOMPLICE

WOMEN MIGHT BE THEIR WORST enemies after all—as in the case of physically disabled victim Dezrin, who has been treated with so much neglect even by her fellow gender.

Ottawa Judge, Justice Sylvia Corthorn in a recent ruling on an Urgent Motion request, utterly dismissed the civil rights of the disabled woman and her son Raymond, who is seeking to visit his mother to ensure her welfare and safety. This is after Justice Callum Macloed, on 24 March 2017, gave an injunction due to his apparent concerns for the safety of the elderly woman. He implored that a religious envoy—consisting of a rabbi, go along with the Defence Counsel's lawyer, Mr. John Summers, for independent verification to ensure that the woman "has not been held, prisoner".

While Justice Macloed—a male, showed much empathy for Dezrin, Justice Corthorn, on the other hand completely disregarded this sanction. Quite surprisingly, her final ruling was in favour of the abusive husband who had subjected her to inhumane conditions and secluded her from her son. Raymond had attempted to rescue his mother from the hands of her captive, but met a brick wall, as Justice Corthorn blocked his attempt.

It is quite disturbing that despite the fact that Dezrin's husband had abused her to the point in which she is unable to talk, write, or even walk anymore—with all access to acquiring proper medical treatment and a proper meal equally inhibited, Justice Corthorn during her ruling determined that the situation was apparently not sufficient to be termed an "urgent matter".

One would think that the elevation of women into positions of high authority—where they are shouldered with the responsibility of making major decisions, would greatly promote the better treatment of women who are victims of insensitivity and immense discrimination. Yet the specific case of Justice Sylvia Corthorn has proven that it's never a matter of gender, as a female judge can be just as (or even more) oppressive as their male counterpart against other women.

This case has shown that women, who find themselves in high political, judicial, and corporate positions, may become the female agents of oppression—just as Judge Corthon, has shown. It's safe to say that the discriminations women face in the Justice system here, and everywhere else in the world—due to callous and tyrannical minds, are not limited to the male gender.

Justice Sylvia's action just goes to show that maybe, just maybe, women can sometimes be their own enemies.

CHAPTER 8

THE SMILING DEMON

The involvement of John Summers in this apparent Mandela Effect orchestration is highly mysterious. Here we have a lawyer working on behalf of his alleged client Horace Carby-Samuels, whose $300/hour rate Horace wouldn't have been even able to afford even when he was working a full-time job—but somehow was able to afford since March 2016? When Raymond asked Mr. Summers, who his 'real client' was who is paying his retainer, he refused to say. When Raymond then asked to meet with him to find out what was going on, Mr. Summers first agreed as long as he could take along three members of his law firm to such a meeting but then he rescinded his offer.

It was further revealed off-the-record by some lawyers in Ottawa that the Bell Baker law firm operates with "backroom connections".

It is apparent, therefore, that Mr. Summers' ability to spread a tissue of lies unchallenged by judges with University of Ottawa affiliations in the lower court is the result of Bell Baker's apparent illicit and clandestine associations with Archons.

CHAPTER 9

The Psychopath

Open Letter

I call on The Honourable Jody Wilson-Raybould. Minister of Justice and Attorney General of Canada to investigate a sordid attack on not only the rights of a woman rendered sick and disabled by the unethical conduct of one lawyer, but the coordinated nature of this attack orchestrated by members of the University of Ottawa community.

Could a mafia-style organization operating from deep within the Faculty of Law at the University of Ottawa be seeking to profit from the manipulation of court cases at the Ottawa courthouse?

Could John Summers provide insight into what could be the greatest conspiracy in the modern history of court systems not only in Canada but of western democracy in general?

Could there ever be a more sick and twisted plot against any known conventions of human decency as the path presented by one Ottawa lawyer?

For many Canadians, hearing about a lawyer being unethical comes to no big surprise.

Indeed, in a CBC Doc Zone documentary, a few years ago, lawyers were "outed" as having an unusual concentration of psychopaths.

But, then there's John Summers who represents the downtown Ottawa law firm of Bell Baker LLP, that is situated right in front of the Ottawa courthouse.

Now, I have seen some treacherous and greedy lawyers in Ontario as someone who has been a member of the legal community.

But, here in Ontario, Mr. Summers could be in a category of his own concerning the apparent evils harboured within the legal community.

Have you wondered in all the experiences you have had with lawyers, just how low can a lawyer stoop on their single-minded focus for money with a lack of respect for human life?

I might have the answer for you now. You see, Mr. Summers and his paymaster had a problem.

Horace, his client was abusing his wife whose name is Dezrin Carby-Samuels; and Raymond, as any responsible son, wanted to protect his Mom from that abuse.

Raymond had sought to ask his Mom whether she wanted to temporarily move to a spare room in his south Kanata place to help expedite her medical recovery, which was not being helped by Horace's worsening pattern of irrational anger and violence at the home Dezrin shares with Horace in Kanata.

However, Mr. Summers didn't want Raymond interfering with the "right" of a man to abuse his woman who he owns as "chattel".

Mr. Summers' simple and effective "solution" to support Horace's apparent right to abuse and torture his woman as he sees fit was to manufacture a litany of lies designed to prevent Dezrin getting the support she desired from her son who had been her primary caregiver in support of her recovery.

Mr. Summers' apparent elaborate and grotesque lies published in his court submissions all sought to maintain and worsen a Hell on Earth for Dezrin.

John Summers' first of many lies that he submitted to the court was that "Raymond suffered from mental illness".

This lie was designed to proselytize the idea to local police that Raymond constituted a "danger".

There was also the lie that "Raymond sought to hold Dezrin and Horace hostage".

This was a lie also denied by Ms. Dezrin in writing, when she could still write.

John Summers then spread the lie to Court that both Dezrin and Horace wanted Raymond evicted back in late April 2015.

John Summers then lied that Raymond was seeking to somehow "force" his Mother to see him.

Mr. Summers further asserted the "medical competence" of Dezrin after more than three years of abuse at her Kanata-Katimavik area home without one shred of medical evidence to support his assertion.

When Justice Callum Macloed asked for independent verification of Dezrin's well-being, Mr. Summers first agreed, but within days reneged on the Agreement with another lie.

Mr. Summers then wrote to Raymond that he would at least obtain some medical information about Dezrin's condition. But that was over a year ago! Yep, you guessed it. Summers lied again.

Mr. Summers in 2017 became even more "creative" by alleging that Raymond got "banned" for calling Ottawa Ambulance Services in an incident that Dezrin credited for saving her life.

Raymond had approached Ottawa Ambulance Services and said there was no such ban.

Mr. Summers even went further by apparently presiding over the forgery of Horace's signature according to two handwriting experts in 2017.

Both handwriting experts assert that there is a 100% certainty that Horace's signature was subject to forgery.

When Summers apparently couldn't get Horace to endorse his lies the determined Summers put pressure on Ms. Gorette Cleroux, his secretary to fraudulently prepare an affidavit of more lies against Raymond concocted by Summers to perpetuate Dezrin not getting the vital assistance she wanted from her son against beat-downs by Horace linked to the abuse Dezrin had described.

However, all the lies of Mr. Summers at the Ottawa courthouse would have gone nowhere if it was not for Mr. Summers calling upon judges at the Ottawa Courthouse who all graduated from the same law school as Mr. Summers–University of Ottawa Faculty of Law.

Is it a coincidence that four judges at the Ottawa courthouse who ignored all of Mr, Summers voluminous lies were all graduates of the same law school Mr. Summers attended and the Judges who had sought to support the affirmation of the rights of Dezrin and her son to see each other were from other law schools?

I don't believe in such "coincidences".

Back on 11 February 2016, Raymond had successfully obtained a court order from Justice Patrick Smith, who is affiliated with the Lakehead University community.

But since that time, the judges who have sought to roll back this ruling are all alumni from the very same Faculty of Law as Mr. Summers. This suggests a coordinated action through a common criminal association with one another.

Justice Callum Macloed is an alumnus of Queens University in Kingston, Ontario.

This Justice had sought to support a path of social justice for both Dezrin and her son, and Justice Beaudoin, who also similarly sought justice in this matter had graduated from the Faculty of Law at the University of Windsor.

The apparent low-life judges who coordinated the seizing of the case from a path of justice for Dezrin Carby-Samuels are Justice Pierre Roger, Senior Justice James McNamara, and Justice Sylvia Corthon who are alumni from the University of Ottawa Faculty of Law along with John E. Summers.

Justice Sylvia Corthorn along with these other judges pursued an apparent criminal conspiracy designed to both ignore evidence presented by Raymond in defence of his Mother and support for Raymond by the non-University of Ottawa judges.

When Justice Beaudoin approved of a Motion to take Justice Sylvia Corthorn off the case, Corthon S simply ignored Beaudoin's approval of Raymond's motion and expedited her Kangaroo Court ruling.

Ms. Dezrin was a retired Registered Nurse who sought to spread charity to whoever she met. But thanks to Mr. Summers, Dezrin can no longer walk, talk or write today under Mr, Summers' lies.

Horace lost no time after Mr. Summers' paymasters had Raymond illegally evicted in late April 2015. Without Raymond there to protect her, the abuse got worse.

Within weeks, Dezrin lost the ability to walk, write or talk

Horace's abuse was confirmed by Dezrin Carby-Samuels, his wife, in her very own handwriting– that is, when she could still write.

This abuse ranged from a beat down to depriving Dezrin of the speech therapy she needed for a medical condition, to profound psychological torture.

Horace is so violent that one day on January 29, 2013, when Raymond had expressed concern in the kitchen to his father's abuse, seeing his Mom cry after another round of abuse, Horace decided to grab a kitchen knife to stab Raymond. In the process, Raymond, who sought to grab his knife to prevent him from stabbing Raymond in the stomach had one of his fingers almost severed by the knife.

It's plainly apparent here that Mr. Summers has sought to orchestrate a false flag conspiracy against Dezrin and her son with the organized support of the University of Ottawa Faculty of Law "mafia", which have sought to preside over a Kangaroo Court at its worse, and I ask readers to send emails and letters to the Attorney General to demand an immediate investigation.

Dezrin has been physically weakened by Horace's abuse and John Summers' coordinated conspiracy in this matter.

[Original letter was sent to the Office of the Attorney General of Canada and Minister of Justice Canada]

CHAPTER 10

THE PARANORMAL AND EXTRA-DIMENSIONAL

My fellow human beings, let's talk about this so-called "Mandela Effect".

The Mandela Effect has not only been linked to all kinds of divergent experiences of pop culture like logos, but nowadays to changes in geography, histories like the JFK assassination and even to, changes in family members.

But, what if you were able to notice that one of your family members seemed to be in the process of being "replaced" by a "different person" as it began to happen in some kind of transition to a "new alternative reality"? In this "new alternative reality," the Statute of Liberty is on "Liberty Island" instead of Ellis Island, where it ought to be situated for having had a historical role the welcoming of new immigrants to the shores of America. In this "reality" instead of simply 'Starbucks' there is "Starbucks Coffee" among many other well-documented discrepancies.

Have you been wondering what the "Mandela Effect" is all about, and who might be able to provide some critical insights on it?

If so, you might wish to consider asking one particular Ottawa lawyer. This very bright and clever lawyer is John Summers and he represents Bell Baker LLP.

You see, when Horace Carby-Samuels and his wife Dezrin began to experience what we now appreciate as the "Mandela Effect", his son worked to countervail its efforts to change through various naturopathy treatments — *And it was working.*

This somehow caught the attention of "a Group" who hired John Summers to pose as Horace's lawyer to fabricate court documents that Raymond "suffered from mental illness" to instigate the severing of contact with his parents.

Mr. Summers' paymasters wanted the experiments against the Ottawa couple to continue without Raymond's "interference" as part of Mandela Effect testing before expediting the Effect to the much wider population that we observe today regarding documented experiences of changes to family members.

Mr. Summers used his apparent connections with operatives to prevent Dezrin from seeing her son since 12 June 2015 to enable the "Mandela Effect" to continue. Dezrin essentially became a "Mandela Effect guinea pig".

This would have not occurred if Dezrin was able to talk, walk and write. However, it became apparent that the paymasters for John Summers did not see it in their interest Raymond's effort to protect the well-being of his parents.

After the paymasters of John Summers orchestrated an eviction against Dezrin's son, this poor woman lost her ability to talk, walk and write under apparent medical experiments associated with Mandela Effect intelligent design.

The Mandela Effect is the product of apparent intelligent design which began to be expedited in January 2013 with the help of the data from this couple associated with the work of the late Dr. Jerry Tenenbaum against Dezrin.

When Dezrin began to experience apparent symptoms of the Mandela Effect, she had been pushed to Dr. Tenenbaum, who for years collected data, but sought to provide no kind of treatment which would improve Dezrin's condition.

Dr. Tenenbaum's operatives got furious when Dezrin's condition began to substantively improve as a result of Raymond's intervention.

Since that time, Mr. Summers with the apparent support of a rich "Third Party" has sought to use lies to continue to prevent Raymond from rescuing his parents from an apparent effort to exploit an elderly Ottawa couple.

When Raymond asked Mr. Summers, who is paying his Retainer that he works for because his father in no way could afford to pay for years a more than $300/hour lawyer, Mr. Summers refused to disclose his paymaster.

Mr. Summers and his paymasters without any written endorsement by this Ottawa couple was even able to simply reply on an Affidavit supplied by Gorette Cleroux, his very own secretary, to pursue a new claim against Raymond as being a "Vexatious Litigant" simply because Raymond sought to verify the well-being of his Mother. Dezrin had suffered profound abuse, thanks to the efforts of Ottawa Police Detective Robert Griffin Jr., who conspired in Raymond's illegal eviction that was then enforced by the court as the result of lies presented by John Summers.

Finding out who is paying Mr. Summers retainer bills as part of apparent extensive collusion may be key to appreciating the involvement of Archons, in prevailing "Mandela Effects".

It was the ancient Pagan Gnostics who sought to warn humanity about the Archons as the humanized face of a demonic alien artificial intelligence. The Pagan Gnostics simply referred to this threat as "artificial man" in texts that Christian elites under the influence of these demons would seek to cover-up.

It is, therefore, no apparent coincidence that when Horace sought to warn everyone during his apparent Mandela Effect experience that his apparent warnings were related to the "Fallen Angels" which the Pagan Gnostics link to "artificial man".

However, it is notable that the clever activities of Mr. John Summers to manipulate the Superior Court of Justice in Ottawa designed to perpetuate a Mandela Effect against an Ottawa couple who needed assistance from their son wouldn't have been successful if it was not reinforced by the corrupt activities of an apparent clandestine University of Ottawa alumni network which apparently includes Ottawa Judges and the Office of the Chief of Police.

Ottawa Police Chief Charles Bordeleau shares a past University of Ottawa affiliation to an apparent clique that has brutally victimized Dezrin to reinforce Mandela Effect related experiments against her.

Judges who were not graduates of the Faculty of Law at the University of Ottawa at the Superior Court of Ottawa all supported Raymond's efforts to get the support that Dezrin has sought from Raymond. In contrast, Justices McNamara, Corthorn and Roger, who are all University of Ottawa, Faculty of Law alumni, all sought to play their apparent roles in a "Mandela Effect" against Dezrin. Horace had begun to experience a rather violent alien presence seeking to "override" his human matrix with an alternative persona starting from January 2013. At the end of January 2013, the apparent alien presence of Horace took out a kitchen knife and held it against Raymond's stomach after Raymond expressed concern to Horace for having witnessed his mother being abused by him. As a result of trying to prevent himself from being stabbed, Raymond was sent to the Emergency Room as a result of his finger being nearly severed-off due to this violent act.

The alternative persona of Horace was violent and fixated on making humanity "members of a Bio-Electrical Union" as Horace began to rant about in his writings.

A spiritual medium in Ottawa alleged that Horace was taken over by a reptilian entity that sought to experience a human body.

This spiritual medium also alleged that Marcella Carby-Samuels (who conspired with John Summers in perpetuating Raymond's eviction against the explicit demands of Dezrin, to see her son) had also been taken over by the same entities.

Marcella also began to betray extremely violent tendencies in efforts to enforce apparent medical experiments against Dezrin.

Indeed, more and more families have reported loved ones being replaced by characters with a different recalling of family memories.

Horace, who had previously described his encounters with aliens through "out of body experiences" began to warn his son and anyone who he thought would listen about an imminent *Extraterrestrial threat* against Earth and humanity.

As Horace began to be taken over more and more, his true human identity could no longer make the same warnings against Archons.

It's becoming more and more apparent that Ottawa lawyer John Summers may be a key link to appreciating organized elite complicity in the "Mandela Effect".

There seem to be more and more representatives these days coming out about how an alleged "Mandela Effect" is creating rifts among family members. That is to say, it seems that family members from "the real Earth" are being foisted on identically appearing family members in this "new or simulated Earth", and who have a different recalling of past associations. The Mandela Effect traces its name from divergent experiences of when Nelson Mandela had died among people and ensuing discrepancies in experiences among people of material reality as suggesting evidence of human experiences of "alternative realities".

More and more people are noticing that some family members seem to be changing into different people right before their eyes, which naturally is causing alarm among those people who are referring to this phenomenon as a "Mandela Effect".

The role and relationship of Mr. Summers with well-financed paymasters suggest that the Mandela Effect supports an orchestrated elite agenda.

Horace's hysterical fears against aliens and the "Fallen Angels" in his spiritual struggles against the Mandela Effect suggest that it is part of an agenda that is alien and that is linked to a lower and cross-dimensional "artificial intelligence" referred to by the ancient Pagan Gnostics as the Archons.

Whether or not the damage caused by the Mandela Effect can be reversed to enable the reuniting of family members may very well depend on humanity discovering the role of John Summers and his paymasters against the activities of an Ottawa couple.

CHAPTER 11

THE TREACHEROUS LIAR

JUST WHEN YOU THOUGHT THE law profession could not get any lower in matters pertaining to professional ethics, you might wish to think again. On Ontario Superior Court File 15-66772, Defence Counsel John Summers prepared a rather interesting affidavit that "ambulance services have placed a block" against Raymond, the plaintiff in this case. At *The Canadian*, we reviewed a note in response to Raymond's inquiry to Ottawa Ambulance Services, which completely denied any existence of such a 'blacklist.' This is yet again, one other apparent mischievous allegation spread by Mr. Summers in affidavits he has prepared.

Apparently, according to Mr. Summers, Raymond was being a nuisance because he had called Ottawa paramedics a couple of years ago when he saw his Mother lying beside her bed not breathing. Raymond called his father, who became the Defendant in this case, who was not the least bit worried.

Thankfully, Raymond had the good sense to call 9-1-1 and Ottawa Paramedics had given Raymond instructions on exactly how to revive his Mother. These instructions included putting her on her side. Raymond, followed these instructions, and soon after Raymond's mother started breathing again, just before paramedics arrived.

Raymond's Mom was very grateful to her son as she described in a written note as 'saving her life'. However, it appears John Summers and his client have been 'not so grateful' by electing to slander Raymond for having sought to save his Mother's life in the face of a bizarre passive indifference by Raymond's father.

However, this is not even the biggest lie that Mr. Summers has sought to spread.

You see, since 12 June 2015, Raymond has not been able to see his Mother.

Raymond's Mother back in spring 2015, handed a note to her son that her husband had been abusing her. Specifically, the note read, "Dad Abuses Me." Raymond's mother had hoped that by putting her abuse in writing, Raymond could then carry it to the police to relieve her situation of abuse.

However, the alien persona of Raymond's father had a plan in mind, and that was to spread the lie that Raymond 'suffers from mental illness' which he used to get the police to remove him from looking after his Mother anymore, and since that time John Summers has spread the lie that 'Raymond's parents don't want to see him anymore.' On 24 March 2017, Justice Macloed asked for what he described as 'independent verification' of Raymond's mother's wishes to ensure that she was 'not being held a prisoner'. However, this endorsement was blocked under the auspices of John Summers who has continued to spread the apparent fraudulent representation concerning the wishes of Raymond's Mother.

You might ask why doesn't Raymond's Mother just run away from the situation of abuse and meet with her son? Well, unfortunately, that's not possible, because Raymond's Mother can no longer walk, write or talk, as a result of being forcibly separated from Raymond, who had been her caregiver who had also sought to protect his Mom from the abuse and neglect. Within weeks of being forcibly separated from her son in late April 2015, Dezrin, who is Raymond's Mom lost the ability to talk, walk and write in early June 2015 according to the Nepean, Rideau and Osgoode Community Centre. And, thanks to John Summers, conditions of abuse have been perpetuated under a plethora of misrepresentation.

CBC-TV's Doc Zone had once named lawyers as having a relatively high concentration of psychopaths. A psychopath is an ego-driven entity committed to pursuing a singular objective in pursuit of an objective for "success" irrespective of empathy in general or, specifically, how many lives along the way are destroyed. Unfortunately, John Summers has sought to pursue his activities in the courtroom regardless of the civil rights of Dezrin – a now chronically ill and disabled Mom – whose living Hell has been perpetuated by the tactics of deception lacking in a moral or ethical conscious associated with human decency as described by Raymond who we interviewed. We were told that John Summers has reportedly sought to "refrain from any comment" regarding the "Hell on Earth" that a sick and disabled elderly woman is being subjugated.

CHAPTER 12

The Attack Against Motherhood

There are moments when behaviours of certain individuals tend to undermine the basic principle of humanity. However, when such behaviour is displayed by someone who is supposed to know better, then, eyebrows should be raised.

Ms. Dezrin Carby-Samuels, and her son, Raymond have both had to deal with countless abuse of their basic human rights and just when everyone thought that justice will be served, John E. Summers stepped in with his callous disregard for the desires of Dezrin and her enforced isolation by his client.

John E. Summers, a Bell Baker lawyer has gone to the extent of preparing a fraudulent affidavit and using other deceptive methods to deny Dezrin and Raymond the chance to even see each other since 12 June 2015.

The evil being perpetuated by John Summers clearly shows that people who are supposed to know better with regards to the application of the laws of the land can even stoop so low as to use lies and fraud to commit crimes against humanity. If nothing at all, John Summers should have realized that Dezrin Carby-Samuels is an aged, elderly woman who deserves nothing less than respect and reverence from society.

There is one thing that John Summers' callous disregard for the rights of Dezrin further proves and that is the fact that there is a very big difference between being human and a human being. This goes to show that one can be a human being alright and still behave in a way that is alien to humans who embrace empathy for each other. For a lawyer to be able to fabricate lies against an elderly woman and her son is simply a slap right in the face of law enforcement and our humanity.

Even though on the 11th of February, 2016, Justice Patrick Smith's Superior Court of Ontario made a ruling that Raymond should be allowed to pay daily visits to his sick and bedridden mother. However, John Summers in collaboration with Dezrin's husband, Horace, and daughter, Marcella have used dubious ways and means to prevent Raymond from seeing his sick mother. They even went to the extent of fraudulently tagging Raymond as not being sound mentally.

When a lawyer, in his right senses, decides to deceive the court to frustrate an elderly woman like Dezrin Carby-Samuels, then it is about time that well-meaning humans team up to support a petition for the disbarment of John Summers from further practicing law in the Province of Ontario.

John Summers: Ottawa Lawyer Undermines Justice for Elderly Women

Thanks to the activities of John Summers from the law firm Bell Baker in Ottawa an elderly woman's hope of ever seeing her son before she dies is fading. Ms. Dezrin Carby-Samuels had sought to see her son since 12 June 2015.

Raymond Carby-Samuels, who had witnessed the infliction of abuse and neglect by his father, Horace Carby-Samuels, who got Raymond evicted from his parents' home so that he would not be able to further defend his elderly Mom from that abuse.

Justice Patrick Smith granted a court order giving mutual access to Raymond and his Mother seeing each other on 11 February 2016. The abuse against Dezrin Carby-Samuels that worsened with the forcible removal of Raymond worsened the abuse and resulted in Dezrin not being able to talk, walk and write.

John Summers through unethical activities which is the current subject of a complaint to the Law Society of Upper Canada has managed to frustrate Dezrin's access to seeing Raymond, her son. John Summers' unethical activities include preparing a fraudulent affidavit that falsely accused Raymond of suffering from "mental illness". Mr. Summers has sought to support other such accusations without one iota of independently verifiable evidence as Dezrin's health has deteriorated.

As John Summers' deceit, deception and lies mount, Dezrin's health has gotten worse.

We ask for members of the public to take a stand against Bell Baker's lawyer oppressing the civil rights of a defenceless elderly woman and her son seeing each other through free speech that will help liberate Ms. Dezrin Carby-Samuels, from the elder spousal abuse that is being perpetuated by Mr. John Summers.

The law profession is supposed to be honourable and not to be used as a tool to deprive a mother of ever seeing her son protect an abuser who has seized control of her money to perpetuate abuse against her with the help of a lawyer who seems willing to support the lies that undermines the course of justice.

Ms. Dezrin Carby-Samuels, had been made an apparent prisoner of her own home thanks to the assistance of John Summers and his dishonourable activities.

CHAPTER 13

The Perpetuator of Domestic Abuse and Terror

It is widely accepted that physically disabled Canadians are entitled to equal rights and the affirmation of the human rights. This has been enshrined in our *Canadian Charter of Rights and Freedoms*.

That is why Ontario Superior Court Justice Macloed in an Ottawa on 24 March 2017 direction on a Motion asked John Summers to go with a religious envoy to visit the physically disabled client of his abusive client to find out who she wants to see to break her isolation.

For more than 500 days (as of this chronicle), John Summers' client has blocked visitation access and made his wife essentially a prisoner in her own home.

After consulting with his client, John Summers replied that his client would not allow either him or the court endorsed envoy to see his wife. Rather than Mr. Summers demanding that his client respects the court's direction as a condition of his continued service and in the interest of respecting the rights of a physically disabled person, John Summers elected to perpetuate his client's *de facto* criminal interference.

Thanks to John Summers, Dezrin's life has been made into a Hell in her own home for more than 500 days. She can no longer walk, write and talk thanks to the abuse involving forced isolation. Watch the above video for more information.

John Summers has helped to embellish the lies of "his client" which have included the fraudulent misrepresentation that Dezrin's son "suffers from mental illness" to justify her husband's desire to block Dezrin and Raymond, her son's desire to see each other.

CHAPTER 14

Non-Humans in Our Midst?

Today, I'm going to tell you very shocking news about a lawyer in Ottawa. His activities beg the rather alarming question on whether he's part of a group of 'Archons' identified by Alex Collier that is part of an effort to sell-out fellow humans to manipulative aliens for commercial profit.

John Lash revealed on Metahistory.org that the 'Archons' appear as "regular people" but are controlled by a collective demonic alien artificial intelligence mind matrix which has been responsible for orchestrating wars and countless human suffering on our planet Earth.

These entities are not from our universe, but originate from a lower dimension that has reportedly sought to use its artificial intelligence to divide, rule, conquer and exploit spiritual-biological beings like humans who possess souls that endows us with higher dimensional consciousness.

The truly shocking activities of John Summers reveals apparent "fifth columns" in strategic positions of local police and among Judges who appear to be part of a "new slave trade" involving humans seeking to sell-out humans to the nefarious activities of Archons.

The most vulnerable members of human society which include "missing children", the homeless and the elderly are reportedly being exploited by alleged alien interests, and it appears that John Summers has aided and abetted a hostile agenda.

When Ottawa man Horace Carby-Samuels began to complain to friends and family about an "Extraterrestrial threat" his son sought to come to both his father's and his mother's rescue. Horace began to complain of aliens seeking to take control of his body through his mind.

The result of these reported alien incursions was that a normally mild-mannered Horace began to suffer from increasing apparent episodes where an alien mind would seize control of him which resulted in that alien persona inflicting sadistic abuse against his wife.

Raymond reported seeing his father's eyes roll in his head every time this apparent psychotic alien presence took over. During one of these episodes, the apparent alien that seized control of Horace held a knife against Raymond's stomach, which sent him to the Emergency Room when Raymond had sought to protect his mother from the apparent abusive alien presence.

An informer revealed that Horace was taken over by an officer of an alien military command structure that sought to experience human emotions through Horace.

According to Alex Collier, the souls of humans are being "bottled-up" while aliens are seizing control of the bodies of human hosts. Horace appears to be one of the latest victims and it appears that we, as humans, have John Summers to thank in his continued efforts to "protect" Horace and Dezrin as the property of the aliens that have sought to use these two humans.

John Summers entered the picture just when Raymond sought to get help for both his father and mother who were being subjected to a violation of their human sovereignty.

Mr. Summers claimed to be working for Horace Carby-Samuels to keep Raymond away from both his father and mother. But after Raymond told Mr. Summers that this was not credible because his now-retired father couldn't even afford a lawyer working at over $300/hour, when his father was working, Mr. Summers then revealed that he was "not at liberty" to say who he was being retained by.

Similarly Africans used to sell fellow Africans as slaves for commercial profit. Alex Collier reveals that ultra-insiders are selling out other humans to enable demonic aliens to subject humans to various sadistic experiments.

Both Horace and Dezrin Carby-Samuels appear to have been subjected to alien abduction and related experiments and it appears that at least one Ottawa lawyer's job is to ensure that these experiments continue without any further interference from humans like Raymond.

John Summers' key role in all this has been to make up a tissue of lies that would then be reinforced by fellow Archons working at Ottawa Superior Court. These include Justices MacNamara, Roger and Corthorn who together used their mutual ties to an apparent "University of Ottawa" clique to sabotage efforts by other judges to support Raymond's efforts.

When Raymond back in February 2016 obtained an Order from Justice Patrick Smith to protect his Mom from the sadistic alien personae that had seized control of his father's body, John Summers and his apparent Archon associates expedited a false flag operation against Raymond to ignore all evidence of abuse by

Horace while also seeking to declare Raymond to be a "Vexatious Litigant" for seeking to reinstate Justice Patrick Smith's Order.

John Summers' published lies in court documents include fraudulent claims of Raymond "suffering from mental illness" and being "blacklisted by Ottawa Ambulance Services." These lies would then be treated as "fact" by his fellow Archons operating as Judges.

John Summers' activities are a wake-up call to all humans of how our planet is being destroyed as a result of those humans who seek to support an apparent alien agenda against other humans who seek commercial profit and power under the hegemony of demons.

CHAPTER 15

The False Affidavit

The heights of wickedness that can be shown by a human being towards another person can only be imagined. There have always been reported cases of people putting others through various degrees of torture. However, those people mostly had certain things in common and that includes not being well-informed, the incidence of some mental disorder, and many others. It is therefore very rare to come across an individual who is well-informed, educated and expected to be an example for others in the society stooping so low to spread false information in affidavits just to win a case against a man and her mother.

The woman, Dezrin, has had to endure a very torrid time at the hands of her husband. Ms. Dezrin thought that her only hope of getting out of the house alive and kicking was to let her son Raymond know of what was going on. She, therefore, wrote a note for her son that read "Dad Abuse Me" and gave it to her son. Raymond also took the matter up and decided to involve law enforcement agencies and the legal system. However, things just went from bad to worse as his dream of seeing his mother happy and lively again was squashed by certain criminal elements within the police service.

John Summers, the lawyer hired by Dezrin's husband, has made it a point that mother and son must lose the case either by hook or by crook. He started by making claims that Raymond "suffered from mental illness" and as such shouldn't be allowed to be visiting Dezrin. He peddled this falsehood until Raymond was barred from visiting his mother in June 2015. Raymond has since that time not been allowed to even see his mother even after obtaining permission from the courts.

Currently, there has also been another development in the case that all help in proving how diabolic John Summers can be.

In an affidavit that Mr. Summers prepared, he claimed that Raymond had been blacklisted by the ambulance service for some time now. However, upon further investigation, it was found out to be completely untrue.

Raymond had called for an ambulance when he found his mother lying in a supine position and not breathing. According to the 9-1-1 call that he placed at that time, he even stayed on the line for some time as the paramedics gave him instructions on what to do to resuscitate his mother. By the time that the ambulance came, the mother had already gained consciousness and up to this day, she says she will forever be indebted to her son for what he did that day.

For a mother to appreciate something that her son did for her, it comes as a hit below the belt to realize that John Summers has decided to falsify what happened on that day to win a case against an elderly woman whose constant abuse at the hands of her husband has rendered her immobile. This is surely the height of wickedness that can be shown by a human being towards another human.

CHAPTER 16

Contempt for Human Decency

Is it true that the world is coming to an end?

THIS IS THE MILLION-DOLLAR QUESTION that many people have been asking for a very long time now and conspiracy theorists will straight away answer in the affirmative. A look at the situation involving an elderly woman, Dezrin Carby-Samuels and her son, Raymond being subjected to all forms of abuse both at home and even in the presence of the justice system makes it a bit difficult to dispute the fact that the life in this world may actually be about to come to an end.

For some time now, Dezrin has been at the receiving end of abuse involving enforced isolation by Horace Carby-Samuels and daughter, Marcella Carby-Samuels. The cruelty that father and daughter showed to Dezrin was even enough to send her to her early grave. However, her willing spirit has kept her alive even though she can no longer speak, write or walk. This notwithstanding, a lawyer by the name John Summers seems to be the last straw that breaks the camel's back if something is not done immediately to correct the harm being caused to Dezrin.

John Summers, a Bell Baker lawyer, created an affidavit containing the fraudulent assertion that Raymond suffers from "mental illness". This lie was made to ensure that Raymond never gets the chance to visit his sick and bedridden mother.

What will compel a lawyer under oath to blatantly embellish lies against an elderly, sick lady and her son's desire to see each other? There are so many things that come into play when the apparent wickedness of John Summers towards Dezrin is discussed, and all points to the fact that society is losing its direction with regards to the acceptable practices. Old age is a stage in a person's life that is revered all over the world by both the young and the elderly in society. So it comes as a shock when a lawyer decides to connive with a father and daughter to execute abuse involving psychological trauma against an elderly woman.

John Summers' lies further came to light when the court found out that Horace Carby-Samuels had not filed his defence in 2016. Summers simply claimed that his client was not very conversant with the practices and procedures of the courts. This shouldn't have raised any eyebrows since not everyone knows what to do when it comes to dealing with the courts. However, Horace is a man who had the effrontery to dismiss his lawyer to present his account in a court case in the year 1990. So how can someone claim that such a person is a novice when it comes to court procedures?

Whatever John Summers hopes to achieve by subjecting Dezrin to such psychological traumas can never be understood. This is a crime against society and the earlier it is curbed the better it will be for humanity.

CHAPTER 17

The Twisted Ego

John Summers will be the first to tell you that he supports the integrity of and the commitment to family. However, he has an interesting way of showing it. For about one year now, John Summers has fought to ensure that Dezrin, a mother, and Raymond, her son—who love each other, as close-knit mothers and sons tend to do—never see each other again.

However, a lack of reasons for preventing a law-abiding son and mother from seeing each other has not stopped John Summers.

Mr. Summers has championed an unlawful effort by Horace to prevent Dezrin, his wife, and Raymond, her son, from seeing each other. To this end, Mr. Summers has shown great skill in the use of lies and deception. These include John Summers' submission to the Ontario Superior Court in Ottawa that Raymond suffers from 'mental illness' that's a threat to his mother. After all, why rely on evidence when you can make it up?

Back in spring 2016, John Summers also lied about his client being ignorant of court procedure, causing him to not file a defence. This is the same client who was so confident about his legal skills that, back in the 1990s, he fired his lawyer at the time, and represented himself in Federal Court.

Most recently, on March 24, 2017, John Summers admitted to Justice MacLeod at the Ottawa Courthouse that he has never even met Dezrin. In response, Justice MacLeod asked that he and an envoy from a very established local religious organization meet with Ms. Dezrin, to reconfirm her desire to see her son that she has historically maintained since their forcible separation by her husband back in April 2015.

Due to Horace's apparent fear that such a meeting would lead to Dezrin and her son seeing each other again, John Summers reported back, saying that his "client" doesn't want either him, his own lawyer, nor this envoy seeing Dezrin.

If John Summers were a lawyer of integrity, he would insist to his client that he and the envoy endorsed by the court would be allowed to meet with Dezrin to confirm her interest in seeing her son, a condition of his legal services. However, Mr. Summers instead decided that he would accept his client's apparent perpetuation of abuse, neglect, and forcible isolation, which has resulted in conditions of profound psychological trauma against Dezrin.

Although Dezrin has been physically disabled under a pattern of abuse and neglect by his client, John Summers also admitted to Justice MacLeod that Dezrin remains mentally capable. However, John Summers has sought to ignore Dezrin's mental capability by going along with his client's desire to pursue what could be described as the criminal denial of Dezrin's right to see her son.

Is it okay for someone to abuse a spouse or significant other to the point of physical incapacity, and then for that person to ignore the independent will of that human being? Is it okay for a lawyer to turn a blind eye to the cries of that human being who has been essentially forcibly confined by his client? Don't physically disabled people have rights in Canada? Don't lawyers have a professional responsibility to the court for the testimony of their clients based on integrity, and especially so when human lives are at stake?

How does a lawyer who claims to support the values of integrity, commitment to family, and the rule of law required of his profession then participate in what could be described as a *de facto* criminal conspiracy to ignore the civil rights of a mentally capable person that is affirmed by the *Canadian Charter of Rights and Freedoms*?

Does Mr. Summers have any empathy for Dezrin's plight and sovereignty as a human being, and Raymond's efforts to defend his mom's rights? Or is Mr. Summers primarily concerned about getting his next legal retainer fees from his client, even if those fees could be construed as a form of 'blood money'?

We, the undersigned, united, say that no person who is so willing to ignore the pleas and cries of a defenceless elderly woman who had documented her abuse in writing when she could still write is fit to be practicing law in Ontario, Canada, or anywhere else.

John Summers doesn't have the integrity to ensure that the rights of a mother are respected in his effort to prevent a sick and elderly mother and her son from ever seeing each other again. In the process, John Summers has turned his back on both human suffering and basic professional ethics.

We, the undersigned, deplore the professional behaviour of John Summers as an attack against the loving relationship of mothers and their children everywhere that cannot be ignored.

Lawyers should not be allowed to support the possible criminal actions of their clients that threaten quality-of-life or the lives of fellow human beings based upon a pattern of verifiable lies and deception.

The defence of a client's interest shall not include participation in either an apparent criminal conspiracy or support for activities that threaten lives through the calculated use of clients and tactics of macabre deception.

We, the undersigned, say that John Summers has thrown the legal profession into disrepute by being willing to perpetuate the infliction of conditions of torture and psychological trauma by his client against another human being, against the better judgment of the court that has sought to endorse the importance of establishing the independent will of an abused woman.

We, the undersigned, support the Law Society of Upper Canada disbarment of Mr. John Summers from further practicing law as a result of having breached professional ethical standards that have endangered and/or oppressed human life concerning fundamental rights and freedoms.

[Signatories appeared in original petition]

CHAPTER 18

No Rights for Disabled People

Do physically disabled people have a right to see who they want?

Or, can someone essentially seize control of a physically disabled person and block visitation access that the disabled person desires?

John Summers is one Ottawa lawyer who appears to have perpetuated abuse against a disabled woman in Ottawa. Since June 12, 2015, Dezrin's sought visitation access has been blocked by her abusive husband, and John Summers has used lies to perpetuate conditions of profound abuse involving psychological trauma for more than 500 days.

On March 24, 2017, at a Court Motion hearing in Ottawa, Justice C. MacLeod stated, "I think it would be in everyone's best interest for there to be independent verification that she's not being held prisoner."

Since that time, John Summers has failed to provide the requested information to the court.

CHAPTER 19

THE ABOMINATION: CRIMES AGAINST HUMANITY

For how long will certain elements continue to tarnish the highly esteemed image of the law profession? One would have thought that, aside from the constant reports of certain law professionals being influenced so as to prevent justice from being served, nothing more can be done to raise eyebrows. However, it turns out the complete opposite is the case, as a lawyer by the name of John Summers has done something that almost the entire world's population would frown upon.

Human beings are created in such a way that they always have a feeling of sympathy whenever another human is going through some form of pain. It is therefore very rare to realise that a professionally trained lawyer, who has sworn to ensure that justice is always served, can stoop so low as to connive with Dezrin's husband in preventing the right thing from being done. People are known to always do certain things when there is something better at the end. However, when one decides to think about what would force a professional lawyer like John

Summers to do what he is doing, the realization is that it is just sheer wickedness.

Dezrin has had to endure all sorts of maltreatment at the hands of her husband, and when she couldn't take it any longer, she made it known to her son, Raymond.

Raymond then decided to use legal means to ensure that such constant abuse against his mother was stopped. However, John Summers has been a stumbling block to Raymond's desire to seek justice for his mother.

Among the numerous things that John Summers has been doing to ensure that justice is never served, he submitted a fraudulent disinformation affidavit claiming that Raymond had been blacklisted by the ambulance service. Previously, this same lawyer had gone to various lengths just to make people would believe that Raymond was "suffering from mental illness," and this led to Raymond being barred from even visiting his mother.

For a human being to perpetuate a chronically ill elderly woman's constant abuse by her husband, one is left to wonder what the fate of the world is going to be in some years to come. Dezrin has now been rendered bedridden and cannot talk or even write. This is a woman who was full of life even at an old age, but has now become a shadow of herself as she suffers in silence. This is a direct result of John Summers turning his back on Judge MacLeod's request on March 24, 2017, to verify that Dezrin "has not been held prisoner."

Wickedness to the elderly has and will always be something that society frowns upon. Therefore, this should have been enough to jolt even John Summers from his slumber. But the knowledge that he was actually perpetuating a heinous crime against an elderly woman and humanity as a whole has seemingly not phased him.

The sad part of Dezrin's case is the fact that her source of joy and happiness, Raymond, has been barred from seeing her for over two years now. And John Summers, along with the lies that he has sought to proselytize in court, has served to perpetuate Dezrin's abuse.

Epilogue

TWO INDEPENDENT WITNESSES ALLEGE THAT as of around February 2020, Dezrin Carby-Samuels died, under the horrific abuse of her torturer, and in isolation, thanks, in part, to the evil deeds of John E. Summers and his psychopathic confederates in the legal system. Raymond never got to see his "Mother" thanks to a kangaroo court system controlled by John Summers and his handlers.

In seeking to support an apparent cabal at the University of Ottawa, judges at the Ontario Court of Appeal and the Supreme Court of Canada, without a visible minority member among them, acted without any mercy in seeking independent verification of Dezrin's desire to see her son before her death.

Every single judge who has played a role in this debacle, along with John Summers, should be kicked-out of the law profession for their complicity in this *Devil's Pact*. They have no business making any adjudication decisions involving humans. They are without an ounce of the human decency that should be at the core of their professional responsibilities.

The editor of this book has not discovered any evidence that Horace Carby-Samuels and John Summers' paymasters even provided Dezrin with a funeral.

With that said, the editor of this book maintains that the apparent abuse and torture of Dezrin by Horace was a regressive alien simulation, within the rubric of the so-called "Mandela Effect", which John Summers sought to facilitate.

The Mandela Effect is not the product of poor memory, as the Archons would have us believe, but is the product of real manipulation, which is the manifestation of interference by extra-dimensional Artificial Intelligence (AI) in our human space-time continuum. This has been voluminously documented by David Icke, African Elders like Credo Mutwa and independent scholarly researchers who include Dr. Michael Salla.

Haven't you noticed that the sun is now white rather than yellow, and appears larger than its former glory, along with other bizarre alternations of history, geographic relationships and even aspects of popular culture?

Thanks to the entities that John Summers appears to serve, our sense of reality is being turned into an artificially induced state of consciousness of consciousness, as described in John Carpenter's "They Live".

Certain people seemed to have opened-up our reality of the Gates of Hell, and this book has shown John Summers' apparent role in facilitating a dimensional doorway, which has now destroyed Dezrin Carby-Samuels and replaced Horace Carby-Samuels with an alien persona, which the legal system seeks to protect. As humans, we may be witnessing an effort to take-over our world by manipulative aliens, with the legal systems providing the cover for that take-over process.

This book provides a window on this repressive society, under the control of demons, that we as humans must collectively oppose if we seek to evolve into the kind of society that most of us would want to be part of.

Appendix

Supreme Court of Canada: File Number SCC 38391

File No._____

IN THE SUPREME COURT OF CANADA

(ON APPEAL FROM THE COURT OF APPEAL OF ONTARIO)

BETWEEN:

RAYMOND CARBY-SAMUELS

APPLICANT (Appellant)

AND:

HORACE CARBY-SAMUELS

RESPONDENT (Respondent)

APPLICATION FOR LEAVE TO APPEAL

(Pursuant to s. 40 of the Supreme Court of Canada Act and Rule 25(1), 43.1 Of the Rules of the Supreme Court of Canada)

Raymond Carby-Samuels	John E. Summers
Self-Represented Litigant	Counsel for the Respondent
Tel: (514) 712-7516	Tel: (613) 237-3444 / Fax: (613) 237-1413
Email: cosmopolita_rc@yahoo.com	Email: Jsummers@bellbaker.com
B.P. 24191 – 300 Eagleson Rd.	**BELL BAKER LLP**
Kanata, Ontario K2M 2C3	#700 – 116 Lisgar Street
	Ottawa, Ontario K2P OC2

File No. _____

IN THE SUPREME COURT OF CANADA

(ON APPEAL FROM THE COURT OF APPEAL OF ONTARIO)

BETWEEN:

RAYMOND CARBY-SAMUELS

APPLICANT (Appellant)

AND:

HORACE CARBY-SAMUELS

RESPONDENT (Respondent)

APPLICATION FOR LEAVE TO APPEAL

(Pursuant to s. 40 of the Supreme Court of Canada Act and Rule 25(1), 43.1
Of the Rules of the Supreme Court of Canada)

Raymond Carby-Samuels	John E. Summers
Self-Represented Litigant	Counsel for the Respondent
Tel: (514) 712-7516	Tel: (613) 237-3444 / Fax: (613) 237-1413
Email: cosmopolita_rc@yahoo.com	Email: Jsummers@bellbaker.com
B.P. 24191 – 300 Eagleson Rd.	**BELL BAKER LLP**
Kanata, Ontario K2M 2C3	#700 – 116 Lisgar Street
	Ottawa, Ontario K2P 0C2

TABLE OF CONTENTS

Tab	Document	Page
1	Notice of Application, dated September 20, 2018	1
2	**Formal Judgements of Lower Courts**	
	A Transcript Excerpts, Superior Court of Justice, 14 August 2017	10
	B Memorandum of Superior Court, Madam Justice S. Corthorn	51
	C Order of Superior Court, Hon. Madam Justice S Corthorn	67
	D Order of Court of Appeal for Ontario, 20 July 2018	70
3	**Memorandum of Argument**	74
	Part I: Overview and Statement of Facts	77
	Part II: Statement of Issues	86
	Part III: Statement of Argument	87
	Part IV: Costs	93
	Part V: Order Sought	93
	Part VI: Table of Authorities	96
	Part VII: Statutory and Constitutional Provisions ["Schedule B"]	98
	A *Ontario Courts of Justice Act*, R.S.O. 1990, c C. 43	99
	B *Family Law Act*, R.S.O. 1990, c. F.3.	100
	C. *Ontario Good Samaritan Act*, S.O. 2001	101
	D. *Criminal Code of Canada* (R.S.C., 1985, c C-46)	103
	E *Ontario Rules of Civil Procedure* (Mandatory Mediation Provision)	106

	F	*Supreme Court Act*, RSC, 1985, C S-26	*109*
	G	*Canadian Charter of Rights and Freedoms* (Constitution Act, 1982)	112
4		**Other Documents Relied Upon**	
	A	Default Motion, December 2014	114
		- Contains original Statement of Claim and effort to amend Statement of Claim	
	B	Default Order of Ontario Superior Court of Justice	132
		- Justice Patrick Smith's Endorsement – 11 February 2016	
		Superior Court of Ontario File Number – 15 – 66772	
	C	Letter from Superior Court on Recusal Motion	134
		- Issued by Tina Johanson - Dated 5 October 2017	
	D	Recusal Motion Against Corthorn, J	135
		- Superior Court of Ontario File Number 15 – 66772	
		Dated 10 October 2017	
	E	Appellant's Factum on Appeal from Superior Court	165
		- ONCA – Court of Appeal for Ontario File C-64716	
	F	Affidavits of Raymond Carby-Samuels citing Defendant's Torts	195
		- Dated 9 May 2017 and Issued to Superior Court	
	G	Murray v Toth, 2012 ONSC 5815 [Orchestrated Eviction]	208
		- Superior Court File – 15-66772	
		Sazone v Schechter et al, 2016 OCNA 566	211
	H	Dezrin Carby-Samuels confirms in writing that she has been Subjected to Domestic Violence / Abuse by Respondent	225
		Note written in early to mid 2015	
	I	Legal Demand Letter from Counsel for Raymond Carby-Samuels	226
		Todd Ji - Dated 10 June 2015	

J	Counsel for Raymond Carby-Samuels documents abuse Todd Ji - Dated 10 June 2015	228
K	Other Letters from Lawyer in support of Appellant's actions	230
L	Direction of Justice MacLeod -Transcript – 24 March 2017	234
M	Motion for Leave to Amend Statement of Claim [Excerpted]	237
N	Law of Equity – Clean Hands Definition	252
O	Article on Older Victims of Domestic Violence	253
P	Defence Counsel Notifies of Intent to File Summary Judgement over a Year After Default and After Plaintiff's Lawyer Sought Mandatory Mediation Dated 27 January 2017	257
Q	Dezrin Carby-Samuels writes in defence of her Raymond Carby-Samuels, when she could still write - Winter 2015 Court of Appeals Assertion on 20 July 2018 of being "compelled" to see her son is false	259

File No._____

IN THE SUPREME COURT OF CANADA

(ON APPEAL FROM THE COURT OF APPEAL OF ONTARIO)

BETWEEN:

RAYMOND CARBY-SAMUELS

APPLICANT (Appellant)

AND:

HORACE CARBY-SAMUELS

RESPONDENT (Respondent)

APPLICATION FOR LEAVE TO APPEAL

(Pursuant to s. 40 of the Supreme Court of Canada Act and Rule 25(1) of the Rules of the Supreme Court of Canada)

Raymond Carby-Samuels

Self-Represented Litigant

Tel: (514) 712-7516

Email: cosmopolita_rc@yahoo.com

B.P. 24191 – 300 Eagleson Rd.

Kanata, Ontario K2M 2C3

John E. Summers

Counsel for the Respondent

Tel: (613) 237-3444 / Fax: (613) 237-1413

Email: Jsummers@bellbaker.com

BELL BAKER LLP

#700 – 116 Lisgar Street

Ottawa, Ontario K2P OC2

File No._____

IN THE SUPREME COURT OF CANADA

(ON APPEAL FROM THE COURT OF APPEAL OF ONTARIO)

BETWEEN:

RAYMOND CARBY-SAMUELS

APPLICANT (Appellant

AND:

HORACE CARBY-SAMUELS

RESPONDENT (Respondent

APPLICATION FOR LEAVE TO APPEAL

(Pursuant to s. 40 of the Supreme Court of Canada Act and Rule 25(1) of the Rules of the Supreme Court of Canada)

Raymond Carby-Samuels	John E. Summers
Self-Represented Litigant	Counsel for the Respondent
Tel: (514) 712-7516	Tel: (613) 237-3444 / Fax: (613) 237-1413
Email: cosmopolita_rc@yahoo.com	Email: Jsummers@bellbaker.com
B.P. 24191 – 300 Eagleson Rd.	**BELL BAKER LLP**
Kanata, Ontario K2M 2C3	#700 – 116 Lisgar Street
	Ottawa, Ontario K2P OC2

File No._____

IN THE SUPREME COURT OF CANADA

(ON APPEAL FROM THE COURT OF APPEAL OF ONTARIO)

BETWEEN:

RAYMOND CARBY-SAMUELS

APPLICANT (Appellant

AND:

HORACE CARBY-SAMUELS

RESPONDENT (Respondent)

NOTICE OF APPLICATION FOR LEAVE TO APPEAL

(Pursuant to s. 40 of the Supreme Court of Canada Act and Rule 25(1) of the Rules of the Supreme Court of Canada)

TAKE NOTICE that Raymond Carby-Samuels (the "**Applicant**") applies for leave to appeal to the Court, under s. 40 of the *Supreme Court Act* and rule 25 (1) of the Rules of the Supreme Court of Canada, from the judgement of the Court of Appeal for Ontario, Court File No. C64705, made July 20, 2018, and for an order:

1. Granting leave to appeal;
2. If leave to appeal is granted, ordering costs to the Applicant; and
3. Any further or other order that the court may deem appropriate.

AND FURTHER TAKE NOTICE that this application for leave is made on the following grounds:

1. Guidance is required if it prejudicial or in breach of equity for someone who has demonstrable experience as an experienced self-represented litigant to be granted a set-aside Motion request for the filing of court materials after they not only didn't file a Statement of Defence but any paperwork to the lower court which showed any interest in eventually filing a Defence.
2. Guidance on the appropriate and potentially inappropriate timing during a litigation process for Mandatory Mediation in Ontario, as defined in the Ontario Rules of Civil Procedure and specifically the appropriate timing for a litigant to launch Summary Judgement. Can Summary Judgement be launched at any time or must it be launched prior during a specific period of a litigation process?
3. Guidance is required on whether the lower Courts are obliged to provide an adjournment for a self-represented litigant, when that adjournment is being sought by Counsel that is present who is acting on behalf of the self-represented litigant, and who is seeking that adjournment in an inherently complex matter such as preparing a defence against an effort of opposing Counsel who seeks Summary Judgement? Guidance is therefore required on what is the right of a self-represented litigant to seek the representation from Counsel for specific areas of litigation when that self-represented litigant deems it necessary in a matter of civil rights; and when that self-represented litigant can afford it? Should Counsel who asks for an adjournment to enable legal representation for a self-represented litigant expect the court to grant that adjournment?
4. Guidance is required if a litigant who seeks Summary Judgement must have "clean hands" as defined by the Law of Equity, or can a litigant who has verifiably

engaged in unethical conduct against the opposing litigant render their Summary Judgement application as breaching equity guidelines which a Court must follow?

5. Guidance is required if someone who has committed some form of documented bodily assault supported by a police report can then appropriately quash through the legal device of Summary Judgement the effort of the victim to file for civil damages and compensation for that assault.

6. Guidance is required if someone can orchestrate an eviction which leads to the seizing of personal and/or professional belongings for a period of days, many weeks or more can then appropriately quash through the legal device of Summary Judgement the effort of the victim to file for civil damages and compensation for not only a potentially unlawful eviction but also the seizure of property.

7. Guidance is required if someone can admittedly seize personal and/or professional belongings for a period of days, many weeks or even years can then appropriately quash through the legal device of Summary Judgement the effort of the victim to file for civil damages and compensation for not only a potentially unlawful eviction but also the seizure of property.

8. Guidance is required if someone can spread public mischief involving the filing of fraudulent reports to the police which leads of eviction or other hardships or emotional distress as a result of those fraudulent police reports can then appropriately quash through the legal device of Summary Judgement the effort of the victim to file for civil damages and compensation.

9. Guidance is required if a Good Samaritan who is seeking to act to save someone's life or at least safeguard their well being can be blocked in that act by a Third Party against the will of individual who has sought the support or intervention of the Good Samaritan. In the case of someone who suffers from a physical disability which prevents them from attending court, is the court required to independently verify the desires of the individual whose life the Good Samaritan sought to safeguard before the Court can support a Summary Judgement. What's

the inherent jurisdiction of the court to protect profoundly physically disabled people who are as vulnerable as mentally non-competent individuals?

10. Guidance is required on what obligations, if any, lower courts have in giving the appearance of providing self-represented litigants with due process by ensuring that any ruling demonstrates that the materials prepared by the self-represented litigant were thoroughly read. This includes the court citing references to those materials including case law which has been identified by the self-represented litigant as supporting his or her affirmations to the Court in any ruling? Or can a court simply state that there is "no basis to intervene in a decision of the lower court" in spite of possibly numerous bases identified in submitted materials by the self-represented litigant. Correspondingly, does the absence the treatment by the appellate court of case law identified by the self-represented litigant as bases of overturning the decision of a "lower court" suggest a lack of constitutionally required due process and that the self-represented litigant is justified in having a "reasonable apprehension of bias" against an appellate court for a failure to provide critical review and oversight? Could the lack of such treatment in a ruling suggest that his or her status as a self-represented litigant might have coloured the Court's equitable treatment of the self-represented litigant that the *Canadian Charter of Rights and Freedoms* guarantees? What proof can a self-represented litigant rely on that his or her documents were even read if supporting case law, evidence, judicial rulings or statutes were not mentioned in the subsequent ruling of an appellate Court?

11. Guidance is required as to how much assistance courts should give to vulnerable self-represented litigants in making sure that their substantive legal rights reinforced by Sections 24(1) of the *Canadian Charter of Rights and Freedoms* are protected. How should courts understand or interpret issues raised by self-represented litigants in chambers or at trial or on an appeal in an unconventional fashion or that may not be fully or clearly articulated. In other words, what leeway should courts provide self-represented litigants who have a civil right as a

Canadian to represent themselves but who lack the legal training of a lawyer to present substantive legal issues.

12. Have lawyers whose fees which are often out of reach for middle-income, the working poor and people who are without income unjustly created classes of people who may be impaired in seeking to avail their rights as self-represented litigants by a court-driven legal system that overly relies on the knowledge and experience that Counsel has in representing substantive legal matters? In order to help ensure that all Canadians can avail themselves of their Charter rights without financial barriers imposed by having to retain Counsel to exercise those rights under Section 24(1) of the *Canadian Charter of Rights and Freedoms,* should our legal system be reformed to simplify court processes and procedure to the comprehension level of the average Canadians to ensure that Courts will better focus on substantive legal issues that will not be distorted by Counsel's superior knowledge of court rules, procedures and conventions which may be used by Counsel to frustrate the ability of self-represented litigants assert civil rights against *prima facie* infringements? Should the Canadian court system be redesigned to make sure that growing numbers of self-represented litigants who cannot afford Counsel will not be subjected to the practice of "lawyering" in which Counsel uses their knowledge of nuanced technical procedures to undermine a self-represented litigant's assertion of civil rights? Or should self-represented litigants get protected access to lawyers including the time when Counsel might seek an adjournment in behalf of a self-represented litigant? Should courts require Duty Counsels to assist with all matters of litigation from the preparation of legal documents to being present in Court to confront serious challenges by Opposing Counsel which include a "Vexatious Litigant" claim?

13. Additional guidance is required as to how courts should interpret and apply court rules and procedures to vulnerable self-represented litigants. Should courts apply a contextual approach that recognizes self-represented litigants' lack of

understanding of court rules and procedures, or should court rules and procedures be applied identically to all litigants?

14. Additional guidance is required on the how much effort lower courts are required to ensure that the appearance of equity and matters of due process is maintained. When the presiding Superior Court Judge was faced with a recusal Motion that was approved to proceed by the administrative Judge of the Superior Court was that presiding judge obliged to wait for the outcome of that recusal motion before rendering a decision on 'Summary Judgement'? By not waiting, can it be construed by a fair and impartial third party observer that Summary Judgement rendered by the Court which was made after the administrative Judge thought the self-representing litigant had solid grounds to make a recusal Motion, has the appearance of being retaliatory against the complainant self-represented litigant; and did the Court of Appeal miss a valuable opportunity to respond to that enquiry made by the self-represented litigant which this Court can now speak to? Did the appellate court err by firstly declaring a "strong presumption" of impartiality which ignored the fact that the administrative judge of the lower court had evaluated the grounds established for the judges recusal as worthy of a Motion; and then failing to review those grounds held as substantive by the administrative judge? Does the appellate court's subsequent characterization of the presiding judge of the lower court's decision as "thorough and compelling" give the appearance of side-stepping the procedural rights of the appellant in favour of a deference to the presiding judge that is not consistent with Supreme Court of Canada's case law view on the significance of a 'reasonable apprehension of bias'.

15. Institutionalized racism is a well-established historical fact in Canadian society and in Ontario a *Royal Commission* under The Hon Stephen Lewis documented how our legal system has worked against perceived young black males. The existence of institutionalized racism in Canadian society in general and in the Canadian court system specifically has also been acknowledged by the Supreme Court of

Canada. Guidance is therefore required to deal with the obligations of the Court to eradicate itself from any appearance of further impairing self-represented litigants who are young black males or other marginalized racialized populations who have been statistically proven to face on-going inequitable treatment. Was the lower court obliged pursuant to *stare decisis* to ensure that self-represented litigant's case law in support of their Appeal was referred to in their rendering of a decision on the self-represented litigant's Appeal? Does the failure of the Appellate Court to do this give the appearance of so much deference to Counsel that the Court would see no need to thoroughly read a self-represented litigant's perfected Appeal who is from a demographic group that can encountered systematic discrimination which has been acknowledged by this Court?

16. Guidance is required on how visible minority groups which this Court along with various learned studies has confirmed have verifiably faced systemic discrimination within our court system and society in general, be protected from such constitutional infringements or cultural and religious insensitivities to a moral conscience if they seek to avail themselves of the constitutional protected civil rights with the Canadian court system, in light of growing numbers of self-resented litigants and the increasing diversity of Canada as a vibrant and multicultural society whose value systems may be different from the presiding judges but are nevertheless equally legitimate pursuant to the *Canadians Charter of Rights and Freedoms* and its clause which affirms the freedoms of religion, conscience and the multicultural heritage of Canada.

Dated at Ottawa, Ontario this 19th day of September 2018

SIGNED BY: _____

Raymond Carby-Samuels, Self-Represented Litigant

B.P. 24191 — 300 Eagleson Rd.

Kanata, Ontario K2M 2C3

Tel: (514) 712-7516

E-mails: lawsociety.carby.samuels@utoronto.ca / cosmopolita_rc@yahoo.com

ORIGINAL TO: THE REGISTRAR

COPIES TO:

BELL BAKER LLP

#700 – 116 Lisgar Street

Ottawa, Ontario   K2P OC2

John E. Summers

Tel: (613) 237-3444

Fax: (613) 237-1413

Email: Jsummers@bellbaker.com

Counsel for the Respondent

NOTICE TO THE RESPONDENT OR INTERVENER: A respondent or intervener may serve and file a memorandum in response to this application for leave to appeal within 30 days after the day in which a file is opened by the court following the filing of the application for leave to appeal or, if a file has already been opened, within 30 days after the service of this application for leave to appeal. If no response is filed within that time, the Registrar with submit this application for leave to appeal to the Court for consideration under section 43 of the *Supreme Court Act*.

Court File Nos. CV-15-66772/CV-17-00071624

SUPERIOR COURT OF JUSTICE

BETWEEN:

RAYMOND CARBY-SAMUELS

Applicant

-and-

HORACE CARBY-SAMUELS II

Respondent

PROCEEDINGS

BEFORE THE HONOURABLE JUSTICE S. CORTHORN
on August 14th, 2017, at OTTAWA, Ontario

APPEARANCES:

Raymond Carby-Samuels   In Person
J. Summers   Counsel for the Respondent

right. And then for the application which is 17-71624, I have an application record.

MR. SUMMERS: Yes.

THE COURT: And I have a factum. Just give me a moment. That is dated May 2017.

MR. SUMMERS: Yes.

THE COURT: Okay. All right. So those are all your client's materials.

MR. SUMMERS: Yes.

THE COURT: All right. Thank you.

MR. SUMMERS: Your Honour, I think Mr. Carby-Samuels wants to address Your Honour. He - he indicates he has a lawyer outside. I've asked him to bring the lawyer into the courtroom. He wants to speak to Your Honour first...

THE COURT: Sure.

MR. SUMMERS: ...before he brings his lawyer into the courtroom.

THE COURT: Okay. Thank you. Okay, thank you. You can have a seat.

MR. SUMMERS: Thank you, Your Honour.

THE COURT: Okay. And Madam Registrar, I'm also just going to give you back the confirmation form for today. I don't need that. Well, actually, no, I will take that back, sorry. All right. Thank you. All right.

So, Mr. Carby-Samuels, I just also first want to make sure that I have your materials. So, I'll - I'll take the same kind of time with you that I've just taken with Mr. Summers. So, I have from you an affidavit sworn May 16, 2017, and then I have -

[handwritten annotations in left margin: "Plaintiff's Lawyer present" / "Travelled from Toronto"] sorry; I have an affidavit from you sworn, hold on, May 9, 2017, and then I have an affidavit sworn by you, and it was filed over the bench with me, I remember getting it, sworn June 21, 2017. And then I also have a factum from you on the motion. So I have three documents from you, and they are all in the 15-66772. Those are the materials that you've filed, correct?

MR. R. CARBY-SAMUELS: Yes, Your Honour, those are the...

THE COURT: Okay.

MR. R. CARBY-SAMUELS: ...materials that I've filed.

THE COURT: Okay. Great. Thank you. And then in the application, which is 17-71624, I don't have any materials from you. So, there's the motion to dismiss your action started in 2015, and you've confirmed to me that the materials we just reviewed are all of your materials on that motion, correct?

MR. R. CARBY-SAMUELS: Which motion are we talking about - summary judgment or vexatious litigation?

THE COURT: The motion for summary judgment.

MR. R. CARBY-SAMUELS: Okay, yeah, because I filed materials for both summary judgment and vexatious litigation.

THE COURT: All in the - all in the same thing.

MR. R. CARBY-SAMUELS: But the materials are not completed because my lawyer has not had an opportunity to file an appropriate response to those particular motions because....

[handwritten margin note: plaintiff's lawyer had not enough time to prepare]

THE COURT: Okay. So, I just - I just want to stop you there...

MR. R. CARBY-SAMUELS: Yes.

THE COURT: ...for one second, if you don't mind, because I have - okay, let me just look at the 17. Okay, I have a factum in 17. Okay. Okay.

So, in the 2017 - so thank you for pointing that out because by going through the file I have found the materials that you filed in the 2017. And what I have found is an affidavit in your name, and it was sworn on May - in May of this year. Then I have a factum from you that was also dated early May of this year. And I have a letter and factum relating - also dated in May - also relating to the application about the vexatious litigate. So, and I have a draft judgment, it would appear, from you.

MR. R. CARBY-SAMUELS: I....

THE COURT: So, those are all the materials you've filed, correct?

MR. R. CARBY-SAMUELS: Those are...

THE COURT: To date.

MR. R. CARBY-SAMUELS: ...materials I've filed to date, but my lawyer needs to - I'm - I'm here to ask permission of Your Honour for my lawyer to be here before I can make - because he wants to ask for an adjournment...

THE COURT: Okay.

MR. R. CARBY-SAMUELS: ...and I need to ask Your Honour's permission first for that.

THE COURT: Okay. Is your lawyer here today?

[Handwritten annotation: Plaintiff's lawyer sought to ask for adjournement]

MR. R. CARBY-SAMUELS: Okay. I'll have to text him.
THE COURT: Okay.
MR. R. CARBY-SAMUELS: Okay. Thank you, Your Honour.
THE COURT: Okay. Thank you.

RECESS
UPON RESUMING

[handwritten note: Mr. Singh present to ask for adjournm^t]

THE COURT: Good morning.
MR. SINGH: Good morning, Your Honour.
THE COURT: So we took a brief break, and I apologize, I was on a professional call when our CSO came up to get me, so, I apologize for the delay in getting back down.

Mr. Singh, you're here, as I understand it from Mr. Carby-Samuels, you're here as a friend of the court?
MR. SINGH: That's correct, Your Honour.
THE COURT: Okay. So let me just see if I can - I may have given those materials back to Madam Registrar. In any event, I did see - I just wanted to get a letter. There was a letter from you that I believe was filed with the Court earlier. It was addressed to Mr. Summers. And that may be in the materials that I gave back to you, Madam Registrar. I'll just flip through, thank you. Here we are. Okay. Thank you.

So, and I'm sorry, I've lost - the letter's from you Mr. Singh. It's undated, and it's to Mr. Summers, and it begins, "Please be advised that I have been recently retained by Mr. Carby-Samuels" and it goes on to speak to a request that Mr. Summers contact your office, and it talks about the passage of time since. And I'm going to call your client, Mr. Carby-Samuels. And Mr. Summers, I'll refer to your client as Horace, H-O-R-A-C-E, just for the sake of clarity, given that we have the same last name. So where it refers to Mr. Carby-Samuels not having been able to see his mom since June. So I don't know the date of your letter, and I don't know if you have a copy of that letter in front of you. Or maybe Mr. Summers, you would be able to tell me....

MR. SUMMERS: I received it June the 1st, Your Honour.

THE COURT: Okay. Thank you. In any event, that's of some help. So that's - I just wanted to understand the date of - of that letter. And so, as I understand it, Mr. Singh, you have some submissions that you want to make as a friend of the court this morning.

MR. SINGH: The, the only - I was speaking to Mr. Samuels outside. He has requested me to help him seek an adjournment for this - this matter. He hasn't filed defence materials to this motion. He - he has had some financial, from what he's told me, he's had some financial issues where he couldn't retain counsel to either act, I mean, act on the motion and make the submissions, or even

[handwritten annotation: Adjournment sought]

APPENDIX 119

MR. SINGH: Those are all for my submissions, Your
Honour.
THE COURT: Okay. So I'll hear from you briefly
Mr. Carby-Samuels.
MR. R. CARBY-SAMUELS: Okay. Your Honour, I
attempted to fulfill the request of Your Honour
with exactitude. The retainer with Mr. Singh was
signed, and I could provide it if Your Honour so
requires it, but I don't have it with me right
here, but a retainer was signed July 7th. Since -
on the wisdom of Justice, Senior Justice McNamara,
and Justice Roger, required and suggested,
vehemently, that I seek a lawyer to fill out the
paperwork, I had to be at the behest of the
schedule of Mr. Singh, who has his own schedule
with respect to clients, and although I - although
I was - signed an agreement on July 7th, with - for
the preparation of the documentation, these
documentation was only delivered, officially,
today, so based upon the vehemence that I get
documentation prepared by a lawyer, I would have
prepared the documentation in a more timely way,
but based upon the wisdom of the court, I had to
wait until Mr. Singh was able to get that
documentation to me. So if Your Honour wants me
to prove to you - to the Court, that I took steps
to get the limited scope retainer signed, then I
can do so. But I had signed - signed everything
with Mr. Singh on July 7th, so it seems to me that
my - I made every effort to comply with Your
Honour's request, and I should not be held in - in
a disadvantage because my efforts to get a lawyer

Registrar, maybe I could have those. And maybe they're in your materials, Mr. Summers.

MR. SUMMERS: I can assist, Your Honour. If you take the application record.

THE COURT: Its okay, Madam Registrar, it's okay. Where would I find those?

MR. SUMMERS: So, exhibits - I'm just confirming the exhibits. With respect to Justice McNamara, it's Exhibit H - sorry, not H, G as in George.

THE COURT: Okay. And I found Roger at Exhibit E.

MR. SUMMERS: Yes.

THE COURT: All right. So, I'm going to ask you both - thank you - to sit down, and I want to read those for a moment.

MR. SUMMERS: Just as further assistance, Your Honour, with Justice McNamara it's in on his last - paragraph 16 is where he addresses the issue of legal advice.

THE COURT: Sorry, paragraph 16. Thank you.

MR. SUMMERS: Sixteen, which is on the last page.

THE COURT: Okay. Thank you. All right.

So, what I see is that Justice Roger recommended in December of 2015 that Mr. Carby-Samuels, and I quote, "should seek legal assistance". It's not shall, but should. And then at page four of the endorsement of Justice McNamara, in concluding his endorsement, he says, "I would echo the comments of Roger, J. that it might prove helpful to the plaintiff to seek some legal advice." And again, it's not mandatory, it's a - it's a recommendation. And so that advice was given in

Reasons for Decision
Corthorn, J.

THE COURT: Okay. Thank you. Could I get the exhibits from you, Madam Registrar, please? That's great. Thank you. All right. I will be back, hopefully no later, no longer than half an hour, and then we can - you'll get my decision. Thank you.

MR. SUMMERS: Thank you, Your Honour.

R E C E S S
U P O N   R E S U M I N G

THE COURT: So I'll give you my reasons on the request for an adjournment.

REASONS FOR DECISION
CORTHORN, J. (Orally):

The parties to these matters are father and son. I refer to the represented party, the father, as Horace, and to the unrepresented party, the son, as Mr. Carby-Samuels.

Mr. Carby-Samuels seeks an adjournment of the motion for summary judgment and the application to have him declared a vexatious litigant. He does so for a number of reasons including the following:

    a) He wishes to file additional materials on both the motion and the application;

    b) He would like to proceed with a motion, sorry, with an urgent motion for interim relief; and

Reasons for Decision
Corthorn, J.

c) He explains his delay with respect to the urgent motion on the basis that he has followed the recommendation of Regional Senior Justice McNamara and Justice Roger that he obtain the assistance of counsel.

On the request for an adjournment, I heard submissions from Mr. Carby-Samuels and from Mr. Singh, a lawyer acting as a friend of the court on Mr. Carby-Samuels behalf.

This is Mr. Carby-Samuels' third request for an adjournment of both the motion for summary judgment, and the application. The first request was made on May 16, 2017, and was granted by Justice Ryan Bell. The adjournment granted at that time was peremptory to Mr. Carby-Samuels. The terms of the adjournment addressed Mr. Carby-Samuels retaining counsel and the availability of counsel retained by him to appear on the new date for the motion, June 21.

At no time prior to June 21 was counsel for Horace advised that Mr. Carby-Samuels had retained counsel, or that counsel, if retained, would not be available to proceed on June 21. The matters came before me on that date. They were adjourned because of a scheduling issue, which resulted in less than sufficient time being available for the matters to be heard. They were also adjourned because Mr. Carby-Samuels, once again indicated that he was in the process of retaining counsel.

Reasons for Decision
Corthorn, J.

I remained seized of the matters, and scheduled both the motion and the application to be heard by me today.

On June 21, Mr. Carby-Samuels stated his intention to proceed with an urgent motion. In adjourning the matters on that date, I included in my endorsement a direction to Mr. Carby-Samuels that if he wished to seek urgent relief, "He shall seek same bye scheduling an urgent motion in the usual manner". No such motion was scheduled by Mr. Carby-Samuels prior to August 14, 2017.

Today he presented in court with a set of materials drafted by Mr. Singh, and delivered to Mr. Carby-Samuels today. I am told that the materials relate to an urgent motion for interim relief.

Mr. Singh advises the court that he is on a limited retainer, in particular to assist Mr. Carby-Samuels by making a demand letter, Exhibit 1 to the motion, and by preparing materials for an urgent motion. Exhibits 2, 3, and 4 to the motion clearly demonstrate that Mr. Singh was made aware of the June 21 return date for the matters, the contents of my endorsement from that date, and the August 14 return date for the matters.

Mr. Singh acknowledges that at no time did he respond to either of the letters, Exhibits 2 and 3, he received from Mr. Summers. To his credit,

… PETER TREMBLAY

Reasons for Decision
Corthorn, J.

he has apologized for not responding. I fully understand that a client is not to be negatively impacted by the conduct of his or her counsel in the event that conduct falls short of professional standards that lawyers are required to meet. I do not rely on Mr. Singh's lack of response in determining the outcome of Mr. Carby-Samuel's request for an adjournment.

I note the recommendations made by Justice Roger, in his December 2015 endorsement, and by RSJ McNamara, in his 2016 endorsement, that Mr. Carby-Samuels seek or obtain the assistance of counsel. Those endorsements were made in the context of the 2015 action commenced by Mr. Carby-Samuels. They were made before the 2017 application on Horace's behalf was issued.

I also emphasize that the contents of both endorsements amount to recommendations only. Mr. Carby-Samuels was not ordered by either Justice Roger or RSJ McNamara to retain counsel to represent him in the 2015 action. There is nothing in the way of an order in either the 2015 action or the 2017 application requiring Mr. Carby-Samuels to be represented.

It has taken Mr. Carby-Samuels since June 2016, if not December 2015, to reach the stage of retaining a lawyer on a limited basis. I am not confident that if Mr. Carby-Samuels is given further time, he will retain counsel to represent him on either the motion for summary judgment or the application.

The word "urgent" must be given meaning in the context of the delays incurred in this matter. Mr. Carby-Samuels has had since May 16, 2017, and since June 21 to arrange for an urgent motion to be scheduled. Mr. Carby-Samuels has not been alone in responding to the May 16 and June 21 endorsements of Justice Ryan Bell, and me, respectively.

Mr. Singh was made aware in a timely manner of the endorsements made on those dates. There has been no communication from either Mr. Carby-Samuels or Mr. Singh to counsel for Horace, advising of Mr. Carby-Samuels intention to:
    a) Seek an adjournment of the motion and the application; and
    b) Proceed with an urgent motion after today's date.

Neither Mr. Carby-Samuels nor Mr. Singh provided counsel for Horace prior to today with a copy of the materials for the proposed urgent motion, even in draft form.

I note that neither Mr. Singh nor Mr. Carby-Samuels identified what, if any, additional materials Mr. Carby-Samuels intends to file on either the motion or the application. Before the request for an adjournment was heard, I reviewed

126 PETER TREMBLAY

Reasons for Decision
Corthorn, J.

with Mr. Carby-Samuels the various materials he has filed to date on the motion, and on the adjournment. Those materials include records and facta.

In his endorsement dated June 2016, RSJ McNamara said, "In view of the nature of the allegations, it is hoped that the parties will move this matter forward as expeditiously as possible." That endorsement was made in the context of Mr. Carby-Samuels' action commenced in 2015. It is more than 1.5 years since that action was commenced. I find that in all of the circumstances, Mr. Carby-Samuels is not entitled to a further adjournment of the motion or the application. I am satisfied that he is not prejudiced by the lack of an adjournment. If the motion for summary judgment is granted, then his action is without merit, and he is not entitled to interim relief. If the motion for summary judgment fails, then the action remains alive, and Mr. Carby-Samuels will be in a position to pursue a motion for interim relief. Similarly, if the application succeeds and Mr. Carby-Samuels is declared a vexatious litigant, then he is not entitled to further interim relief from the Court. If the application is not successful, then Mr. Carby-Samuels is not precluded from proceeding with a motion in the context of his 2015 action for interim relief.

We will proceed first with the motion for summary judgment, and then with the application for a

MR. R. CARBY-SAMUELS: Your Honour, I'm objecting without making of some statements in reply to Your Honour's not granting adjournment. Your Honour made nuances between should and shall, which a civilian ought not to be...

THE COURT: Okay. So...

MR. R. CARBY-SAMUELS: ...required to have.

THE COURT: ...Mr. Carby-Samuels, if you have any issues with my endorsement, the avenue that you have is to - I'm, I'm not sure, depending on what I do, either seek leave to appeal, or appeal it if that's your choice, but I've made my decision and we go with it at this point in time. The avenues of relief that you have arising from my decision are something for you to consider after today.

MR. R. CARBY-SAMUELS: Well, Your Honour...

THE COURT: So....

MR. R. CARBY-SAMUELS: ...that's not possible. If Your Honour declares me a vexatious litigant, I will have no [indiscernible], so because of the gravity, I would like to first comment on these motions being completely inadmissible. And I want to be...

THE COURT: So, I'm...

MR. R. CARBY-SAMUELS: ...treated fairly.

THE COURT: ...going to ask you to - to sit down Mr. Carby-Samuels, and what you will be able to do, is during your submissions, you'll be able to address what you are concerned about in terms of the contents of each of the records. So, I'm going to ask you to sit down, and I'm going to ask Mr. Summers to make his submissions. You'll have

128 PETER TREMBLAY

Submissions by Mr. Summers

his submissions. You'll have the lunch break to speak with Mr. Singh about whatever it is you wish to speak with him about, including any procedural issues, and then after lunch we will deal with your submissions on the motion for summary judgment. But for now...

MR. R. CARBY-SAMUELS: Your Honour, that's a breach of procedure.

THE COURT: ...we're going ahead.

MR. R. CARBY-SAMUELS: Your Honour, that's a breach of procedure. This - the matter cannot be....

THE COURT: I'm going to ask you to sit down Mr. Carby-Samuels, and when Mr. Summers is finished, we'll take a break.

MR. SUMMERS: Thank you, Your Honour. So, Your Honour, I won't go through the case law in any great extent. I know Your Honour is fully aware of the extensive case law regarding motions for summary judgment, and especially the *Court of Appeals* decision in Herniak.

THE COURT: *Supreme Court*.

MR. SUMMERS: I'm sorry, *Supreme Court*, yes. So, I will - I'll just address mainly the facts in my submission on the - on the facts.

SUBMISSIONS BY MR. SUMMERS:

So this action brought by Mr. Carby-Samuels, essentially only seeks to require his father to allow his mother - or to allow him to see his mother.

[annotations in margin: Court interruption [14]; summary judgement ignored complexity of Plaintiff's claim; Best evidentiary foot not put forward.]

Submissions by Mr. Summers

MR. SUMMERS: And so the statement of claim dated December 4, 2015 and is – is no worry that the defendant is Horace Carby-Samuels, the father, and not the mother, who he's seeking access to. And the relief he's seeking, is simply an order directing his father to cease and desist interfering with his ability to see his – his mother. And he sets out the three or four paragraphs to support that.

[handwritten margin: erroneous]

Now, my position in terms of the motion for summary judgment is, first of all, the Court does not have the jurisdiction to order mentally competent individuals interact with anybody, or to allow an adult to allow someone to interact with another adult. There's no dispute that Mr. Carby-Samuels' mother Dezrin, spelled D-E-Z-R-I-N, for the record, is mentally competent.

[handwritten margin: Defence counsel mischaracterizes claim – no affidavit provided on any competence heresay.]

So the question is, is whether the Court....
THE COURT: When you say there is no dispute, I take it you mean that there is no allegation made...
MR. SUMMERS: Yes.
THE COURT: ...that she's mentally incompetent.
MR. SUMMERS: Yes, there's no allegation that she's mentally incompetent.
THE COURT: And I take it there's no – there's no evidence, otherwise, filed on the motion that she's not mental – or that she's mentally incompetent. Am I correct?
MR. SUMMERS: That's correct.

Submissions by Mr. Summers

THE COURT: Okay.
MR. SUMMERS: And that was going to be my next point with respect to the - or with respect to the onus. The onus would be on Mr. Carby-Samuels to bring evidence forth to suggest that his mother was, is mentally incompetent, and that as a result requires court - the Court to become involved in allowing his relief. However, I would submit to you the proper avenue would have been to bring an application under the *Substitute Decisions Act*, if in fact, he did feel that she was mentally incompetent, at which point he would have had to have named her as the - as a respondent as well as the public guardian and trustee.
THE COURT: Okay. Just give me a moment. The public guardian and trustee have to be named as a respondent, or simply be served?
MR. SUMMERS: Simply be served. I apologize, Your Honour.

And I would point out that this fact was brought to Mr. Carby-Samuels' attention at the motion before Justice McNamara when a motion was brought to set aside the - the judgment, and....
THE COURT: Is that reflected in his endorsement?
MR. SUMMERS: It is reflected in his endorsement because at the time Mr. Carby-Samuels had filed - filed a, what seemed to be a notice of motion suggestive of guardianship - or of a request for guardianship of his mother, and Justice McNamara pointed out at that time that the appropriate avenue would have - he'd have to file an

Submissions by Mr. Summers

application for that - for guardianship, name his mother and serve the public guardian and trustee.

So the question becomes is based upon the pleadings and based upon the evidence presented by Mr. Carby-Samuels, is there a genuine issue for trial? Is there something that the court could provide relief for? And it's my respectful submission that there isn't - there is not a genuine issue for trial, and even if all the facts accepted by Mr. Carby - even if all the facts plead in the statement of claim, and or the affidavit material that he submitted were taken as accurate....

THE COURT: I'm just going to stop you for a second.

MR. SUMMERS: Yes.

THE COURT: Mr. Carby-Samuels, are you able to wait until one o'clock to do whatever it is you're doing?

MR. R. CARBY-SAMUELS: No, Your Honour, because - no, Your Honour, because I don't have counsel here, and right now I'm being lynched in a courtroom by - by a lawyer who is being funded by people other than my father who's manipulating in the court process. This whole process is *ultra vires* and unconstitutional, and a - and a lynching. So, I don't consent to this process. If this process is not stopped, then I'm going to be making a complaint to the respective parties because I'm, my rights are not being respected here.

[Handwritten margin notes: Plaintiff objects to not having counsel. Appeals — Virt has counsel]

132   PETER TREMBLAY

Submissions by Mr. Summers

THE COURT: Okay. So, I'm just...
MR. R. CARBY-SAMUELS: It's unconstitutional.
THE COURT: ...asking you Mr. Carby-Samuels, could you just stop whatever it is you're doing, because it's just a little bit distracting and so it's important for me to hear what Mr. Summers has to say, and similarly, when you're making your submissions this afternoon, I'm - I'm certain that Mr. Summers is not going to be making movement or doing things that are distracting. So I'm simply asking you to extend him the same courtesy.
MR. R. CARBY-SAMUELS: I don't - I want to discontinue the whole process. I have to use the washroom, and I'm - this whole process is *ultra vires*. The Court has no authority to hear the inadmissible representation of Mr. Summers. And if it continues...
THE COURT: So....
MR. R. CARBY-SAMUELS: ...this Court - this Court will - you're going to - Your Honour is bringing the matter into dispute by not allowing me to have counsel, and by making distinguishes between should and shall that me, as a self-represented litigant ought not to know. I am being prejudiced by...
THE COURT: Okay, I've heard...
MR. R. CARBY-SAMUELS: ...Your Honour.
THE COURT: ...I've heard you Mr. Carby-Samuels, and I've made my....
MR. R. CARBY-SAMUELS: And this matter cannot continue, and I'm asking you to discontinue this process because it's unconstitutional and *ultra*

[handwritten margin notes: Denial of Legal Counsel / erroneous. / nuances. / to legitimate.]

JOHN SUMMERS - APPENDIX   133

Submissions by Mr. Summers

we'll turn to the application, and we'll go in the same order on that.
MR. SUMMERS: Thank you, Your Honour.
THE COURT: Okay. Thank you.

SUBMISSIONS (CONTINUED) BY MR. SUMMERS:

So, Your Honour, as I was saying before - before the break, there is no genuine issue to be tried in that there's - there's nothing in the, in the record to suggest that the Court even has the jurisdiction, if it were to accept all the facts, as plead by Mr. Carby-Samuels to award any relief that he is - that he is seeking, and....
THE COURT: So, let me just stop you there. So, in terms of, I guess - when you say I - I don't have jurisdiction, or this Court wouldn't have jurisdiction to do what he wants to do, it doesn't have jurisdiction within the context of the claim as framed?
MR. SUMMERS: Yes.
THE COURT: Okay.
MR. SUMMERS: As the uncontested facts are that my client required the assistance of the police to remove his son from his house as a result of the abusive behaviour which both he and his wife were enjoying at the hands of their son.
THE COURT: So, now you're at the - at the affidavit of Horace?
MR. SUMMERS: Yes.
THE COURT: Okay, just a moment.
MR. SUMMERS: And you'll find that affidavit at Tab 2 of the motion record.

134 PETER TREMBLAY

Submissions by Mr. Summers

THE COURT: I have it. Thank you.

MR. SUMMERS: And the - my client had to seek and get the assistance of the Elder Abuse Unit from the city - from the Ottawa Police Force to have their son removed from - from the home. And then he tried to arrange access between Mr. Carby-Samuels, their son, and the mother through the Nepean, Rideau, Osgoode Community Resource Centre, but that resource centre terminated the relationship with Mr. Raymond Carby-Samuels because of his continued - his harassing phone calls to the staff.

THE COURT: Okay. So, when I look at the - the evidence in paragraph ten...

MR. SUMMERS: Yes.

THE COURT: ...that evidence is based on information and belief from somebody at the Nepean, Rideau, Osgoode Community Centre.

MR. SUMMERS: Yes.

THE COURT: But it doesn't say who.

MR. SUMMERS: Yes, you're correct in that, Your Honour, in that I don't have the name of the individual who - who gave that information to - to my client, other than that they were terminating the relationship with - with, or - or no longer supervising the visits.

I guess the one item that you could take from that is that my client has community support, and so....

JOHN SUMMERS – APPENDIX   135

Submissions by Mr. Summers

THE COURT: Well, I may not be able to inasmuch as the affidavit - it doesn't actually comply with the rule regarding affidavit...
MR. SUMMERS: Yes.
THE COURT: ...evidence on information and belief. So....
MR. SUMMERS: And, I mean, you can disregard that paragraph, Your Honour. I don't think it's - it's necessarily germane to the - to the issue because if we're dealing with the motion for summary judgment, again, if you - if you accept all the facts as presented before you, is that Mr. Carby-Samuels lived with his adult parents, both of his adult parents are mentally competent. His parents removed him from the home. They had to seek the assistance of the police to remove him from the home, and no longer want access to him. Now, I....
THE COURT: Well, I guess more properly put, no longer want him to have access to them.
MR. SUMMERS: Yes. Yes, fair enough.
THE COURT: Okay.
MR. SUMMERS: And again, to go back to a point I made earlier, in that, the named defendant is my - is the father, not - not the mother. And so, the issue is whether there's any supporting evidence to suggest that the father has to be compelled to allow his son to see his wife.

Now the onus, I would submit, Your Honour is on Mr. Carby-Samuels to present you with some evidence to support why, first of all the - the

Submissions by Mr. R. Carby-Samuels

[Handwritten margin notes:
Dissembling.
mother's expression of will prevented.
+Evidentiary not forward
failed verifiable.
Fictions or no evidence.
counsel
Heresay
Speculation]

facts that - that would suggest he should be
entitled to see his mother, and more importantly
the law in which she may rely upon to - to support
his position, and he's not done so. And so the
rules provide that summary judgment shall be
granted. If there is no genuine issue for trial,
and I would respectfully submit that since there
is no genuine issue for trial and that Mr. Carby-
Samuels has failed to provide any evidence to
support why his claim as pled would lead to any
award from this Court that the action should be
dismissed.

THE COURT: Thank you.

MR. SUMMERS: Subject to any questions, Your
Honour, those are my submissions.

THE COURT: Okay. Thank you. Okay. So Mr.
Carby-Samuels, I'll hear from you on the motion.
And so this is just the motion. We'll get to the
application later.

MR. R. CARBY-SAMUELS: The motion is for summary
judgment, Your Honour.

THE COURT: Yes.

SUBMISSIONS BY MR. R. CARBY-SAMUELS:

Yes. First I'd like to apologize for the outburst
in part contributing to my needing the washroom
before. It was not intended as a disrespect to my
honourable friend, or Your Honour, but I
apologize. The perception as it might have been
disrespectful, and I wanted to also express my
gratitude to Your Honour for allowing me the, at
least, the opportunity of being able to prepare

Submissions by Mr. R. Carby-Samuels

the urgent motion when you did on a discretionary basis, so I wanted to make sure that Your Honour would - would not - did not receive that my outburst, which is just an internal frustration and using the washroom, and these things that were not intended at all to be disrespectful to Your Honour, which has taken the time out of her valuable schedule to - to hear our motion, and my - my learned friend, not in any respect to both you or the court, which I have sought to respect as much as I could.
THE COURT: Okay. Thank you. Apology accepted. And I'm happy to hear your submissions.
MR. R. CARBY-SAMUELS: Okay. Your Honour, the first thing I would like to say with respect to access to my mom. If I knew for a fact that my mom didn't want to see me, and my father didn't want to see me, I would not be wasting the time of the Court, or my learned friend's time and the expenses associated with his retainer to proceed, but on the matter of access to my mom, all the information which I have is that she still wanted to see me. If I can qualify an answer, Your Honour, directly to what my learned friend was saying, he had said, I believe, Your Honour, you can correct me if I'm wrong, that they arranged for a Nepean, Rideau Community Centre having access to my mom, but the Nepean, Rideau Community Centre only intervene because I had sent a demand letter by my lawyer at the time Todd Ji...
THE COURT: Okay.
MR. R. CARBY-SAMUELS: Todd Ji...

Submissions by Mr. R. Carby-Samuels

THE COURT: So I just...

MR. R. CARBY-SAMUELS: Sorry, Your Honour.

THE COURT: ...want to stop you for a second - oh, no you can stay standing, thank you. I just want to stop you for a second, but I need to know where the evidence is in that regard. So you filed a reply...

MR. R. CARBY-SAMUELS: Yes, Your Honour.

THE COURT: ...and it has all these documents attached...

MR. R. CARBY-SAMUELS: Yes.

THE COURT: ...one to fifteen.

MR. R. CARBY-SAMUELS: Yes, Your Honour.

THE COURT: So in your reply, I would anticipate finding your evidence, and there's - I don't see an affidavit. Oh, yes, I do. Okay, here we are.

MR. R. CARBY-SAMUELS: It should be there, Your Honour.

THE COURT: Number three. It is. And so I'm....

MR. R. CARBY-SAMUELS: It should be there.

THE COURT: And it was - there's an affidavit dated April of 2016. In any event, there's another document - it's not signed, but I need to know where the evidence is that you're relying on. So it needs to come from something that you've filed with the court.

MR. R. CARBY-SAMUELS: Yes, Your Honour. I apologize again to the Court again, I didn't anticipate that I was not going to get an adjournment, so because of that, I don't have any - I don't have that material in front of me to tell you when, but I know, as a fact, Your Honour,

JOHN SUMMERS – APPENDIX 139

Submissions by Mr. R. Carby-Samuels

I could leaf through the material and find the exact letter, but I know as a fact, Your Honour, that I did submit demand letters, Your Honour, from – issued by my lawyer in June, early June 2015, Your Honour, saying that – saying – observing that abuse is taking place in a home that I reported to my lawyer at the time, and saying, and giving him until my father, until a certain period of time in order to release my belongings, Your Honour, and for me to see my mom, and it was based upon, the letter was – I had submit it among some material in – in that I submitted to the court. I could go and – and – and retrieve it, because I'm 100 percent sure I submitted it Your Honour, but...

THE COURT: Okay. And so...

MR. R. CARBY-SAMUELS: ...it was a demand letter.

THE COURT: ...it's a letter from who to who?

MR. R. CARBY-SAMUELS: It was a letter from Todd Ji sent to my father asking him to – giving him a certain period of time for me to see my mom, and to at least my personal and professional belongings, which is a part of my statement of claim, because my father would for weeks, would not....

THE COURT: Okay. That's fine. I just wanted to know...

MR. R. CARBY-SAMUELS: Sorry, Your Honour.

THE COURT: ...from whom to whom.

MR. R. CARBY-SAMUELS: Yes.

THE COURT: So there's a letter from your lawyer to your father...

140   PETER TREMBLAY

                  Submissions by Mr. R. Carby-Samuels

MR. R. CARBY-SAMUELS: Yes.
THE COURT: ...and it's dated June, 2015.
MR. R. CARBY-SAMUELS: It's June - June something
Early June 2015.
THE COURT: Okay. I'll search for it.
MR. R. CARBY-SAMUELS: Yes.
THE COURT: That's fine. Okay. So I've heard
from you in regard to that letter. What's your
next point?
MR. R. CARBY-SAMUELS: My next point, Your Honour
is that my learned friend keeps insinuating, Your
Honour, that it's my parents who wanted me to
remove from the home, but my mom protested
vehemently that - if I can just - let me get that
Your Honour. Sorry for the crinkling. My mom
protested - let me just get that, Your Honour. M
protested vehemently against the actions that wer
taking place to report me to the police.
THE COURT: And are you looking at your - your
materials in the 2015 action, it's titled, Reply
to Applicant's Motion Record, is that what you're
looking at?
MR. R. CARBY-SAMUELS: Well, I - well, Your
Honour, I noted a previous motion, you had - I ha
submitted materials in my mom's handwriting, and
you had told me that I should write the materials
out, so this - where I'm getting, retrieving this
from is from a document entitled, Motion for
Interim Injunction Mandatory Order Ex-Parte...
THE COURT: Okay.
MR. R. CARBY-SAMUELS: ...under....

[Handwritten margin note: Court fails to acknowledge that evidence mom didn't support actions of father.]

JOHN SUMMERS – APPENDIX 141

Submissions by Mr. R. Carby-Samuels

THE COURT: I don't have that in front of me on this motion, and so, what I'm required to rely on in deciding this motion is what you've filed on this motion. So, you've – but if you give me a moment, we'll see what we can do. How many – how many documents are attached to that record?

MR. R. CARBY-SAMUELS: This particular record, well, yeah this record includes....

THE COURT: How many tabs? What's the highest number on the tabs in that document?

MR. R. CARBY-SAMUELS: There's fifteen tabs, oh yeah, but the letter from the – the letter from the lawyer is – one letter, let me see if it's the same one. Just one letter.

THE COURT: Madam...

MR. R. CARBY-SAMUELS: There's 15 tabs here, Your Honour.

THE COURT: ...there's another record with the coloured tabs in there – you'll see it at the back. No, it's at the back. Right. I'll just take a look at that. Thank you.

MR. R. CARBY-SAMUELS: There are 15 tabs and there's one letter from the lawyer, but the other letter is with the courtroom in a statement in other documents. The letter – the demand letter is not in this document. It was another letter in here from my lawyer about the abuse that I had reported.

THE COURT: What tab are you at?

MR. R. CARBY-SAMUELS: Yeah, so the demand – this is the demand letter is among my material, but I wouldn't be able to tell you which....

[handwritten margin note: Letter from Lawyer Tabls]

142   PETER TREMBLAY

                Submissions by Mr. R. Carby-Samuels   (2)

MR. R. CARBY-SAMUELS: So, so if I could ask Your
Honour, because the evidence is not in front of
you, as far as that is, does that preclude me in
your written, whatever you're going to be, to ask
of the Court of submitting it, because I don't
know what's in front of you right now, per se, but
I don't know whether I'm now prohibited from –
from submitting that. If Your Honour is so
[indiscernible] facilitate a decision.

THE COURT: I think there's been ample time, Mr.
Carby-Samuels for you to get materials before the
Court, and I'm not inclined at this point – I'm
not saying I'm ruling it out entirely, but I'm not
inclined at this point to give you additional
time, given that this is the third time this
matter has been before the court.

So, I've got your point about your mother having
written a note to say that she has an interest in
continuing to see you, and I'm going to ask you to
move on to your next point.

MR. R. CARBY-SAMUELS: Okay. My next point, Your
Honour, is that my learned friend, in – in
focusing on summary judgment is based upon the
concept, my understanding that there's no triable
case, and he says that well, I cannot force, you
know, my mom to see me. I would not want to force
my mom to see me, but, so – so my – so my point I
want to move is that my claim is much more complex
than simply accessing my mom.

Submissions by Mr. R. Carby-Samuels

[handwritten margin: unlawful eviction not dealt with]

In my statement of claim, I - part of that was - was not dealt with in the summary judgment is - was in my view, is an illegal eviction, I'm sorry, part of my financial claim, subversion of the *Ontario Landlord and Tenants Act*, illegal and enforcement of eviction, duty of care by evicting me at 2:00 a.m. in the morning without giving me - which put my life in danger to risk in - on terms of the road....

THE COURT: Okay. So, I'm looking at the statement of claim, which is the subject of this motion for summary judgment. And it's the statement of claim that was issued in December 2015 in action number 15-66772. And in it, it is - I'm going to count - it's seven paragraphs long, and it deals only with you being given access to see your mother. It has - it doesn't deal with these other things that you're talking about, making it much more complex.

The only thing the claim that's the subject of this motion deals with, is you having access to your mom.

[handwritten margin: Amended claim dealt with in default judgement]

MR. R. CARBY-SAMUELS: Well, Your Honour, the claim was amended, and this amended documentation - my amended claim was considered by Justice Patrick Smith when he rendered his decision on February - February 11, so all these matters were in my amended claim was submitted to the court. So your court - your court is only getting my first submission. I made a supplementary submission that was made along with the default

Submissions by Mr. R. Carby-Samuels

judgment, which included all the supplementary statements of claim, and as a self-represented litigant, to the best of my knowledge I - I, and the best of my effort, I made it clear that these were amended claims in front of me.

And I have the documentation in front of me, financial claim, Court File 15-66772, which was submitted back in December 2015. The amended statement of claim, which was filed to the best of my knowledge as a self-represented litigant, provides for an itemized list of torts and costs associated with that.

THE COURT: Okay. Just give me a moment. Can you see if there's an amended statement of claim in that box? And you can have a seat. I'm just going to check for the amended statement of claim.

MR. R. CARBY-SAMUELS: It was a part of the default judgment that was submitted to Justice Patrick Smith.

THE COURT: Okay. Well, I've read his judgment and I see that he granted default judgment with respect to access to your mother. It may be, and I see a financial claim in previous materials. It may be that you submitted a document titled Financial Claim, but I don't see a formally amended statement of claim.

MR. R. CARBY-SAMUELS: Your Honour, Patrick Smith awarded access plus $25,000 in costs, and the $25,000 was - in costs, was based upon the amendment that I made which listed all these costs. So he didn't just award access to my mom,

Submissions by Mr. R. Carby-Samuels

he awarded me $25,000 in costs. And I - of costs, which I itemized in my amended statement of claim, which is included in the default motion that I submitted to the Court. So that's why he - the only reason Justice Patrick Smith awarded me $25,000 in costs was because there was the financial claim associated with my mom access - accessing my mom.
THE COURT: Okay. So he didn't award you $25,000 in costs. He awarded you damages of $25,000.
MR. R. CARBY-SAMUELS: Well, it was based upon the $25,000 of itemized costs, which I [indiscernible]. So it wasn't arbitrary, I - my amount of costs which I submitted...
THE COURT: Okay.
MR. R. CARBY-SAMUELS: ...to the judge....
THE COURT: In any event...
MR. R. CARBY-SAMUELS: Yeah.
THE COURT: ...I hear you...
MR. R. CARBY-SAMUELS: Yes.
THE COURT: ...on that, so just give me a moment. All right. Okay. So I have your point that the matter is more complex than simply an issue of access. What's your next point? Can I ask you this? How many more points do you have?
MR. R. CARBY-SAMUELS: I didn't count them. I have a few more, Your Honour. I didn't count them.
THE COURT: Well, I'd like you to tell me how many more you have, because we don't have all afternoon. I've got this matter, the application, and then I have another one, so I don't wish to

Submissions by Mr. R. Carby-Samuels

cut you off, but I also need to deal with this efficiently.

MR. R. CARBY-SAMUELS: I believe I have at least seven or eight more points, Your Honour.

THE COURT: Okay. Well, I need you to go through them quickly.

MR. R. CARBY-SAMUELS: Yes. My - my other point, Your Honour, is that the - based upon Section 96 of the *Court of Justice Act*...

THE COURT: Okay.

MR. R. CARBY-SAMUELS: ...the *Court of Justice Act* deals with equity. And the court being a simultaneously a court of common law and a court of equity. Equity, as - as you might already know, Your Honour, but I'll repeat the points quickly. Equity based upon three particular pillars. Equity will not suffer alone without a remedy. Equity [indiscernible] to do justice and not by [indiscernible] definition and he who comes with equity must come with clean hands. The maxim is expressed by in precision instrument manufacturing corporation, Justice Murphy of the Supreme Court of the United States....

THE COURT: That's okay. I understand the...

MR. R. CARBY-SAMUELS: Okay.

THE COURT: ...concept of...

MR. R. CARBY-SAMUELS: Okay.

THE COURT: ...equity.

MR. R. CARBY-SAMUELS: And so, in terms of clean hands, Your Honour, for more than a year, which is - which is based upon a corresponding claim, my - the defendant lied to police that I suffered from

Submissions by Mr. R. Carby-Samuels

mental illness, as a means of keeping me away from my mom. So, this defendant - and lying to police is a criminal offence. So how, after lying to police that I suffer from mental illness without any remedies, how can a defendant also who - who I reported to police for having stabbed me, and caused me bodily harm back in 2013....

THE COURT: Okay. I'm going to - you're going to need to move on, because I'm looking at the evidence that I have before me, and you don't deal with that in your affidavit. I've, I've made note that you want me to consider equitable principles, and I will do that when I make my decision.

MR. R. CARBY-SAMUELS: Okay.

THE COURT: But you need to move on, because I don't have any evidence regarding - well actually it's in paragraph seven, so I've got it. I've got your point.

MR. R. CARBY-SAMUELS: Okay.

THE COURT: Okay.

MR. R. CARBY-SAMUELS: Okay, but if I could just, as a caveat, Your Honour, my learned friend is being well-financed by - by people, apparently, other than my father. The gravity of summary judgment and vexatious litigant should not - as I can - I can appreciate Your Honour, cannot be taken lightly. I do...

THE COURT: I'm - I'm fully aware of the...

MR. R. CARBY-SAMUELS: Yeah.

THE COURT: ...principles of summary judgment...

MR. R. CARBY-SAMUELS: Yeah.

Submissions by Mr. R. Carby-Samuels

THE COURT: ...and I'm fully aware of the principles of equity. I'm going to ask you for the sake of efficiency...
MR. R. CARBY-SAMUELS: Okay.
THE COURT: ...to move onto your next point.
MR. R. CARBY-SAMUELS: Okay. But....
THE COURT: Thank you.
MR. R. CARBY-SAMUELS: But, I'm just...
THE COURT: No...
MR. R. CARBY-SAMUELS: ...asking you....
THE COURT: ...you've got to move onto your next point.
MR. R. CARBY-SAMUELS: My – my next point with respect to summary judgment, if I – I'll have to – okay. I – I remember what I'm looking – looking for, so I won't bother getting the exact paper, but my next point on summary judgment is that *Rules of Civil Procedure* Section number 20 says that a motion for summary judgment is supposed to be filed after the defence files their statement of defence. After – and the understanding, just as your – Your Honour picked out the nuance of should and shall, after does not mean you wait a year to file a summary judgment. In my view, it's an abuse of process to be waiting a period of approximately a year in order to file a summary judgment as the....
THE COURT: Are you telling me there's no statement of defence in this matter?
MR. R. CARBY-SAMUELS: There's a statement of defence, Your Honour...
THE COURT: Okay.

John Summers – Appendix 149

Submissions by Mr. R. Carby-Samuels

[Handwritten margin note: Summary Judgement not done in a timely manner is required.]

MR. R. CARBY-SAMUELS: ...but they waited over – they waited – the statement of defence was filed, and the – and the summary judgment was filed approximately a year apart, and as the....

THE COURT: So, I'm sorry – so the statement of defence was filed and then a year later they moved for summary judgment?

MR. R. CARBY-SAMUELS: Approximately, yes, Your Honour.

THE COURT: Okay. That's fine. I have the point

MR. R. CARBY-SAMUELS: It was filed a year, and that's after means in a timely manner. After does not mean you wait months and months and months and months in order to file a summary judgment which ends up creating costs.

[Handwritten margin note: mandatory mediation request from lawyer ignored]

My other point with that, Your Honour, to – to, as a supplement to that, my lawyer – lawyer, Ms. Peter (ph) back in January requested that a trial go to mandatory mediation – mandatory....

THE COURT: So I just...

MR. R. CARBY-SAMUELS: Yeah.

THE COURT: ...want to understand...

MR. R. CARBY-SAMUELS: Yeah.

THE COURT: ...with respect to you're – you're concerned about the timing?

MR. R. CARBY-SAMUELS: Yes, Your Honour.

THE COURT: Okay. So, I have your point about Rule 20.01(3), I've got that. What's your next point?

MR. R. CARBY-SAMUELS: My next point – my next point with that, Your Honour, is that Justice

Submissions by Mr. R. Carby-Samuels

David M. Brown of the Superior Court had ruled that - had observed that lawyers are abusing summary judgment to create....
THE COURT: I'm - I'm aware of...
MR. R. CARBY-SAMUELS: Yeah.
THE COURT: ...Justice Brown's comments about the process.
MR. R. CARBY-SAMUELS: Yeah, and they're abusive and they're just racking up costs unnecessarily when - and disrespecting the full appreciation test...
THE COURT: Okay.
MR. R. CARBY-SAMUELS: ...and that is of complex litigation when matters ought to be sent to trial rather than trying to use up the - the summary judgment process to not only...
THE COURT: Okay.
MR. R. CARBY-SAMUELS: ...create more costs, but billable hours for the lawyer.
THE COURT: Okay.
MR. R. CARBY-SAMUELS: That's my point on that.
THE COURT: Got it. Thank you.
MR. R. CARBY-SAMUELS: Abuse of process.
THE COURT: Okay. Thank you.
THE COURT: My other - my other point I want to make in terms of summary judgment is that both in Toronto and Ottawa, both of these jurisdictions require a process of mandatory mediation that - that the lawyer that - that a lawyer wrote to Mr. Summers about, and he in turn replied to the lawyer saying that, "well I'm in the process of

Submissions by Mr. R. Carby-Samuels

preparing a summary judgment so", if I can get that letter, Your Honour. Let me get that letter.
THE COURT: Is your point, Mr. Carby-Samuels that in your view this matter should have gone to mediation before a motion for summary judgment was pursued?
MR. R. CARBY-SAMUELS: Yes, it has...
THE COURT: I have that point.
MR. R. CARBY-SAMUELS: ...because my - because there's a mandatory mediation process based upon the time it should have went into mediation, based upon the time any summary judgment should have been if it was a sincere presentation of summary judgment, should have been made right after and the...
THE COURT: I have your point.
MR. R. CARBY-SAMUELS: ...issue is that, yeah....
THE COURT: I have your point on timing, both in terms of the statement of defence and before or after mediation. Is there anything else?
MR. R. CARBY-SAMUELS: So, so my - so, so just as Your Honour distinguished between should and shall...
THE COURT: Mm-hmm.
MR. R. CARBY-SAMUELS: ...mandatory means there's no flexibility.
THE COURT: Yeah, I have that point.
MR. R. CARBY-SAMUELS: Okay.
THE COURT: I have that point.
MR. R. CARBY-SAMUELS: Okay. You have that point.
THE COURT: So I need you to move on to your next point.

Submissions by Mr. R. Carby-Samuels

MR. R. CARBY-SAMUELS: Okay. So....

THE COURT: If you have one, or perhaps you're done.

MR. R. CARBY-SAMUELS: Okay. And my next point on summary judgment is that it has been ruled in previous decisions that the timing of - timing of summary judgment is a fact for dismissal, so I just want to mention, Your Honour, that Your Honour was aware that judges have ruled against summary judgment surely on the fact that it was a - a....

THE COURT: This is not my first motion for...

MR. R. CARBY-SAMUELS: Okay.

THE COURT: ...summary judgment. I'm well into double digits on motions for summary judgment, and in my decisions on it, I'm fully aware of - of timing and - so no worries about that.

MR. R. CARBY-SAMUELS: Okay. So on my next point on - my next point on summary judgment is that the - the affidavit is inadequate to deal with the complexity of the request of the - of the - my learned friend. My learned friend....

THE COURT: In what way is it inadequate?

MR. R. CARBY-SAMUELS: It's inadequate because the - the - the affidavit is based upon hearsay representation about what my parents want, when - when there's no - there's no independent verification at all what the - what the defendant is asserting regarding the intent of him and my mother - what they want to do. And all the statements he made is pure hearsay inadmissible.

CITATION: *Carby-Samuels II v. Carby-Samuels*, 2017 ONSC 6814
COURT FILE NO.: 15-66772
DATE: 2017/11/16

ONTARIO

SUPERIOR COURT OF JUSTICE

BETWEEN:

Raymond Carby-Samuels II

Plaintiff

– and –

Horace R. Carby-Samuels

Defendant

**RULING ON MOTION
FOR SUMMARY JUDGMENT**

Madam Justice Sylvia Corthorn

Released: November 16, 2017

CITATION: *Carby-Samuels II v. Carby-Samuels*, 2017 ONSC 6814
COURT FILE NO.: 15-66772
DATE: 2017/11/16

ONTARIO
SUPERIOR COURT OF JUSTICE

BETWEEN:

Raymond Carby-Samuels II

Plaintiff

Self-represented

– and –

Horace R. Carby-Samuels

Defendant

John E. Summers, for the Defendant

HEARD: August 14, 2017

RULING ON MOTION FOR SUMMARY JUDGMENT

CORTHORN, J.

Overview

[1] The parties to this action are father (Horace Carby-Samuels) and son (Raymond Carby-Samuels II). This action is one of a number of proceedings pursued by Raymond in 2015, 2016, and 2017 arising from the difficult relationship between him and his parents. On the same date this motion for summary judgment was heard, I heard an application by Horace with respect to vexatious proceedings.

[2] At the heart of the numerous proceedings are:

   a). Raymond's concern for the well-being of his mother (Dezrin Carby-Samuels), now in her mid-eighties; and

   b) The disagreement between father and son as to the nature and quality of care Dezrin requires.

[3] The relationship between Raymond and his parents is difficult and troublesome for all concerned. The question raised by the motion for summary judgment is whether litigation in this court provides a vehicle for resolution of the strife within the Carby-Samuels family.

Issues

[4] The two issues to be determined are:

> *[handwritten: Factually incorrect. fails to acknowledge torts documented to co...]*

1) Is the defendant entitled to summary judgment in the form of an order dismissing the action?

2) Alternatively, is the plaintiff entitled to leave of the court to amend his pleading as per the draft "Financial Claim" included as an exhibit to the plaintiff's responding affidavit?

Disposition

[handwritten: Leeway to self-rep. litigant ignore]

[5] The defendant is granted summary judgment; the action is dismissed.

[6] The plaintiff did not bring either a formal motion or cross-motion for leave to amend his statement of claim. Regardless, I have considered his request for leave to amend his pleading. I find that the plaintiff is not entitled to leave to amend his pleading. The motion for leave to amend the pleading is dismissed.

[handwritten: Reasonable apprehension of bias - ignores Court of appeal ruling. - Sanzone v. Schecke]

Issue No. 1 – Summary Judgment

[7] The existing statement of claim:

- Includes only Horace Carby-Samuels as a defendant;
- Does not include any allegation that Dezrin Carby-Samuels is mentally incompetent; and
- Includes as the relief sought, an order permitting Raymond to see his mother Dezrin.

[8] The specific relief sought is limited to the following single paragraph:

> [A]n Order directing Horace Carby-Samuels to cease and desist interfering in the ability of Raymond Carby-Samuels II and the Plaintiff's disabled and sick Mom, Dezrin Carby-Samuels to see each other; and to immediately enable access to each other, without further delay, at a mutually convenient location for both the Plaintiff and the Plaintiff's mother that takes into consideration the disabilities of the Plaintiff's mother.

[handwritten bottom left: Oral transcripts confirms that...]

[handwritten bottom right: Torts were presently in Default motion and a part of...]

[9] The pleading identifies that the action is brought pursuant to Rule 76 of the *Rules of Civil Procedure*. There are four substantive paragraphs in the pleading. In summary the allegations are:

- Horace treats Dezrin as his "property", forcibly confines her, and prevents her from exercising her right of freedom of association (i.e. to see Raymond);

- Horace's conduct is illegal and in contravention of the *Charter of Rights and Freedoms* and the *Criminal Code*. (No sections of either the *Charter* or the *Code* are specifically cited in the pleading.); and

- Dezrin provided Raymond with documentary evidence of the abuse and neglect she has suffered by reason of Horace's conduct. Dezrin also documented her desire to see her son.

[10] There is no evidence on the motion to support a finding that Dezrin is mentally incompetent with respect to personal care. Horace's evidence is that he and Dezrin have chosen not to see their son because of the difficulties encountered when he spends time with one or both of them. Horace was not cross-examined on his affidavit. I accept his evidence in that regard.

[11] The court does not have jurisdiction to make an order requiring a mentally competent adult (Dezrin) to interact with another individual. Therefore, even if Dezrin were named as a defendant in the action, the court would not be in a position to compel her to see her son.

[12] The court does not have jurisdiction to make an order compelling a mentally competent adult (Horace) to require another mentally competent adult (Dezrin) to interact with a third family member (Raymond).

[13] Based on the statement of claim as currently drafted, there is no genuine issue for trial. I am satisfied, having considered the affidavit evidence and the substance of the pleading, that granting summary judgment is a proportionate, expeditious, and cost-effective means by which to achieve a just result in this matter.

[14] In response to the motion for summary judgment, the plaintiff seeks leave to amend his pleading. Only if the plaintiff is entitled to leave to amend his pleading will the dismissal of the action be avoided.

[18] In support of the proposed amendments to the pleading, the plaintiff filed a 42-paragraph affidavit (sworn on May 9, 2017). The affidavit is deficient in a number of ways:

- It makes reference to statements made or information provided by others, without including any confirmation that the affiant believes the statements or information to be true. To the extent that hearsay evidence is permissible on a motion, the relevant portions of the affidavit do not comply with the requirements of hearsay evidence;

- The plaintiff includes his opinion with respect to Dezrin's medical condition (including Type II Diabetes). The plaintiff is not a medical expert; and

- The affidavit includes entirely unsubstantiated allegations of conspiracy on the part of a number of individuals (Marcella, counsel for Horace, and police officers).

[19] The plaintiff's affidavit includes very limited evidence that is admissible on the motion. Of the proposed claims, the only such claim supported by admissible evidence is that with respect to an assault alleged to have occurred in early 2013. In summary, the plaintiff alleges that as a result of an altercation between him and his father in the kitchen of the family home, the plaintiff suffered an injury to the small finger on his left hand.

[20] Included as an exhibit to the plaintiff's affidavit is a copy of a Civilian Witness Statement from an Ottawa Police Service General Occurrence Report dated January 2013. The statement is handwritten and difficult to read. In the statement, the plaintiff describes the alleged assault by the defendant.

[21] Also included as an exhibit to the plaintiff's affidavit is a copy of a March 2013 letter from a physician. In the letter, the physician refers to surgery conducted in March and identifies that the plaintiff was to remain off work for four weeks (until mid-April). In the proposed pleading it is alleged that the plaintiff missed six months of work because of the injury to the small finger on the plaintiff's left hand. There is no evidence as to the nature of the plaintiff's employment at the time.

[22] I am satisfied that the plaintiff knew by no later than the summer of 2013 (the end of the six-month absence from work) of the matters giving rise to a claim based on the alleged assault in January 2013. More than two years have passed since "the day on which a reasonable person with the abilities and in the circumstances of [the plaintiff] first ought to have known of the matters" giving rise to a claim based on the alleged assault (*Limitations Act, 2002*, S.O. 2002, c. 24, Sched. B, ss.4 and 5(1)(b)). Even allowing for discoverability, the plaintiff's proposed claim with respect to the January 2013 incident is out of time.

[23] The proposed amended pleading is, when considered in its entirety, in keeping with the nature of a vexatious pleading. A general characteristic of vexatious proceedings is that the matters raised from one proceeding "tend to be rolled forward into subsequent actions and repeated and supplemented" (*Lang Michener Lash Johnston v. Fabian* (1987), 59 O.R. (2d) 353, 37 D.L.R. (4th) 685 (H.C.), at para. 20).

[24] When the proposed amended pleading is read together with the pleadings in other actions commenced by the plaintiff in this court, the Small Claims Court, and the Federal Court of Canada, the rolling forward, repetition, and supplementing are obvious. Leaving aside the lack of admissible evidence to support the claims advanced in the proposed amended pleading, and the expiration of the limitation period with respect to the claims arising from the alleged assault, the proposed amended pleading constitutes a vexatious proceeding.

[25] In the companion application by Horace for relief from vexatious proceedings, I found that the plaintiff pursued vexatious proceedings or conducted proceedings in a vexatious manner (*Carby-Samuels v. Carby-Samuels II*, 2017 ONSC 6834). Had I not heard this motion for summary judgment at the same time, the relief granted on the application would have addressed this action. The relief would have included that the plaintiff is not permitted to proceed with this action without obtaining leave of a judge of the Superior Court of Justice in accordance with section 140(3) of the *Courts of Justice Act*, R.S.O. 1990, c. C.43. This action would have been brought to a conclusion in the context of the application to address vexatious proceedings.

[26] The plaintiff's motion for leave to amend his pleading is dismissed.

Summary

[27] I order as follows:

1. The action is dismissed.

2. The plaintiff's motion for leave to amend his pleading is dismissed.

Costs

[28] The history of this proceeding is set out in my decision on the related application. The history includes that a default judgment obtained by the plaintiff was set aside. In his reasons on the motion to set aside the default judgment, Regional Senior Justice McNamara ordered that costs of the motion be in the cause.

[29] The history of this proceeding also includes the plaintiff's motion, heard by me several weeks ago, for leave to bring an urgent motion. The plaintiff's request for leave was denied. There were no costs ordered on the motion.

[30]   I find no reason to deprive the defendant of his reasonable costs of the motion for summary judgment. Given his success on this, the defendant is entitled to his costs of the motion.

[31]   In addressing costs of the action, I therefore consider the costs incurred by the defendant on (a) his motion to set aside the default judgment, and (b) the motion for summary judgment.

a) Scale of Costs

[32]   I have considered the factors in rule 57.01 of the *Rules of Civil Procedure*. I find that the defendant is entitled to costs of both motions on a partial indemnity basis.

b) Amount of Costs

[33]   At the conclusion of the motion for summary judgment, counsel filed a costs envelope. I rely on the contents of that envelope in determining the amount of costs payable.

[34]   Counsel for the defendant has 18 years of experience at the bar; his full indemnity hourly rate is $325. That hourly rate is reasonable for counsel of that level of experience. Therefore, the partial indemnity hourly rate to be used in the context of fixing costs is $195 (0.6 x $325).

- *Motion to Set Aside Default Judgment*

[35]   A copy of the defendant's motion record on the motion to set aside the default judgment is included as an exhibit to the plaintiff's affidavit in response to the motion for summary judgment. As a result, I have documents to assist in assessing the reasonableness of the fees and disbursements claimed with respect to that motion.

[36]   On the motion for default judgment, counsel's total docketed time is 9.7 hours, including attending on the return of the motion. I find that amount of time to be reasonable for the work done. The partial indemnity costs claimed are:

Fees (9.7 x $195)	$ 1,891.50
H.S.T. on fees	$ 245.90
Disbursements (filing fee)	$ 121.00
Total	$ 2,258.40

- *Motion for Summary Judgment*

[37]   On the motion for summary judgment, the total time is 13.5 hours—including attendance on two adjournments and on the return of the motion. My only concern with respect to the amount of time is the inclusion of time for attendance on the adjournments.

[38] The only adjournment of the motion (from June to August, 2017) was the result of judicial time constraints and my inability to hear the motion in the time allotted on the given day. It would not be reasonable to require the plaintiff to pay the costs associated with that adjournment.

[39] On the return of the motion in August, the plaintiff again sought an adjournment. That adjournment was contested and refused. I find that the amount of time required to address the contested adjournment did not result in a significant increase in the amount of time otherwise required on the return of the motion.

[40] I reduce the time on the motion for summary judgment to 11 hours (estimating 2.5 hours in total for the two adjournments).

[41] The partial indemnity costs claimed on the motion for summary judgment are:

Fees (11 x $195)	$ 2,145.00
H.S.T. on fees	$ 278.85
Disbursements	
Filing fee	$ 160.00
Statement of defence	$ 154.00
Total	$ 2,737.85

- *Total Partial Indemnity Costs*

[42] The total partial indemnity costs claimed are $4,996.25 ($2,258.40 + $2,737.85). I round that figure to $4,995.

[43] The plaintiff shall pay to the defendant his costs of this action, on a partial indemnity basis, in the amount of $4,995.

Other Matters

[44] As I did in my decision on the related application, I dispense with the requirement for the approval of the plaintiff to the form and content of the order to be taken out arising from this ruling. The draft order shall be prepared by counsel for the defendant and submitted to the civil counter with the specific direction that the order is for my signature.

Madam Justice Sylvia Corthorn

Released: November 16, 2017

CITATION: *Carby-Samuels II v. Carby-Samuels*, 2017 ONSC 6814
COURT FILE NO.: 15-66772
DATE: 2017/11/16

ONTARIO

SUPERIOR COURT OF JUSTICE

BETWEEN:

Raymond Carby-Samuels II

Plaintiff

– and –

Horace R. Carby-Samuels

Defendant

**RULING ON MOTION
FOR SUMMARY JUDGMENT**

Madam Justice Sylvia Corthorn

Released: November 16, 2017

CITATION: *Carby-Samuels II v. Carby-Samuels*, 2017 ONSC 6814
COURT FILE NO.: 15-66772
DATE: 2017/11/16

ONTARIO

SUPERIOR COURT OF JUSTICE

BETWEEN:

Raymond Carby-Samuels II

Plaintiff

– and –

Horace R. Carby-Samuels

Defendant

Self-represented

John E. Summers, for the Defendant

HEARD: August 14, 2017

RULING ON MOTION FOR SUMMARY JUDGMENT

CORTHORN, J.

Overview

[1] The parties to this action are father (Horace Carby-Samuels) and son (Raymond Carby-Samuels II). This action is one of a number of proceedings pursued by Raymond in 2015, 2016, and 2017 arising from the difficult relationship between him and his parents. On the same date this motion for summary judgment was heard, I heard an application by Horace with respect to vexatious proceedings.

[2] At the heart of the numerous proceedings are:

a) Raymond's concern for the well-being of his mother (Dezrin Carby-Samuels), now in her mid-eighties; and

b) The disagreement between father and son as to the nature and quality of care Dezrin requires.

[3] The relationship between Raymond and his parents is difficult and troublesome for all concerned. The question raised by the motion for summary judgment is whether litigation in this court provides a vehicle for resolution of the strife within the Carby-Samuels family.

Issues

[4] The two issues to be determined are:

1) Is the defendant entitled to summary judgment in the form of an order dismissing the action?

2) Alternatively, is the plaintiff entitled to leave of the court to amend his pleading as per the draft "Financial Claim" included as an exhibit to the plaintiff's responding affidavit?

Disposition

[5] The defendant is granted summary judgment; the action is dismissed.

[6] The plaintiff did not bring either a formal motion or cross-motion for leave to amend his statement of claim. Regardless, I have considered his request for leave to amend his pleading. I find that the plaintiff is not entitled to leave to amend his pleading. The motion for leave to amend the pleading is dismissed.

Issue No. 1 – Summary Judgment

[7] The existing statement of claim:

- Includes only Horace Carby-Samuels as a defendant;
- Does not include any allegation that Dezrin Carby-Samuels is mentally incompetent; and
- Includes as the relief sought, an order permitting Raymond to see his mother Dezrin.

[8] The specific relief sought is limited to the following single paragraph:

> [A]n Order directing Horace Carby-Samuels to cease and desist interfering in the ability of Raymond Carby-Samuels II and the Plaintiff's disabled and sick Mom, Dezrin Carby-Samuels to see each other; and to immediately enable access to each other, without further delay, at a mutually convenient location for both the Plaintiff and the Plaintiff's mother that takes into consideration the disabilities of the Plaintiff's mother.

[9] The pleading identifies that the action is brought pursuant to Rule 76 of the *Rules of Civil Procedure*. There are four substantive paragraphs in the pleading. In summary the allegations are:

- Horace treats Dezrin as his "property", forcibly confines her, and prevents her from exercising her right of freedom of association (i.e. to see Raymond);

- Horace's conduct is illegal and in contravention of the *Charter of Rights and Freedoms* and the *Criminal Code*. (No sections of either the *Charter* or the *Code* are specifically cited in the pleading.); and

- Dezrin provided Raymond with documentary evidence of the abuse and neglect she has suffered by reason of Horace's conduct. Dezrin also documented her desire to see her son.

[10] There is no evidence on the motion to support a finding that Dezrin is mentally incompetent with respect to personal care. Horace's evidence is that he and Dezrin have chosen not to see their son because of the difficulties encountered when he spends time with one or both of them. Horace was not cross-examined on his affidavit. I accept his evidence in that regard.

[11] The court does not have jurisdiction to make an order requiring a mentally competent adult (Dezrin) to interact with another individual. Therefore, even if Dezrin were named as a defendant in the action, the court would not be in a position to compel her to see her son.

[12] The court does not have jurisdiction to make an order compelling a mentally competent adult (Horace) to require another mentally competent adult (Dezrin) to interact with a third family member (Raymond).

[13] Based on the statement of claim as currently drafted, there is no genuine issue for trial. I am satisfied, having considered the affidavit evidence and the substance of the pleading, that granting summary judgment is a proportionate, expeditious, and cost-effective means by which to achieve a just result in this matter.

[14] In response to the motion for summary judgment, the plaintiff seeks leave to amend his pleading. Only if the plaintiff is entitled to leave to amend his pleading will the dismissal of the action be avoided.

Issue No. 2 – Proposed Amended Pleading

[15] The draft amended pleading included in the plaintiff's responding motion record identifies numerous claims not included in the original pleading. The amended portions of the pleading are not underlined; as such, the draft pleading does not comply with the *Rules of Civil Procedure*. Regardless of the technical deficiencies in the proposed amended pleading, I have considered the substance of the proposed allegations.

[16] The plaintiff calls the draft pleading "Financial Claim", presumably in an effort to highlight that he seeks compensation in addition to non-monetary relief. For example, the monetary relief sought includes:

- Damages in the amount of $5,000 for "illegal eviction" from his parents' home in April 2015;

- Damages in the amount of $4,500 from the defendant arising from an assault alleged to have occurred in 2013;

- Damages totalling $1,000 from the plaintiff's sister, Marcella, for an assault and battery alleged to have occurred in early 2015. Marcella is not named as a defendant in the original pleading and her name does not appear in the title of proceeding in the proposed amended pleading;

- Damages in the amount of $2,000 from Marcella because she hired a member of the Ottawa Police Service to harass the plaintiff; and

- Damages in the amount of $3,000 from Horace and Marcella on the basis of intentional infliction of mental distress and/or conspiracy. In that regard, the plaintiff alleges that both Marcella and Horace fall within the definition of "psychopath", based on an episode of CBC Television's "The Doc Zone".

[17] The proposed amended pleading includes a claim in "Detinue / Trover / Rei Vindicatio". The plaintiff alleges that the defendant is denying the plaintiff access to his personal belongings. An allegation is also made that Horace and Marcella conspired with the Ottawa Police Service so as to cause the police to make a "false arrest" of the plaintiff. The plaintiff alleges that the Ottawa Police Service, acting as agents of Horace and Marcella, have defamed and slandered him.

[18]   In support of the proposed amendments to the pleading, the plaintiff filed a 42-paragraph affidavit (sworn on May 9, 2017). The affidavit is deficient in a number of ways:

- It makes reference to statements made or information provided by others, without including any confirmation that the affiant believes the statements or information to be true. To the extent that hearsay evidence is permissible on a motion, the relevant portions of the affidavit do not comply with the requirements of hearsay evidence;

- The plaintiff includes his opinion with respect to Dezrin's medical condition (including Type II Diabetes). The plaintiff is not a medical expert; and

- The affidavit includes entirely unsubstantiated allegations of conspiracy on the part of a number of individuals (Marcella, counsel for Horace, and police officers).

[19]   The plaintiff's affidavit includes very limited evidence that is admissible on the motion. Of the proposed claims, the only such claim supported by admissible evidence is that with respect to an assault alleged to have occurred in early 2013. In summary, the plaintiff alleges that as a result of an altercation between him and his father in the kitchen of the family home, the plaintiff suffered an injury to the small finger on his left hand.

[20]   Included as an exhibit to the plaintiff's affidavit is a copy of a Civilian Witness Statement from an Ottawa Police Service General Occurrence Report dated January 2013. The statement is handwritten and difficult to read. In the statement, the plaintiff describes the alleged assault by the defendant.

[21]   Also included as an exhibit to the plaintiff's affidavit is a copy of a March 2013 letter from a physician. In the letter, the physician refers to surgery conducted in March and identifies that the plaintiff was to remain off work for four weeks (until mid-April). In the proposed pleading it is alleged that the plaintiff missed six months of work because of the injury to the small finger on the plaintiff's left hand. There is no evidence as to the nature of the plaintiff's employment at the time.

[22]   I am satisfied that the plaintiff knew by no later than the summer of 2013 (the end of the six-month absence from work) of the matters giving rise to a claim based on the alleged assault in January 2013. More than two years have passed since "the day on which a reasonable person with the abilities and in the circumstances of [the plaintiff] first ought to have known of the matters" giving rise to a claim based on the alleged assault (*Limitations Act, 2002*, S.O. 2002, c. 24, Sched. B, ss.4 and 5(1)(b)). Even allowing for discoverability, the plaintiff's proposed claim with respect to the January 2013 incident is out of time.

[23] The proposed amended pleading is, when considered in its entirety, in keeping with the nature of a vexatious pleading. A general characteristic of vexatious proceedings is that the matters raised from one proceeding "tend to be rolled forward into subsequent actions and repeated and supplemented" (*Lang Michener Lash Johnston v. Fabian* (1987), 59 O.R. (2d) 353, 37 D.L.R. (4th) 685 (H.C.), at para. 20).

[24] When the proposed amended pleading is read together with the pleadings in other actions commenced by the plaintiff in this court, the Small Claims Court, and the Federal Court of Canada, the rolling forward, repetition, and supplementing are obvious. Leaving aside the lack of admissible evidence to support the claims advanced in the proposed amended pleading, and the expiration of the limitation period with respect to the claims arising from the alleged assault, the proposed amended pleading constitutes a vexatious proceeding.

[25] In the companion application by Horace for relief from vexatious proceedings, I found that the plaintiff pursued vexatious proceedings or conducted proceedings in a vexatious manner (*Carby-Samuels v. Carby-Samuels II*, 2017 ONSC 6834). Had I not heard this motion for summary judgment at the same time, the relief granted on the application would have addressed this action. The relief would have included that the plaintiff is not permitted to proceed with this action without obtaining leave of a judge of the Superior Court of Justice in accordance with section 140(3) of the *Courts of Justice Act*, R.S.O. 1990, c. C.43. This action would have been brought to a conclusion in the context of the application to address vexatious proceedings.

[26] The plaintiff's motion for leave to amend his pleading is dismissed.

Summary

[27] I order as follows:

1. The action is dismissed.

2. The plaintiff's motion for leave to amend his pleading is dismissed.

Costs

[28] The history of this proceeding is set out in my decision on the related application. The history includes that a default judgment obtained by the plaintiff was set aside. In his reasons on the motion to set aside the default judgment, Regional Senior Justice McNamara ordered that costs of the motion be in the cause.

[29] The history of this proceeding also includes the plaintiff's motion, heard by me several weeks ago, for leave to bring an urgent motion. The plaintiff's request for leave was denied. There were no costs ordered on the motion.

[30] I find no reason to deprive the defendant of his reasonable costs of the motion for summary judgment. Given his success on this, the defendant is entitled to his costs of the motion.

[31] In addressing costs of the action, I therefore consider the costs incurred by the defendant on (a) his motion to set aside the default judgment, and (b) the motion for summary judgment.

a) Scale of Costs

[32] I have considered the factors in rule 57.01 of the *Rules of Civil Procedure*. I find that the defendant is entitled to costs of both motions on a partial indemnity basis.

b) Amount of Costs

[33] At the conclusion of the motion for summary judgment, counsel filed a costs envelope. I rely on the contents of that envelope in determining the amount of costs payable.

[34] Counsel for the defendant has 18 years of experience at the bar; his full indemnity hourly rate is $325. That hourly rate is reasonable for counsel of that level of experience. Therefore, the partial indemnity hourly rate to be used in the context of fixing costs is $195 (0.6 x $325).

- **Motion to Set Aside Default Judgment**

[35] A copy of the defendant's motion record on the motion to set aside the default judgment is included as an exhibit to the plaintiff's affidavit in response to the motion for summary judgment. As a result, I have documents to assist in assessing the reasonableness of the fees and disbursements claimed with respect to that motion.

[36] On the motion for default judgment, counsel's total docketed time is 9.7 hours, including attending on the return of the motion. I find that amount of time to be reasonable for the work done. The partial indemnity costs claimed are:

Fees (9.7 x $195)	$ 1,891.50
H.S.T. on fees	$ 245.90
Disbursements (filing fee)	$ 121.00
Total	$ 2,258.40

- **Motion for Summary Judgment**

[37] On the motion for summary judgment, the total time is 13.5 hours—including attendance on two adjournments and on the return of the motion. My only concern with respect to the amount of time is the inclusion of time for attendance on the adjournments.

[38] The only adjournment of the motion (from June to August, 2017) was the result of judicial time constraints and my inability to hear the motion in the time allotted on the given day. It would not be reasonable to require the plaintiff to pay the costs associated with that adjournment.

[39] On the return of the motion in August, the plaintiff again sought an adjournment. That adjournment was contested and refused. I find that the amount of time required to address the contested adjournment did not result in a significant increase in the amount of time otherwise required on the return of the motion.

[40] I reduce the time on the motion for summary judgment to 11 hours (estimating 2.5 hours in total for the two adjournments).

[41] The partial indemnity costs claimed on the motion for summary judgment are:

Fees (11 x $195)	$ 2,145.00
H.S.T. on fees	$ 278.85
Disbursements	
Filing fee	$ 160.00
Statement of defence	$ 154.00
Total	$ 2,737.85

- *Total Partial Indemnity Costs*

[42] The total partial indemnity costs claimed are $4,996.25 ($2,258.40 + $2,737.85). I round that figure to $4,995.

[43] The plaintiff shall pay to the defendant his costs of this action, on a partial indemnity basis, in the amount of $4,995.

Other Matters

[44] As I did in my decision on the related application, I dispense with the requirement for the approval of the plaintiff to the form and content of the order to be taken out arising from this ruling. The draft order shall be prepared by counsel for the defendant and submitted to the civil counter with the specific direction that the order is for my signature.

Madam Justice Sylvia Corthorn

Released: November 16, 2017

Court File No: 15-66772

ONTARIO
SUPERIOR COURT OF JUSTICE

BEFORE THE HONOURABLE MADAM JUSTICE SYLVIA CORTHORN	))	THURSDAY, THE 16th DAY OF NOVEMBER 2017

BETWEEN:

RAYMOND CARBY-SAMUELS II

Plaintiff

- and -

HORACE R. CARBY-SAMUELS

Defendant

ORDER

THIS MOTION made by the Defendant was heard this day at the Court House, 161 Elgin Street, Ottawa, ON.

UPON HEARING the submissions of the parties on Summary Judgment and on reading the parties' materials, filed,

1. THIS COURT ORDERS THAT the action is dismissed.

2. **THIS COURT ORDERS THAT** the Plaintiff's Motion for Leave to amend his pleading is dismissed.

3. **THIS COURT ORDERS THAT** the Plaintiff shall pay to the Defendant his costs of this action, on a partial indemnity basis, fixed in the amount of $4,995.

ENTERED AT OTTAWA
INSCRIT A OTTAWA

ON/LE   AVR/APR 0 5 2018

DOCUMENT # 0411
IN BOOK NO. 73-13
AU REGISTRE NO. 73-13

"THE Registrar"

Defendant

Court File No. 15-66772

ONTARIO
SUPERIOR COURT OF JUSTICE

PROCEEDING COMMENCED AT OTTAWA

O R D E R

BELL BAKER LLP
Barristers and Solicitors
#700-116 Lisgar Street
Ottawa, ON K2P 0C2

Telephone: 613-237-3444
Facsimile: 613-1413
Email: jsummers@bellbaker.com

JOHN E. SUMMERS
LSUC No. 41580K

Lawyers for the Defendant

BOX #35

COURT OF APPEAL FOR ONTARIO

CITATION: Carby-Samuels II v. Carby-Samuels, 2018 ONCA 664
DATE: 20180725
DOCKET: C64705 & C64716

Hoy A.C.J.O., van Rensburg and Pardu JJ.A.

BETWEEN

Raymond Carby-Samuels II

Appellant

and

Horace R. Carby-Samuels

Respondent

Raymond Carby-Samuels II, acting in person

John E. Summers, for the respondent

Heard and released orally: July 20, 2018

On appeal from the judgment and the order of Justice Sylvia Corthorn of the Superior Court of Justice, dated November 16, 2017, reported at 2017 ONSC 6814 and 2017 ONSC 6834 respectively.

REASONS FOR DECISION

[1] The appellant, Raymond Carby-Samuels, appeals (1) the judgment of the application judge granting his father, the respondent Horace Carby-Samuels, summary judgment dismissing the appellant's claim against him, and (2) the order

of the application judge declaring that the appellant had instituted vexatious proceedings and conducted proceedings in a vexatious manner, and prohibiting him from instituting a proceeding, directly or indirectly, in any court in Ontario without first obtaining leave under s. 140(3) of the *Courts of Justice Act*, R.S.O. 1990, c. C.43.

[2] The appellant argues that the court cannot declare a Canadian citizen vexatious "for seeking to ensure the well-being of his Mom as an expression of religious conscience as affirmed by the Charter". He also argues that the court should find that there was a reasonable apprehension of bias because the application judge accepted his father's assertions, failed to refer to evidence that he says supported his position, failed to grant an adjournment, and proceeded in the face of his intention to bring a motion for an order that she recuse herself. Further, he argues that the application judge erred in relying on an affidavit of an administrator in his father's counsel's office. Finally, he also challenges the authority of Mr. Summers to act on behalf of his father and asks that he be ordered to disclose his fees.

[3] There is no basis for this court to interfere with the application judge's order granting summary judgment dismissing the appellant's action against his father seeking an order permitting him to see his mother, who was 85 years of age at the time of the motion. The application judge correctly held that there is no basis for the court to make an order compelling a mentally competent adult (the father)

require another mentally competent adult (the mother) to interact with a third family member (the appellant).

[4] Nor is there any basis to interfere with the application judge's order declaring the appellant a vexatious litigant and prohibiting him from instituting any proceeding in Ontario without leave. The application judge provided thorough and compelling reasons. Further, there is a strong presumption of judicial impartiality and a heavy burden on a party who seeks to rebut this presumption. The test is whether a reasonable, informed person, viewing the matter realistically and practically — and having thought the matter through — would conclude that it is more likely than not that the judge, whether consciously or unconsciously would not decide fairly: see *Children's Aid Society of the Regional Municipality of Waterloo v. C.T.*, 2017 ONCA 931, [2017] O.J. No 6324, at para. 84. The appellant has not discharged the heavy burden of rebutting the strong presumption of judicial impartiality.

[5] The affidavit with which the appellant takes issue does not appear to be in the record. Counsel for the respondent advises that the affidavit merely served to put various court proceedings and other communications between the parties before the court. This is not unusual in vexatious litigant proceedings.

[6] Finally, there is nothing in the record to suggest that Mr. Summers has been acting at any time in these proceedings without the father's authority and there no basis on which the court can compel the disclosure the appellant seeks.

[7] Accordingly, the appeal is dismissed. The father is entitled to costs of the appeal, fixed in the amount of $1,500, inclusive of HST and disbursements.

"Alexandra Hoy A.C.J.C
"K.M. van Rensburg J.A
"G. Pardu J.A

File No._____

IN THE SUPREME COURT OF CANADA

(ON APPEAL FROM THE COURT OF APPEAL OF ONTARIO)

BETWEEN:

RAYMOND CARBY-SAMUELS

APPLICANT (Appellant)

AND:

HORACE CARBY-SAMUELS

RESPONDENT (Respondent)

MEMORANDUM OF ARGUMENT OF THE APPLICANT (APPELLANT)

(Pursuant to Rule 25 of the Rules of the Supreme Court of Canada).

Raymond Carby-Samuels	**Counsel for the Respondent**
Self-Represented Litigant	
B.P. 24191 – 300 Eagleson Rd.	**BELL BAKER LLP**
Kanata, Ontario K2M 2C3	#700 – 116 Lisgar Street
	Ottawa, Ontario K2P OC2
	John E. Summers
	Tel: (613) 237-3444 / Fax: (613) 237-1413
	Email: Jsummers@bellbaker.com

TABLE OF CONTENTS

			Page
PART I		OVERVIEW AND STATEMENT OF FACTS	1 [77]
A.		Overview	1 [77]
B.		Background to the Current Dispute	6 [82]
C.		Judicial History	8 [84]
PART II		STATEMENT OF ISSUES	10 [86]
PART III		STATEMENT OF ARGUMENT	11 [87]
	A.	Guidance required on court relative to vulnerable self-rep. litigants	11 [87]
		The epidemic of self-representation	11 [87]
		Conflicting appellate authority regarding self-representation	12 [88]
	B.	Summary Judgement	16 [92]
	C.	Institutionalized Racism in Society and the Justice System	16 [92]
		Conclusion	16 [92]
PART IV		COSTS	17 [93]
PART V		ORDER SOUGHT	17 [93]
PART VI		TABLE OF AUTHORITIES	20 [96]
PART VII		STATUTORY PROVISIONS	23 [98]
A		*Ontario Courts of Justice Act*, R.S.O. 1990, c C. 43	24 [99]
B		*Family Law Act*, R.S.O. 1990, c. F.3.	25 [100]
C.		*Ontario Good Samaritan Act*, S.O. 2001	26 [101]

D.	*Criminal Code of Canada* (R.S.C., 1985, c C-46)	28 [103]
E	*Ontario Rules of Civil Procedure* (Mandatory Mediation Provision)	31 [106]
F	*Supreme Court Act, RSC, 1985, C S-26*	34 [109]
G	*Canadian Charter of Rights and Freedoms* (Constitution Act, 1982)	37 [112]

PART I OVERVIEW AND STATEMENT OF FACTS

A. Overview

1   This Court has recognized that "[e]nsuring access to justice is the greatest challenge to the rule of law in Canada today." [1] However, for average Canadians, including many self-represented litigants, "access to justice remains and ideal, not a reality". [2] This case offers this Court an opportunity to correct this injustice by providing guidance to lower courts regarding the fair treatment of self-represented litigants in Canada's civil justice system.

2   This Court has also recognized, in R. v S. (R.D.) [1997] 3 SCR 484, "Per Lamer C.J. and La Forest, Sopinka, Gonthier, Cory, Iacobucci and Major JJ.: The courts should be held to the highest standards of impartiality. Fairness and impartiality must be both subjectively present and objectively demonstrated to the informed and reasonable observer. The trial will be rendered unfair if the words or actions of the presiding judge give rise to a reasonable apprehension of bias to the informed and reasonable observer. Judges must be particularly sensitive to the need not only to be fair but also to appear to all reasonable observers to be fair to all Canadians of every race, religion, nationality and ethnic origin."

3   This Court further elaborated in R v S that, "If actual or apprehended bias arises from a judge's words or conduct, then the judge has exceeded his or her jurisdiction. This excess of jurisdiction can be remedied by an application to the presiding judge for disqualification if the proceedings are still underway, or by appellate review of the judge's decision. A reasonable apprehension of bias, if it arises, colours the entire trial proceedings and cannot be cured by the correctness of the subsequent decision. The mere fact that the judge appears to make proper findings of credibility on certain issues or comes to the correct result cannot alleviate the effects of a reasonable apprehension of bias arising from the judge's other words or conduct."

4   In R v S, this Court has also recognized the phenomenon of institutionalized racism in our broader Canadian society and its potential to pervert the course of justice to perceive young black males. It is therefore reasonable to assert that the self-represented litigant who is perceived as young black male and who faces a member of Counsel from the white

majority group could face even more challenges in their pursuit of justice as a self-representative litigant than would a self-represented litigant who is a white Canadian.

5 The particular issue in this case is the legality and appropriateness of decision of the Superior Court to make a declaration of 'Vexatious Litigant' in light of the fact that the self-represented litigant was seeking to enforce a previous ruling and advisement of the Court; and in light of the fact that the administrative judge of the Superior Court believed that there was sufficient grounds to schedule a recusal motion against the presiding Judge based on a "reasonable apprehension of bias". The administrative judge (Beaudoin, J) had furthermore based His Honour's decision in part on the fact that the presiding judge (Corthorn, J) denied the adjournment request made by Counsel present in behalf of Mr. Raymond Carby-Samuels which effectively blocked the ability of the self-represented litigant to be represented by Counsel during the Summary Judgement trial as was the self-represented litigant's civil right to do so which was also advised by other judges (McNamara SJ and Roger J) who advised the self-represented litigant to seek the advice and representation of Counsel. The administrative judge also took into consideration a pattern of documented differential treatment by the presiding judge which also suggested *prima facie* bias. Notably, the presiding Judge also relied upon a document which was deemed to be a forgery by multiple handwriting experts and that materials was part of the Recusal Motion submitted to the court This further begs the question on whether the court can rely on the integrity of a Summary Judgement which lacks integrity. The Applicant respectfully submits that a fair and just civil justice system must answer this question with a resounding "no".

6 Some civil courts have reported that more than 70% of litigants are now self-represented. [3] Members of this Court have observed in speeches to the legal profession that self-represented litigants are increasingly common in Canadian courts and pose special challenges for the administration of justice. A decade ago, Chief Justice McLachlin called the increase in self-represented litigants an "epidemic". [4]

7 Self-represented litigants are often vulnerable people. [5] Among self-represented litigants are disfranchised visible minorities or relatively recent immigrants to Canada. Most self-represented litigants appear to be average and lower income Canadians who simply

cannot afford expensive retainers and per hourly rates, and would not be able to understand all the complexities including rules and conventions of the Court in the same manner as a lawyer with years of professional training and instruction would. According to a relatively recent study, various court workers believe that the "general public has no idea about court procedures, requirements, the language, who or where to go for help." [6]

8   The Applicant, Mr. Raymond Carby-Samuels, shares many characteristics with other self-represented litigants in Canadian courts and the problems that he has faced with the court system are emblematic of those faced by other self-represented litigants, as well as black Canadians who face on-going systemic discrimination in the justice system.

9   Mr. Raymond Carby-Samuels was born in Toronto, Canada with a Caribbean cultural racial heritage in a society that continues to be substantively controlled by white Europeans in spite of the multicultural nature of today's Canadian society. Institutionalized racism has been a well-established historical fact in Canadian society including institutionalized racism that has been practiced within Canada's justice system in general right down to the *modus operandi* of our court rooms. This fact was acknowledged by this court in R. v D.

10   The Court of Appeal for Ontario also erred by ignoring a declaration of "leeway" to self-represented litigants in *Sanzone v Schechter*, 2016 OCNA 566.

11   In Mr. Raymond Carby-Samuels' Statement of Claim, he had sought to damages for an apparent unlawful and orchestrated eviction as elaborated in *Murray v Toth*, 2012 ONSC 5815, and for damages for that unlawful eviction which include the financial loss as a result of being forcibly separated from both personal and professional belongings; and to this day the Defendant has not returned all belongings. Mr. R Carby-Samuels also filed for damages associated with ongoing interference in the efforts of the Defendant / Respondent in interfering in the ability of Mr. R. Carby-Samuels and his Mother, Dezrin Carby-Samuels from seeing each other. Ms Carby-Samuels has sought to see her son, and the Defendant has refused to provide any evidence to the contrary.

12   On 11 February 2016, Raymond Carby-Samuels had received a Default Judgement from the Superior Court which had awarded Raymond Carby-Samuels $25,000 in damages and had recognized Raymond Carby-Samuels and his Mother had been subjected to

improper interference in their ability to see each other. Raymond Carby-Samuels contended that to the best of his legal knowledge that the Defendant engaged in contempt of Court by refusing to enable the access of Raymond Carby-Samuels to see his Mother when he arrived to her home sometime after accompanied by two officers from the Ottawa Police Services.

13   Raymond Carby-Samuels further contends that McNamara, J ought not have allowed Mr. John E Summers to set-aside Justice Patrick's Smith's Order, and ever since has sought to restore his decision which flies in the face of Summary Judgement. Raymond contends that the McNamara JS erred by granting to the set-aside Motion which violated *stare decisis*. Furthermore John E Summers did not appear to have a *bona fide* Legal Retainer Agreement with the Defendant for either Superior Court proceedings and Court of Appeal for Ontario proceedings which Defence Counsel appears to confirm via email correspondence.

14   Raymond Carby-Samuels further contends that both the lower court and the appellate court failed to hold Defence Counsel to an evidentiary burden of proof that there was "no genuine case for trial". Instead the lower court along with the appellate court erred by switching the evidentiary burden of proof to the Appellant.

15   In the recent decision of *Sanzone v Schechter*, the Ontario Court of Appeal had provided insight regarding the evidentiary burden of proof that a defendant must meet in moving to dismiss an action by way of Summary Judgement, and in particular, what expert evidence may be required.

16   Sanzone involved the appeal of a successful Summary Judgement motion brought by the Defendants, who were dentists to dismiss a medical malpractice action. The Summary Judgement Motion was granted at fist instance on the basis of the self-represented plaintiff had not delivered an expert report in support of an allegation that the defendants had breached.

17   The motions judge held that the appellant's "report" didn't comply with the Rules of Civil Procedure surrounding expert reports and was therefore inadmissible.

18   On appeal, the Court of Appeal held that the defendants, as the parties moving for summary judgement, had the burden of persuading the court that there was no genuine issue requiring trial. Noting that **Rule 20.01(3)** allowed a defendant to move for summary

judgement with supporting affidavit materials or other evidence, the Court of Appeal interpreted this to mean that the defendants were required to put their "best evidentiary foot forward" to discharge their evidentiary burden. Only then would onus shift to the plaintiff to prove that the claim had any real chance of success. The defendants couldn't simply rely on the plaintiff's failure to deliver an expert report as a basis for dismissal of the action.

19   The Court of Appeal also took issue with what it described as the defendants' strategy of using Rule 20 against a self-represented litigant to accelerate requirements regarding an expert report. The appeal was ultimately granted and summary judgement was set aside.

20   The decision of the Court of Appeal for Ontario held that –

"The application judge correctly held that there is no basis for the court to make an order compelling a mentally competent adult (the father) to require another mentally competent adult (the mother) to interact with a third family member (the appellant)."

Both the lower court and appellate court erred in its declaration. Counsel presented no evidence to the Court that the mother was being "compelled" as the appellate court improperly affirmed in its Order. On the contrary, the Appellant provided evidence from Ms Dezrin Carby-Samuels that she deeply values the company and support of her son and that the father has been blocking the desires of the mother from seeing the appellant who had sought to shelter his Mother from domestic abuse.

The compassion of the appellant for his Mother was recognized and affirmed in the original order of the lower court regarding the Default Judgment which confirmed that the Court reinforced by *J.J. v Nova Scotia* (2005) SCC 29717, has every right and power to intervene to protect human life from abuse, and declaring the appellant to be "Vexatious" in his efforts to enforce a previous decision of the Court was categorically unjust.

21   The decision of the Court of Appeal for Ontario also held that –

"Nor is there any basis to interfere with the application judge's order declaring the appellant a vexatious litigant and prohibiting him from instituting any proceeding in Ontario without leave. The application judge provided thorough and compelling reasons. Further, there is a strong presumption of judicial impartiality and a heavy burden on a party who seeks to rebut this presumption... The appellant has not discharged the heavy burden of rebutting the strong presumption of judicial impartiality.'

However, this representation by the appellate court ignores the context of a fundamental breach in the appearance of integrity which occurred when the presiding judge's action gave the appearance of escaping a Recusal Motion which basis of substance was already affirmed the by Court's acceptance to allow the Recusal Motion to proceed before that process was truncated by the pre-emptive decision by Corthorn J on Summary Judgement.

B. Background to the Current Dispute

20. Mr. Raymond Carby-Samuels suffered damages as a result of bodily assault executed by the Defendant against him on 29 January 2009; a subsequent loss of professional incoming having sustained the injury, and a subsequent unlawful eviction that was executed by the Defendant / Respondent against Mr. Carby-Samuels in April 2015 at his place of residence since 1990. The Statement of Claim which Mr. Raymond Carby-Samuels thought he had amended to the best of his ability / knowledge as self-represented litigant which was reviewed by the lower courts and awarded an Order on 11 February 2016 had cited the various grounds as basis for his Claim, including:

A) Bodily assault requiring reconstructive surgery and rehabilitation;

B) Intentional infliction of emotional distress;

C) Public mischief related to spreading falsehoods to Ottawa Police;

D) Conspiracy to perpetrate a false arrest

E) Unlawful Eviction

F) Forcible separation from personal and professional belongings

G) Interference / conspiracy against Canadian Criminal Code

H) Defamation / Slander

I) Economic / Financial Loss

J) Publishing Services to the Defendant / Respondent

21. On 29 January 2013, Horace Carby-Samuels subjected Raymond Carby-Samuels to bodily assault with a knife at his parent's home at 30 Jarlan Terrance in Kanata, Ontario after Raymond Carby-Samuels expressed concerns to Horace Carby-Samuels about witnessing at that time his mother crying after another round of abuse perpetrated by Horace Carby-Samuels against his Mother.

22. At the beginning of January 2015 when Horace Carby-Samuels conspired with his daughter, Marcella Carby-Samuels to make a series of specious calls to the Ottawa Police Services, fraudulently alleging, in part, that Raymond "suffered from mental illness" and was holding both him and Dezrin "hostage". Subsequent publicly mischievous phone calls to the police resulted based Raymond being evicted in late April 2015. During that time Raymond observed assault and abuse against his Mother.

23. In early June 2015, Raymond was forced to obtain the services of a lawyer named Todd Ji, who on 12 June 2015 issued a legal demand letter to Horace for the demand of personal and professional belongings which Horace had severed access to and for the enabling of Raymond and his Mother to see each other at a "neutral location".

24. Alison Timons who has been a supervising social worker at the Nepean, Rideau and Osgoode Community Resource Centre consulted with Dezrin who had agreed that she did in fact want to see her son. However, it was during that time that Ms Timons reported to Raymond that as a result of the inflicting of on-going abuse by Horace against Dezrin which involved his severing of support that they sought to provide in Raymond's absence which was blocked by Horace for weeks, Dezrin lost the ability to effectively walk, talk and write.

25. In the face of the Todd Ji's Demand Letter and consultation by Ms Timons with Dezrin, Raymond and his Mother were able to see each other on 12 June 2015. This was the last time that Raymond and Dezrin were able to see each other.

26. It was only after Todd Ji's demand letter that Marcella out of her credit card paid Horace to move much of Raymond stuff into U-Haul which created storage fee costs to Raymond. However, to this day, Horace has refused to return his beige 12 speed bike and his personal photo albums that Dezrin had made for Raymond. In an emailed letter to Raymond, Defence Counsel declared in summer 2018 that these are now Horace's property and would not be returning them.

C. Judicial History

27. In December 2014, after Horace over months continued to frustrate access to the balance of his belongings and continued to hijack Dezrin's expressed desires to see the Appellant, as Dezrin's condition began to worsen under the dysfunctional and abusive conditions that Horace continued to impose against Dezrin, on 7 December 2014, Mr Raymond Carby-Samuels filed his original Statement of Claim in Superior Court.

28. Horace Carby-Samuels didn't file a Defence within the time prescribed by the *Ontario Rules of Civil Procedure* and was subsequently noted in Default.

29. Having been noted in default, Justice Patrick Smith of the Superior Court in Ottawa issued the following order on 11 February 2016:

On the reading of the Statement of Claim in this action and the proof of service on the Statement of Claim on the Defendant, Horace R. Carby-Samuels, having been noted in default,

1. IT IS ORDERED AND ADJUDGED that the defendant, Horace R. Carby-Samuels pay the plaintiff the sum of $25,000 and the sum of $532.00 for the costs of this action.
2. IT IS ORDERED AND ADJUDGED that the defendant, Horace R. Carby-Samuels also immediately facilitate on-going and permanent access by Raymond Carby-Samuels to see his Mother, Dezrin Carby-Samuels at 3 PM on a daily basis to enable him to resume support to her nutritional and related care-giving requirements that Dezrin has documented in writing that she desires...

30. Horace refused to abide by the Order.

31. The attending police officers advised Raymond that, "We would like nothing better than to help you [Raymond] see your Mom. But you need to go back to Court to get and even stronger endorsement to be able to enter the premises…".

32. Raymond filed a Motion of contempt against Horace sometime in early Spring 2016.

33. It was around this time that John E. Summers who is a lawyer with Bell Baker entered the picture, alleging that he was Horace's new lawyer, and got the order "set-aside" in spite of Raymond's objects that were based upon established case law.

34. In January 2017, Raymond consulted with Ms Miriam Vale Peter, a new lawyer.

35. On 24 January 2017, Ms Peters issued in Raymond's behalf, a demand letter for Mandatory Mediation as prescribed by the *Ontario Rules of Civil Procedure*. Ms Peters also advised Mr. Summers of a proposed mediator. However, Opposing Counsel rejected the mediation request and indicated they would pursue Summary Judgement.

37. In August 2017, Corthorn J seized the Summary Judgement file.

38. Following a pattern of apparent differential and unfair treatment by Corthorn J, Raymond Carby-Samuels prepared a Recusal Motion which Justice Beaudoin reviewed in the very late Fall 2017, and approved it to be scheduled because he felt that it was neither frivolous nor vexatious and had a substantive basis in relation to a "reasonable apprehension of bias". However, during the efforts of the court to actively consult with and coordinate the availability schedule the Recusal Motion for sometime after Christmas 2017 into the beginning of January 2018, Corthorn J unjustly truncated the process by rendering her decision on Summary Judgement in a manner that both subverted the administrative authority of Justice Beaudoin and the customs and conventions of the Court that would have required Corthorn J to wait for the recusal motion.

39. In Justice Corthorn's decision, this judge gave the appearance that Raymond Carby-Samuels had never submitted any Recusal Motion for the Superior Court to consider which

flies in the face of documented evidence of having filed a formal recusal Motion with the court that was supported by a signed affidavit authorized by a Commissioner of Oaths.

40. On the question of judicial impartiality in the decision rendered by the Court of Appeal for Ontario on 20 July 2018, the appellate Court erred by failing to take into consider the Supreme Court of Canada ruling in R. *v.* S. (R.D.), [1997] 3 S.C.R. 484.

41. In R. *v.* S. (R.D.), [1997] 3 S.C.R. 484, the Supreme Court of Canada furthermore affirmed that "anti-black racism" may provide a context to any substantive finding of "reasonable apprehension of bias".

PART II. STATEMENT OF ISSUES

42. This case raises questions of public and national importance and questions of law arising therefrom, as set out below:

> a) Guidance is required as to how much consideration and equitable consideration relative to opposing Counsel courts should give to vulnerable self-represented litigants in making sure that their substantive legal rights are protected. How should courts understand or interpret issues raised by self-represented litigants in chambers, at trial or on appeal made either in an unconventional fashion or that are not fully or clearly articulated in a manner that would be expected of Counsel?

> e) Guidance is required on whether the lower Courts are obliged to provide an adjournment for a self-represented litigant, when that adjournment is being sought by Counsel that is present, and who is seeking that adjournment in an inherently complex matter such as preparing a defence against an effort of opposing Counsel to declare summary judgement?

> f) Guidance is required as to how much assistance courts should give to vulnerable self-represented litigants in making sure that their substantive legal rights reinforced by Sections 24(1) of the *Canadian Charter of Rights and Freedoms* are protected. How should

courts understand or interpret issues raised by self-represented litigants in chambers or at trial or on an appeal in an unconventional fashion or that may not be fully or clearly articulated. In other words, what is the nature of leeway should courts provide self-represented litigants -- asserted by the court in *Sanzone vs Schechter*, 2016 OCNA 566 -- who have a civil right as a Canadian to represent themselves but who lack the legal training of a lawyer to present substantive legal issues.

g) Guidance is required on if, whether, or how the Canadian court system can be reformed to universally protect court access for all Canadians through reforms.

h) Additional guidance is required as to how courts should interpret and apply court rules and procedures to vulnerable self-represented litigants. Should courts apply a contextual approach that recognizes self-represented litigants' lack of understanding of court rules and procedures, or should court rules and procedures be applied identically to all litigants?

PART III. STATEMENT OF ARGUMENT

    A. Introductory Issue: Guidance is required on how much equitable consideration should be given to self-represented litigants and how courts should interpret and apply court rules and procedures to vulnerable self-represented litigants.

The *"epidemic" of self-representation*

43. Self-represented litigants are prevalent in Canadian courtrooms. Chief Justice McLachlin explained to the Canadian Bar Association that "[t]he number of litigants who represent themselves is on the rise" and "[t]he justice system must provide citizens a real opportunity to defend or assert their rights, regardless of their resources." [7]

44. Most self-represented litigants lack the understanding of the legal process. But for even those self-represented litigants who have a very broad appreciation of the legal system, almost all lack the training of a lawyer on the rules and conventions on the preparations,

filings and oral presentations which the Court requires. As the Canadian Judicial Council (CJC) observed in its "Statement of Principles on Self-represented litigants and Accused Persons" (the "Statement"):

> Self-represented persons are generally uninformed about their rights and about the consequences of choosing the options available to them; they may find court procedures complex, confusing and intimidating; **and they may not have the knowledge or skills to participate actively and effectively in their own litigation.** [emphasis added]

45. Noel Semple, an assistant professor with Windsor's Faculty of Law and a member of the National Self-Represented Litigants Project (NSRLP) advisory board who was one of the experts who will be part of the panel discussion during the school's Self-Represented Litigants Awareness Day commented on the critical challenges facing self-represented litigants in Ontario:

"The justice system still has work to do in responding to today's reality — self-represented litigants are a majority in some courts and a large and growing proportion of litigants in other courts. The justice system needs to be more accessible and less costly in time and money for those who need to use it. "

Conflicting appellate authority regarding the relevance of self-representation

46. Although judges have publicly acknowledged the issues facing self-represented litigants, the courts have not provided clear guidance on how these issues should be addressed. The CJC's Statement outlines how participants in litigation, including the judiciary, should interact with self-represented litigants. However, courts have struggled with how to reconcile competing principles within the Statement. The Court of Appeal of Manitoba (MBCA) has described the extent to which judges should afford an "unrepresented litigant" additional leeway as "an increasingly vexing problem" for courts of all levels. [8]

47. While the Statement admonishes "[j]udges to ensure that procedural and evidentiary rules are not used to unjustly hinder the legal interests of a self-represented person", [9] it goes on to state that "[j]udges must exercise diligence in ensuring that the law is applied in an even-handed way to all, regardless of representation." [10] The result is that there is

uncertainty on whether a litigant's self-represented status should be a relevant factor in judicial decision-making and in determining whether to provide assistance.

48. There is a general acknowledgement that courts should provide some assistance to an unrepresented litigant. However, issues arise in determining how to balance "the sometime competing imperatives of helping a litigant who is in need of assistance while maintaining impartiality." [11] Provincial appellate courts have differed on adoption of the Statement an principles embodied therein. Some appellate courts have adopted the Statement and its principles in whole or in part (British Columbia, Quebec, Ontario and Manitoba), and other not at all (Alberta).

49. **British Columbia.** The Court of Appeal for British Columbia (BCCA) has suggested that it is right and just to accommodate to self-represented litigants on procedural matters." [12] In support for this position the BCCA cited the Statement for its admonition to the judiciary that "judges should ensure that procedural and evidentiary rules are not used to unjustly hinder the legal interests of self-represented persons." [13] In *Cole v British Columbia Nurses' Union* (2014), this led the BCCA to consider whether a party's self-represented status was related to his inordinate delay is prosecuting his claim (and concluded it was not). [14]

50. **Quebec.** The Quebec Court of Appeal (**QCCA**) has similarly referred to the Statement for its principle that "judges must adopt specific measures to prevent an unfair disadvantage to self-represented persons." [15] In *Deschenes c Valeurs mobilieres Banque Laurentienne* (2010), the court applied this principle to consider whether the self-represented party's lack of legal representation prejudiced her understanding of court procedures (in that case a filing deadline). [16]

51. **Ontario.** In Ontario, the Court of Appeal for Ontario (**ONCA**) in *Toronto Dominion Bank v Hylton* (2010) found self-representation to be a relevant factor in deciding whether to grant for an adjournment. [17] The ONCA viewed this as part of the Court's obligation to assist a self-represented party to ensure they can present their case to the best of their ability [18]

In the Maclean's article entitled "When lawyers are only for the rich -- SPECIAL REPORT: Fees are soaring, and thousands are being left behind" published on 14 January 2009 by Kate Lunau, she documents many people "find themselves unable, mainly for financial reasons, to access the Canadian justice system," Beverley McLachlin, the chief justice of Canada, said in a recent speech. "Hard hit are average middle-class Canadians."

52. **Manitoba.** In Manitoba, the MBCA reasoned in *Coleman v Pateman Farms Ltd.* (2001) -- decided prior to the CJC's issuance of the Statement – that a self-represented litigant should not be denied the chance to present their case due to a strict application of the court procedure rules. [19] However, the same court has also held more recently that it is an error to consider a litigant's self-represented status as an overriding consideration in determining the consequences of an improperly served statement of claim. [20]

53. **Alberta.** In contrast to its counterparts in other provinces, the Court of Appeal in Alberta has cited the Statement [21] but us "generally in favour of equal application of the rules to the represented and self-represented litigant alike, with limited, appropriate guidance from the Court to assist the self-represented litigant in his efforts to stay with the parameters of the rules." [22]

54. By way of example, in *K (P.E.) v K (B.W.)* (2004), the Court of Appeal directed that "[i]n the absence of special provisions, our courts will apply the same legal principles, rules of evidence, and standards of procedure regardless of whether litigants are represented by Counsel or are self-represnted. [23]

55. Further, in *Koerner v. Capital Health Authority* (2011), the Court of Appeal rejected the Appellant's argument that, as a self-represented litigant, she was entitled to lenience regarding the legal process. The Court of Appeal reasoned that "[t]he Rules of Court make it clear that the same rules apply to all litigants, even if self-represented." [24] As support for this conclusion, the Court of Appeal cited Rule 1.1(2) of the Alberta Rules of Court, which provides: "[t]hese rules also govern all persons who come to the Court for resolution of a claim, whether the person is a self-represented litigant or is represented by a lawyer." [25]

56. However. The *Alberta Rules of Court* don't require courts to ignore self-representation in the exercise of judicial decision-making under the *Rules of Court*.

(iii) The majority in this case gave no weight to Mr. Raymond Carby-Samuels' self-representation

In this case at hand, the majority expressly rejected the relevance of Mr. Raymond Carby-Samuels' self-represented status, and didn't mention the Statement [26] and furthermore did not mention the relevance or lack thereof of any case law which Raymond Carby-Samuels had relied upon to support his Appeal. The prejudice to Mr. Raymond Carby-Samuels was legally fatal for at least two reasons.

First, the Court of Appeal made no apparent effort to understand Mr. Raymond Carby-Samuels' solid grounds in relation to case law which also relied on human rights law; constitutional law and provisions related to the Canadian Criminal Code in addition to violations of equity and court administrative law / rules for making his Appeal which were thoroughly presented in his Perfected Appeal. Furthermore, the Court of Appeal ignored the fatal implications that the failure to provide a request for adjournment by Counsel acting for Raymond Carby-Samuels had in denying the right that Canadians have to seek Counsel and the total lack of experience Raymond Carby-Samuels had in defending himself in a Vexatious Litigation Trial relative to Mr. John Summers as Defence Counsel who was admitted to the Bar in 1999, and failed to acknowledge that Raymond Carby-Samuels has sought to obtain Counsel based upon the advisement of both Roger J and McNamara J.S.. Instead the Court took an apparent narrow view simply describing Raymond Carby-Samuels as an "appellant" and failed to bear any weight on previous legal cases decided upon by the Court of Appeal which affirmed that self-represented litigants are to be provided with leeway.

Second, the appellate court having declared that "Nor is there any basis to interfere with the application judge's order declaring the appellant a vexatious litigant and prohibiting him from instituting any proceedings in Ontario without leave," is an assertion which deprecates from the strong basis fully described and supported by case law which suggests that the

Court of Appeal only sought to be deferent to the judgements of the application judge which were tainted by the evasion of the Recusal Motion process at per the standards of this Court and that this deference denied Raymond Carby-Samuels, a self-represented litigant, his constitutionally protected right to be availed with due process which would have required a thorough examination of his Perfected Appeal which provides an ample outline of bases "to interfere with the application's judge's order".

A contextual approach to the Rules would acknowledge that self-representation is often not a "choice", but a result of circumstance. Here, a contextual approach, including the leeway that the Court of Appeal for Ontario has declared in case law that self-represented litigants are entitled to received would have enabled Mr. Raymond Carby-Samuels grounds of appeal and interpretation which would have allowed Mr Raymond Carby-Samuels the fair opportunity to advance his position.

B) **Summary Judgement**

Guidance is require on affirming the legal conditions for imposing declarations of **Summary Judgement** in a manner which respect recognizes the absence of formal statutes on this matter and the needs to ensure the affirmation of civil rights in relation to guarantees affirmed by the *Canadian Charter of Rights and Freedoms* as the 'supreme law' of the law.

C) Institutionalized Racism

Guidance is required to ensure that in multicultural diversity which Canada represents, the pursuit of a moral conscience which is based on good will be respected by the courts as a civil right and that Canadians will enjoy the equal benefit of case law precedents.

C - Conclusion

57. The issue of self-representation is a significant one. A decision on the presented issues would affect the application of court rules, procedures and the treatment of self-represented litigants courts. Furthermore, with the increase of self-represented litigants in the court system there will be increasing desires by lawyers to truncate the pursuit of the

substantive rights of self-represented litigants by unfairly taking advantage of their lack of knowledge of legal processes, rules and conventions to have them subjected to Summary Judgement as Mr Raymond Carby-Samuels, by judges who having experienced frustration in overall increases of self-represented litigants "consuming court resources" in their eyes may be tempted to side with opposing Counsel in their Summary Judgement litigant claims in a manner which ignores the evidentiary burden of proof on the defendant(s) as affirmed in the *Sazone* case that was before the Ontario Court of Appeal; and that would be detrimental to the affirmation of civil rights regarding due process and equitable treatment which all Canadians are entitled to enjoy whether they can or cannot afford the services of a lawyer.

It is furthermore unfortunate that the lower court refused to provide an adjournment to Counsel present who have driven from Toronto, when all Canadians have an implicit right to be defended by Counsel if resources become available to a self-represented litigant, and then relied upon an affidavit supplied by Counsel's secretary to declare the Raymond Carby-Samuels to be a self-represented litigant. It is furthermore unfortunate that the Court of Appeal erred by not taking the time to review opposing Counsel's improper affidavit before rendering a decision as grave as declaring someone to be a Vexatious Litigant; and correspondingly failed to consider the implications of a failure to provide due process of the Motion that the Court had granted to proceed on the Recusal of Corthon J.

Given all the foregoing, Mr. Raymond Carby-Samuels submits that the Court of Appeal for Ontario erred in making the CA Decision and that the leave to appeal should be granted on the basis that this case raises issues of national and public importance.

PART IV   COSTS

104. Mr Raymond Carby-Samuels requests that he be granted costs of this Application in any event of the cause.

PART V   ORDER SOUGHT

105. Mr. Raymond Carby-Samuels respectfully requests that the leave application be granted, with costs or, in the alternative, an order pursuant to subsection 43 (1.1) of the

Supreme Court Act remanding the case back to the Court of Appeal for consideration based upon the principles of equity outlined is Section 96 of the *Ontario Courts of Justice Act;* and that the Court of Appeal erred in failing to demonstrate judicial review in its ruling of all issues raised in in the Appeal submitted by Raymond Carby-Samuels to that Court.

ALL OF WHICH IS RESPECTFULLY SUBMITTED, this 20th of September 2018.

RAYMOND CARBY-SAMUELS

Self-represented Litigant

Per: _____

ENDNOTES:

[1] Hryniak v. Mauldin, [2014] 1 SCR 87, 2014 SCC 7, 1: Book of Authorities ("BA"), TAB 11.

[2] The Right Honourable Chief Justice McLachlin, "Remarks of the Right Honourable Beverly McLachlin, P.C. Chief Justice of Canada" (Remarks to the Council of the Canadian Bar Association delivered at the Canadian Legal Conference, St. John's, Newfoundland and Labrador, August 12, 2006) [unpublished] ("McLachlin, C.J.C., Remarks to the CBA) , P. 4: BA, Tab 29

[3] Julie Macfarlane, "The National Self-Represented Litigants Project: Identifying and Meeting the Needs of Self-Represented Litigants" (2013), p. 34: *BA*, Tab 26.

[4] "Chief Justice warns against self-representation in courts" Times Colonist (August 13, 2006: BA, Tab 30.

[5] Trevor CW Farrow et al, "Addressing the Needs of Self-Represented Litigants in the Canadian Justice System" (2012), p. 4, BA, Tab 31.

[6] Alison Crawford, "Justice system can't wait for judicial appointments review, say judges" CBC News (May 9, 2016: BA Tab 20, Robson Flether, "Alberta's judge shortage at 'crisis' level but feds have no timeline for resolution", CBC News (April 12, 2016) online, BA, tab 28; Meghan Grant, "Alberta judge shortage at "breaking point", causing trial delays" CBC News (October 26, 2015) online: CBC news: BA, Tab 27; *Weatherford Canada Partnership v Kautschuk,* 2016 ABCA 173, Paragraph 7, BA Tab 17,

[7] McLachin CJC, Remarks to the CBA, above note 2, pp 4- 5, BA, Tab 29

[8] *Manitoba (Director of Child and Family Services),* v A(J), 2004 MBCA 184, Paragraph 32, BA. Tab 15.

[9] Statement of Principles, above, note 32, p. 7: BA, Tab 21.

[10] Id, p 5, BA, Tab 21.

[11] *Manitoba (Director of Child and Family Service)*, above, note 37, Paragraph 32, BA, Tab 15.

[12] Cole v British Columbia Nurses' union, 2014 BCCA 2, Paragrarph 36, BA, Tab 4.

[13] Id, Paragraph 3: BA, Tab 4

[14] Id, Paragraphs 35, 38, BA, Tab 4.

[15] *Deschenes c Valeurs mobilieres Banque Laurentienne*, 2010 QCCA 2137 (CanLII), Paragraph 37, BA Tab 7.

[16] Id, Paragraphs 36 – 39: BA, Tab 7.

[17] Toronto Dominion Bank v. Hylton, 2010 ONCA 752, Paragraphs 39 – 42, BA , Tab 16.

[18] Id, Paragraph 39, BA, Tab 16

[19] *Coleman v Pateman Farms Ltd.*, 2001 MBCA 75, Paragraph 15, BA, Tab 5

[20] Fegol v National Post Co et al, 2007 MBCA 27 (CanLII), Paragraph 27: BA, Tab 8

[21] See e.g. Williams v Williamss, 2015 ABCA 246, Paragraph 38, BA, Tab 18; Malton v Attis, 201 ABCA 130, Paragraph 31, BA, Tab 14.

[22] *Judge P.A. Demong & Jane Wotten*, "Self-Represented Litigants: An Overview", Law Society o Saskatchewan Continuing Professional Development, Page 8: BA, Tab 25.

[23] *K(P.E.) v. K(B.W.)*, 2004 ABCA 289, Paragraph 7, BA, Tab 13

[24] *Koener Capital Health Authority*, 2011, ABCA 289, Paragraph 7, BA, Tab 12

[25] Id. BA, Tab 12

[26] *Court of Appeal Decision, Pintea v Johns*, 2016, ABCA 99.

PART VI TABLE OF AUTHORITES

Case Law **Paragraphs**

1. *R v S* (RD) [1997] 3 SCR 484   2, 3, 41

2. *Cole v British Columbia Nurses' Union*, 2014 BCCA 2   49

3. *Coleman v. Pateman Farms Ltd*, 2001 MBCA 75   52

4. *Deschenes c. Valeurs mobilieres Banque Laurentienne* 2010, QCCA 50

5. *Fegol v National Post co et al*, 2007 MBCA 27   52

6. *Hryniak v Mauldin*, [2014] 1 SCR 87   1

7. *Koerner v Capital Health Authority*, 2011 ABCA 289   55

8. *K(P.E.) v K(B.W.)*, 2004 ABCA 135   54

9. *Toronto Dominion Bank v. Hylton*, 2010, ONCA 752   51

10. *Williams v Williams*, 2015 ABCA 246   53

11. *Khan v. Krylov & Co LLP*, 2017 OCNA 625   [axiomatic]

12. *Sanzone v Schecheter*, 2016 OCNA 566   10, 15, 61, 42

13. *J.J. v Nova Scotia* (2005) SCC 29717   20

PART VII. STATUTORY PROVISIONS

A   Ontario Rules of Civil Procedure [Excerpt]

B   Ontario Courts of Justice Act [Excerpt]

C   Supreme Court of Canada, RSC, 1985, C 2-26, s. (443 (1.1) [Excerpt]

D   Ontario's Good Samaritan Act, 2001

Schedule B

Courts of Justice Act, R.S.O. 1990, c. C.43

Common Law and Equity

Rules of law and equity

96 (1) Courts shall administer concurrently all rules of equity and the common law. R.S.O. 1990, c. C.43, s. 96 (1); 1993, c. 27, Sched.

Rules of equity to prevail

(2) Where a rule of equity conflicts with a rule of the common law, the rule of equity prevails. R.S.O. 1990, c. C.43, s. 96 (2); 1993, c. 27, Sched.

Jurisdiction for equitable relief

(3) Only the Court of Appeal and the Superior Court of Justice, exclusive of the Small Claims Court, may grant equitable relief, unless otherwise provided. 1994, c. 12, s. 38; 1996, c. 25, s. 9 (17).

Family Law Act, R.S.O. 1990, c. F.3

Obligation of child to support parent

32 Every child who is not a minor has an obligation to provide support, in accordance with need, for his or her parent who has cared for or provided support for the child, to the extent that the child is capable of doing so. R.S.O. 1990, c. F.3, s. 32.

Good Samaritan Act, 2001

S.O. 2001, CHAPTER 2

Consolidation Period: From April 27, 2001 to the e-Laws currency date.

No amendments.

Definition

1. In this Act,

"health care professional" means a member of a College of a health profession set out in Schedule 1 to the *Regulated Health Professions Act, 1991*. 2001, c. 2, s. 1.

Protection from liability

2. (1) Despite the rules of common law, a person described in subsection (2) who voluntarily and without reasonable expectation of compensation or reward provides the services described in that subsection is not liable for damages that result from the person's negligence in acting or failing to act while providing the services, unless it is established that the damages were caused by the gross negligence of the person. 2001, c. 2, s. 2 (1).

Persons covered

(2) Subsection (1) applies to,

(a) a health care professional who provides emergency health care services or first aid assistance to a person who is ill, injured or unconscious as a result of an accident or other emergency, if the health care professional does not provide the services or assistance at a hospital or other place having appropriate health care facilities and equipment for that purpose; and

(b) an individual, other than a health care professional described in clause (a), who provides emergency first aid assistance to a person who is ill, injured or unconscious as a result of an accident or other emergency, if the individual provides the assistance at the immediate scene of the accident or emergency. 2001, c. 2, s. 2 (2).

Reimbursement of expenses

(3) Reasonable reimbursement that a person receives for expenses that the person reasonably incurs in providing the services described in subsection (2) shall be deemed not to be compensation or reward for the purpose of subsection (1). 2001, c. 2, s. 2 (3).

3. Omitted (provides for coming into force of provisions of this Act). 2001, c. 2, s. 3.

4. Omitted (enacts short title of this Act). 2001, c. 2, s. 4.

Criminal Code (R.S.C., 1985, c. C-46)

Unlawfully causing bodily harm

269 Every one who unlawfully causes bodily harm to any person is guilty of

    (a) an indictable offence and liable to imprisonment for a term not exceeding ten years; or

- (b) an offence punishable on summary conviction and liable to imprisonment for a term not exceeding eighteen months.

- R.S., 1985, c. C-46, s. 269;
- 1994, c. 44, s. 18.

Theft

- 322 (1) Every one commits theft who fraudulently and without colour of right takes, or fraudulently and without colour of right converts to his use or to the use of another person, anything, whether animate or inanimate, with intent
    - (a) to deprive, temporarily or absolutely, the owner of it, or a person who has a special property or interest in it, of the thing or of his property or interest in it;

Public mischief

- 140 (1) Every one commits public mischief who, with intent to mislead, causes a peace officer to enter on or continue an investigation by

- (i) is unable, by reason of detention, age, illness, mental disorder or other cause, to withdraw himself from that charge, and
- (ii) is unable to provide himself with necessaries of life.

- **Offence**

(2) Every one commits an offence who, being under a legal duty within the meaning of subsection (1), fails without lawful excuse, the proof of which lies on him, to perform that duty, if

- (a) with respect to a duty imposed by paragraph (1)(a) or (b),
    - (i) the person to whom the duty is owed is in destitute or necessitous circumstances, or
    - (ii) the failure to perform the duty endangers the life of the person to whom the duty is owed, or causes or is likely to cause the health of that person to be endangered permanently; or
- (b) with respect to a duty imposed by paragraph (1)(c), the failure to perform the duty endangers the life of the person to whom the duty is owed or causes or is likely to cause the health of that person to be injured permanently.

- **Punishment**

(3) Every one who commits an offence under subsection (2)

- (a) is guilty of an indictable offence and liable to imprisonment for a term not exceeding five years; or

- (b) is guilty of an offence punishable on summary conviction and liable to imprisonment for a term not exceeding eighteen months.

Assault

- **265** (1) A person commits an assault when
    - (a) without the consent of another person, he applies force intentionally to that other person, directly or indirectly;
    - (b) he attempts or threatens, by an act or a gesture, to apply force to another person, if he has, or causes that other person to believe on reasonable grounds that he has, present ability to effect his purpose;

Forcible Confinement

279 (1) Every person commits an offence who kidnaps a person with intent

(2) Every one who, without lawful authority, confines, imprisons or forcibly seizes another person is guilty of

- (a) an indictable offence and liable to imprisonment for a term not exceeding ten years; or

R.R.O. 1990, Reg. 194: RULES OF CIVIL PROCEDURE

under *Courts of Justice Act, R.S.O. 1990, c. C.43*

DISPOSITION WITHOUT TRIAL
19	Default Proceedings
20	Summary Judgment
21	Determination of an Issue Before Trial
22	Special Case
23	Discontinuance and Withdrawal
24	Dismissal of Action for Delay
24.1	Mandatory Mediation

RULE 20 SUMMARY JUDGMENT

WHERE AVAILABLE

To Plaintiff

20.01 (1) A plaintiff may, after the defendant has delivered a statement of defence or served a notice of motion, move with supporting affidavit material or other evidence for summary judgment on all or part of the claim in the statement of claim. R.R.O. 1990, Reg. 194, r. 20.01 (1).

(2) The plaintiff may move, without notice, for leave to serve a notice of motion for summary judgment together with the statement of claim, and leave may be given where special urgency is shown, subject to such directions as are just. R.R.O. 1990, Reg. 194, r. 20.01 (2).

To Defendant

(3) A defendant may, after delivering a statement of defence, move with supporting affidavit material or other evidence for summary judgment dismissing all or part of the claim in the statement of claim. R.R.O. 1990, Reg. 194, r. 20.01 (3).

Courts of Justice Act

R.R.O. 1990, REGULATION 194

RULES OF CIVIL PROCEDURE

RULE 24.1 MANDATORY MEDIATION

PURPOSE

24.1.01 This Rule provides for mandatory mediation in specified actions, in order to reduce cost and delay in litigation and facilitate the early and fair resolution of disputes. O. Reg. 453/98, s. 1; O. Reg. 198/05, s. 2; O. Reg. 438/08, s. 15.

NATURE OF MEDIATION

24.1.02 In mediation, a neutral third party facilitates communication among the parties to a dispute, to assist them in reaching a mutually acceptable resolution. O. Reg. 453/98, s. 1.

DEFINITIONS

24.1.03 In rules 24.1.04 to 24.1.16,

"defence" means,

(a) Revoked: O. Reg. 457/01, s. 5.

(b) a notice of intent to defend,

(c) a statement of defence, and

(d) a notice of motion in response to an action, other than a motion challenging the court's jurisdiction; ("défense")

"mediation co-ordinator" means the person designated under rule 24.1.06. ("coordonnateur de la médiation") O. Reg. 453/98, s. 1; O. Reg. 627/98, s. 2; O. Reg. 457/01, s. 5.

APPLICATION

Scope

24.1.04 (1) This Rule applies to the following actions:

1. Actions that were governed by this Rule immediately before January 1, 2010.

2. Actions that are commenced in one of the following counties on or after January 1, 2010:

i. The City of Ottawa.

ii. The City of Toronto.

iii. The County of Essex.

3. Actions that are transferred to a county listed in paragraph 2 on or after January 1, 2014, unless the court orders otherwise. O. Reg. 438/08, s. 16 (1); O. Reg. 231/13, s. 7.

Exceptions

(2) Despite subrule (1), this Rule does not apply to,

(a) actions to which Rule 75.1 (Mandatory Mediation — Estates, Trusts and Substitute Decisions) applies;

(b) actions in relation to a matter that was the subject of a mediation under section 258.6 of the *Insurance Act*, if the mediation was conducted less than a year before the delivery of the first defence in the action;

(c) actions placed on the Commercial List established by practice direction in the Toronto Region;

(d) actions under Rule 64 (Mortgage Actions);

(e) actions under the *Construction Lien Act*, except trust claims; and

(f) actions under the *Bankruptcy and Insolvency Act* (Canada). O. Reg. 438/08, s. 16 (1).

Exceptions, Class Proceedings Act, 1992

(2.1) Despite subrule (1), this Rule,

(a) applies to an action commenced under the *Class Proceedings Act, 1992* only if certification as a class proceeding has been denied; and

(b) does not apply to actions certified as class proceedings under the *Class Proceedings Act, 1992*. O. Reg. 438/08, s. 16 (1).

CANADA

CONSOLIDATION

CODIFICATION

Supreme Court Act

Loi sur la Cour suprême

R.S.C., 1985, c. S-26

L.R.C. (1985), ch. S-26

Current to June 21, 2016

À jour au 21 juin 2016

Last amended on December 12, 2013

Dernière modification le 12 décembre 2013

OFFICIAL STATUS
OF CONSOLIDATIONS

Subsections 31(1) and (2) of the *Legislation Revision and Consolidation Act*, in force on June 1, 2009, provide as follows:

Published consolidation is evidence
31 (1) Every copy of a consolidated statute or consolidated regulation published by the Minister under this Act in either print or electronic form is evidence of that statute or regulation and of its contents and every copy purporting to be published by the Minister is deemed to be so published, unless the contrary is shown.

Inconsistencies in Acts
(2) In the event of an inconsistency between a consolidated statute published by the Minister under this Act and the original statute or a subsequent amendment as certified by the Clerk of the Parliaments under the *Publication of Statutes Act*, the original statute or amendment prevails to the extent of the inconsistency.

NOTE

This consolidation is current to June 21, 2016. The last amendments came into force on December 12, 2013. Any amendments that were not in force as of June 21, 2016 are set out at the end of this document under the heading "Amendments Not in Force".

CARACTÈRE OFFICIEL
DES CODIFICATIONS

Les paragraphes 31(1) et (2) de la *Loi sur la révision e codification des textes législatifs*, en vigueur le 1er j 2009, prévoient ce qui suit :

Codifications comme élément de preuve
31 (1) Tout exemplaire d'une loi codifiée ou d'un règlem codifié, publié par le ministre en vertu de la présente loi support papier ou sur support électronique, fait foi de ce loi ou de ce règlement et de son contenu. Tout exempla donné comme publié par le ministre est réputé avoir été ai publié, sauf preuve contraire.

Incompatibilité — lois
(2) Les dispositions de la loi d'origine avec ses modificati subséquentes par le greffier des Parlements en vertu de la *sur la publication des lois* l'emportent sur les dispositions compatibles de la loi codifiée publiée par le ministre en ve de la présente loi.

NOTE

Cette codification est à jour au 21 juin 2016. Les derniè modifications sont entrées en vigueur le 12 déce bre 2013. Toutes modifications qui n'étaient pas vigueur au 21 juin 2016 sont énoncées à la fin de ce do ment sous le titre « Modifications non en vigueur ».

Supreme Court
Appellate Jurisdiction
Sections 42-43

No appeal from discretionary orders

42 (1) No appeal lies to the Court from a judgment or order made in the exercise of judicial discretion except in proceedings in the nature of a suit or proceeding in equity originating elsewhere than in the Province of Quebec and except in *mandamus* proceedings.

Exception

(2) This section does not apply to an appeal under section 40.

R.S., 1985, c. S-26, s. 42; 1993, c. 34, s. 117(F).

Applications for leave to appeal

43 (1) Notwithstanding any other Act of Parliament but subject to subsection (1.2), an application to the Supreme Court for leave to appeal shall be made to the Court in writing and the Court shall

(a) grant the application if it is clear from the written material that it does not warrant an oral hearing and that any question involved is, by reason of its public importance or the importance of any issue of law or any issue of mixed law and fact involved in the question, one that ought to be decided by the Supreme Court or is, for any other reason, of such a nature or significance as to warrant decision by it;

(b) dismiss the application if it is clear from the written material that it does not warrant an oral hearing and that there is no question involved as described in paragraph (a); and

(c) order an oral hearing to determine the application, in any other case.

Remand of case

(1.1) Notwithstanding subsection (1), the Court may, in its discretion, remand the whole or any part of the case to the court appealed from or the court of original jurisdiction and order any further proceedings that would be just in the circumstances.

Mandatory oral hearing

(1.2) On the request of the applicant, an oral hearing shall be ordered to determine an application for leave to appeal to the Court from a judgment of a court of appeal setting aside an acquittal of an indictable offence and ordering a new trial if there is no right of appeal on a question of law on which a judge of the court of appeal dissents.

Cour suprême
Juridiction d'appel
Articles 42-43

Exclusion des ordonnances discrétionnaires

42 (1) Ne sont pas susceptibles d'appel devant la Cour les jugements ou ordonnances rendus dans l'exercice d'un pouvoir judiciaire discrétionnaire, sauf dans les procédures de la nature d'une poursuite ou procédure en equity nées hors du Québec et sauf dans les procédures de *mandamus*.

Exception

(2) Le présent article ne s'applique pas aux appels interjetés aux termes de l'article 40.

L.R. (1985), ch. S-26, art. 42; 1993, ch. 34, art. 117(F).

Demande d'autorisation d'appel

43 (1) Malgré toute autre loi fédérale et sous réserve du paragraphe (1.2), la demande d'autorisation d'appel est présentée par écrit à la Cour, qui, selon le cas :

a) l'accueille, s'il ressort des conclusions écrites qu'elle ne justifie pas la tenue d'une audience et, compte tenu de l'importance de l'affaire pour le public, ou de l'importance des questions de droit ou des questions mixtes de droit et de fait qu'elle comporte, ou de sa nature ou de son importance à tout autre égard, qu'elle devrait en être saisie;

b) la rejette, s'il ressort des conclusions écrites qu'elle ne justifie pas la tenue d'une audience et que les questions soulevées ne sont pas visées à l'alinéa a);

c) ordonne, dans les autres cas, la tenue d'une audience pour en décider.

Renvoi d'une affaire

(1.1) Malgré le paragraphe (1), la Cour peut renvoyer une affaire en tout ou en partie à la juridiction inférieure ou à celle de première instance et ordonner les mesures qui lui semblent appropriées.

Audience

(1.2) Sur demande du requérant, la Cour ordonne la tenue d'une audience pour décider d'une demande d'autorisation d'appel dans le cas où la Cour d'appel a annulé un acquittement à l'égard d'un acte criminel et ordonné un nouveau procès, s'il n'y a pas de droit d'appel sur une question de droit au sujet de laquelle un juge de Cour d'appel est dissident.

CONSTITUTION ACT, 1982 (80)

PART I

CANADIAN CHARTER OF RIGHTS AND FREEDOMS

Whereas Canada is founded upon principles that recognize the supremacy of God and the rule of law:

Guarantee of Rights and Freedoms

Marginal note:Rights and freedoms in Canada

1. The *Canadian Charter of Rights and Freedoms* guarantees the rights and freedoms set out in it subject only to such reasonable limits prescribed by law as can be demonstrably justified in a free and democratic society.

Fundamental Freedoms

Marginal note:Fundamental freedoms

2. Everyone has the following fundamental freedoms:

- (*a*) freedom of conscience and religion;
- (*b*) freedom of thought, belief, opinion and expression, including freedom of the press and other media of communication;
- (*c*) freedom of peaceful assembly; and
- (*d*) freedom of association.

Democratic Rights

Marginal note:Democratic rights of citizens

3. Every citizen of Canada has the right to vote in an election of members of the House of Commons or of a legislative assembly and to be qualified for membership therein.

Marginal note:Maximum duration of legislative bodies

- **4.** (1) No House of Commons and no legislative assembly shall continue for longer than five years from the date fixed for the return of the writs at a general election of its members. (81)
- Marginal note:Continuation in special circumstances

    (2) In time of real or apprehended war, invasion or insurrection, a House of Commons may be continued by Parliament and a legislative assembly may be continued by the

legislature beyond five years if such continuation is not opposed by the votes of more than one-third of the members of the House of Commons or the legislative assembly, as the case may be. (82)

Marginal note:Annual sitting of legislative bodies

5. There shall be a sitting of Parliament and of each legislature at least once every twelve months. (83)

Enforcement

Marginal note:Enforcement of guaranteed rights and freedoms

- **24.** (1) Anyone whose rights or freedoms, as guaranteed by this Charter, have been infringed or denied may apply to a court of competent jurisdiction to obtain such remedy as the court considers appropriate and just in the circumstances.
- Marginal note:Exclusion of evidence bringing administration of justice into disrepute

(2) Where, in proceedings under subsection (1), a court concludes that evidence was obtained in a manner that infringed or denied any rights or freedoms guaranteed by this Charter, the evidence shall be excluded if it is established that, having regard to all the circumstances, the admission of it in the proceedings would bring the administration of justice into disrepute.

Court File No: 15-66772

ONTARIO SUPERIOR COURT OF JUSTICE
COURT OF EQUITY

BETWEEN

RAYMOND CARBY-SAMUELS II

Plaintiff

– and –

HORACE R CARBY-SAMUELS

Defendant

MOTION RECORD

INDEX

Description	Tab
Requisition for Default Judgement	1
Default Motion – Particulars	2
Bill of Costs	3
Affidavit 1	4
Affidavit 2	5
Statement of Claim	6
Affidavit of Service – Statement of Claim	7

Description	Tab
Affidavit of Service – Motion	8
Note of Default	9
Judgement / Order	10

Court File No: 15-66772

ONTARIO SUPERIOR COURT OF JUSTICE

BETWEEN

RAYMOND CARBY-SAMUELS II

Plaintiff

–and–

HORACE R CARBY-SAMUELS

Defendant

REQUISITION FOR DEFAULT JUDGEMENT

TO THE LOCAL REGISTRAR AT OTTAWA

I REQUIRE you to note the defendant Horace R Carby-Samuels in default in this action on the ground that he has failed to file a Statement of Defence within the time required by the *Rules of Civil Procedure.*

I REQUIRE default judgment to be signed against the defendant Horace R. Carby-Samuels.

Default judgement may properly be signed in this action because the claim is for:

[X] a debt or liquidated demand in money

[ ] recovery of possession of land

[ ] recovery of possession of personal property

[ ] foreclosure, sale or redemption of a mortgage

[X] special order

(Debt or liquidated demand)

[ ] There has been no payment on account of the claim since the statement of claim was issued. *(Complete Parts B and C.)*

OR

[ ] The following payments have been made on account of the claim since the statement of claim was issued. *(Complete Parts A and C.)*

(Complete this part only where part payment of the claim has been received. Where no payment ha been received on account of the claim, omit this part and complete Part B.)

1. Principal

   Principal sum claimed in statement of claim (without interest) $ ....

Date of Payment	Amount of Payment	Payment Amount Principal	Applied to Interest	Principal Sum Owing
TOTAL	$................	$................	$................	A $................

2. Prejudgment interest

   (Under section 128 of the Courts of Justice Act, judgment may be obtained for prejudgment interes from the date the cause of action arose, if claimed in the statement of claim.)

   Date on which statement of claim was issued ....

   Date from which prejudgment interest is claimed ....

   The plaintiff is entitled to prejudgment interest on the claim, calculated as follows:

   (Calculate simple interest only unless an agreement relied on in the statement of claim specifies otherwise. Calculate interest on the principal sum owing from the date of the last payment. To calcula the interest amount, count the number of days since the last payment, multiply that number by the annual rate of interest, multiply the result by the principal sum owing and divide by 365.)

Principal Sum Owing	Start Date	End Date (Date of Payment)	Number of Days	Rate	Interest Amount

(The last End Date should be the date judgment is signed.)

TOTAL B.................................$

Principal Sum Owing (Total A above) $................................
Total Interest Amount (Total B above) $................................
SIGN JUDGMENT FOR $................................

PART B — NO PAYMENT RECEIVED BY PLAINTIFF

(Complete this part only where no payment has been received on account of the claim.)

1. Principal

   Principal sum claimed in statement of claim (without interest)....... $ 25,000.00

2. Prejudgment interest

   (Under section 128 of the Courts of Justice Act, judgment may be obtained for prejudgment interes from the date the cause of action arose, if claimed in the statement of claim.)

   Date on which statement of claim was issued ....

Date from which prejudgment interest is claimed ....

The plaintiff is entitled to prejudgment interest on the claim, calculated as follows:

(Calculate simple interest only unless an agreement relied on in the statement of claim specifies otherwise. To calculate the interest amount, count the number of days and multiply that number by the annual rate of interest, multiply the result by the principal sum owing and divide by 365.)

Principal Sum Owing	Start Date	End Date (Date of Payment)	Number of Days	Rate	Interest Amount
$ 25,000.00					

TOTAL B .... $

Principal Sum Owing (Total A above) $......25,000.00..............
Total Interest Amount (Total B above) $............................
SIGN JUDGMENT FOR $......25,000.00..............

PART C — POSTJUDGMENT INTEREST AND COSTS

1. Postjudgment interest

    The plaintiff is entitled to postjudgment interest at the rate of   per cent per year,

    [ ] under the *Courts of Justice Act*, as claimed in the statement of claim.

    OR

    [ ] in accordance with the claim made in the statement of claim.

2. Costs

    The plaintiff wishes costs to be,

    [X] fixed by the local registrar.

    OR

    [ ] assessed by an assessment officer.

Date ....4 February 2016.................   ....
                                                     (Signature of plaintiff's lawyer or plaintiff)

H. Raymond Carby-Samuels II
B.P. 24191 – 300 Eagleson Rd
Kanata, Ontario K2M 2C3

Tel: (613) 599-5344

Court File No: 15-66772

ONTARIO SUPERIOR COURT OF JUSTICE

BETWEEN

RAYMOND CARBY-SAMUELS II

Plaintiff

–and –

HORACE R CARBY-SAMUELS

Defendant

FINANCIAL CLAIM

The Plaintiff makes Claims against the Defendants for the following torts:

1. **Illegal Eviction [$5,000]** – The Defendant, Horace Carby-Samuels was legally obliged to obtain the consent of both co-property owners of 30 Jarlan Terrace in Kanata, Ontario. The name of these co-property owners are Horace Carby-Samuels and Dezrin Carby-Samuels. The said Defendant only and improperly relied upon his own direction to perpetrate the eviction of the Plaintiff. Horace Carby-Samuels only has 50% control of the property. The said Defendant therefore required the correspondent authority from Dezrin Carby-Samuels that he did not obtain pursuant to law pertaining to the eviction of *even a relatively casual "guest" in-law*. The said Defendant's after 2 AM eviction carried out in late April 2015 was therefore illegal.

2) **Subversion of Ontario's Landlord and Tenants Act** - A family member or friend occupying a

been associated with their torts. The Plaintiff emphasizes that he has continued to be possessed of additional belongings that remain under the control of Marcella and Horace Carby-uels. These include his 12-speed bicycle.

- **Battery [$4,500]** – Horace Carby-Samuels attacked the Plaintiff with a kitchen knife that he had pointed to the Plaintiff's stomach in a spate of anger than in the process ended up almost severing the small finger of the Plaintiff. The said Defendant's action caused the Plaintiff to have to go into physiotherapy for about six months requiring him not to work; and losing 6 months of potential income. Ottawa Police Service took an official report from the Plaintiff concerning the said Defendant's tort of battery against the Plaintiff.

- **Battery 2 [$500]** – Marcella Carby-Samuels physically pinned down and accosted the Plaintiff at the kitchen sink on 8 January 2015 before mischievously calling the Ottawa Police Services to allege along with Horace Carby-Samuels that the Plaintiff was "causing a domestic dispute"; was ""holding the household hostage" which were vehemently denied by the Plaintiff's Mom, Dezrin Carby-Samuels in writing after this incident. Just before the battery, when the Plaintiff said he would call the police if Marcella did not "back-off, the said Defendant, Marcella, boasted that the Ottawa Police would never believe that a "female" "beat-up" the Plaintiff.

- **Assault [$500]** – Marcella Carby-Samuels during the winter of 2015 assaulted the Plaintiff by threatening the Plaintiff with imminent violent behaviour which involved AGGRESSIVELY impeding the ability of the Plaintiff to create space away from the said Defendant Marcella Carby-Samuels.

- **Tort of Nuisance / Harassment [$2,000]** - Marcella Carby-Samuels hired Robert Griffin who then subjected the Plaintiff to months of harassment that has also included illegal warnings directed by Marcella to this apparent "dirty cop" as her agent that resulted in harassing texting and other means of communications by the agents of the Defendants that sought to threaten the Plaintiff to refrain from contacting Plaintiff's relatives against the Plaintiff's constitutional rights. The Defendants have correspondingly illegally interfered with the Plaintiff and his own

Mom being able to see each other as their civil right to do so. Marcella's hired agent also threatened representatives of the Nepenthe, Rideau and Osgoode Resource Centre on 15 June 2015, who had offered to testify in court against the nefarious activities of the Defendants.

6. **Intentional Infliction of Mental Distress / Conspiracy [$3,000]** – CBC's Doc Zone estimated that there are about 600,000 'psychopaths' in Canada alone and both Defendants are consistent with the description in that investigative report of what constitutes a psychopath. Marcella in particular has been the apparent lead Defendant in engineering the ruthless forcible separation of the Plaintiff and his own Mom resulting in mental distress / anguish. The Defendants have conspired to use the Ottawa Police Services and the corresponding hiring of apparent "dirty cops" named Robert Griffin and Scott Fenton to execute an organized conspiracy of intimidation against the Plaintiff and his witnesses against the oppressive activities of Marcella and Horace Carby-Samuels. The Defendants have also sought to perpetuate mental stress about his Mom's declining health which is the result of the conditions of abuse and neglect by the Defendants that have been enforced by the efforts of the Defendants to illegally block rge Plaintiff's access to seeing his own Mom, Dezrin Carby-Samuels

7. **Tort of Deceit and Fraud** involving **infliction of mental distress [$3,000]** – Marcella has continued to make unsubstantiated allegations concerning the "mental health" of the Plaintiff that have no medical substantiation and allegations that the Plaintiff has sought to "kidnap" his Mom that are not corroborated with any criminal record. The Plaintiff has no criminal record and has never "kidnapped" anyone. Furthermore, the Plaintiff has never sought to "kidnap" anyone. The complaints that the Defendants have made against the Police have been malicious and constitute public mischief as further defined by the Canadian Criminal Code and do little more than substantiate the Defendants' psychopathic state of mind.

8. **Conspiracy** to solicit a false arrest from the Ottawa Police Services through fraudulent misrepresentation and malicious unsubstantiated hearsay allegations.

and illegally enforced separation of the Plaintiff from his own Mother. The Plaintiff had previously never been out of contact with his Mother for more than three days for over 45 years. The illegal eviction also resulted in the Plaintiff being denied access to his personal and professional belongings which incurred the Plaintiff both financial costs and inconvenience amounting to over $10,000 in costs / financial losses related to missed contract opportunities that the Plaintiff could not fulfill. These include the Plaintiff having to buy a bed and mattress to replace the bed and mattress that the Plaintiff was denied access to without warning that had cost the Plaintiff more than $2,000 to having to buy a new one.

10. **Aggravated Damages** – The Plaintiff has been living with the the worsening daily trauma as to the quality of survival of the Plaintiff's Mom having witnessed neglect and abuse that was directed by the Plaintiff "father" against his Mom in late April and the evidence of continued neglect / abuse that the Plaintiff saw his Mom as having been subjected to as of 12 June 2015. The Defendants made themselves agents of the continued abuse and neglect of the Plaintiff's Mom by unlawfully denying the Plaintiff's ability to care for his own Mom resulting in the Plaintiff's Mom now not being able to talk, walk or write. Thanks to the illegal interference by the Defendants in the relationship of the Plaintiff with his Mother, the Plaintiff will no longer be able to her his own Mother talk to him again. Police reports also corroborate the biasing / contempt of the Ottawa Police Services against the civil rights of the Plaintiff.

Punitive Damages. The subversion of the inviolable civil rights of the the Plaintiff by the Defendants has been egregious. At common law, punitive damages can be awarded in any civil suit in which the plaintiff proves that the defendant's conduct was "malicious, oppressive and high-handed [such] that it offends the court's sense of decency": *Hill v. Church of Scientology of Toronto*, [1995] 2 S.C.R. 1130 at para. 196. "The test thus limits the award to misconduct that represents a marked departure from ordinary standards of decent behaviour": *Whiten v. Pilot Insurance Co.*, 2002 SCC 18 at para. 36. The malicious conduct of the Police was further evident in Police reports including 15-5493 on January 015 which shows that Ottawa Police Services acted with egregious contempt against the Plaintiff which involved barely allowing him to speak while accepting the representation of Horace and Marcella Carby-Samuels *ad nauseum*.

i) **Defamation and Slander** - Ottawa Police agents of the Dfendants also instructed neighbours to call the police if they saw the Plaintiff in the neighbourhood which in effect maliciously subjected the aintiff to public ridicule and treatment as if the Plaintiff was a convicted criminal.

OTHER COSTS

Professional Services [$5000] – Horace Carby-Samuels owes money for professional services vided by the Plaintiff for book publishing and related services in relation to his book entitled *Quality-of-Living and Human Development as the Outcome of Economic Progress*, ISBN: 30978190616

- Comprehensive Copy and Substantive Editing $2,000.00
- Typesetting / Layout / Book cover design $1,000.00
- Printing $1,000.00
- Advertising and Internet Marketing $1,000.00

rcise Machine [$1,000.00] – The Plaintiff bought an exercise machine to help his Mom get tically needed exercise and then the Defendants presented the Plaintiff from using the machine to him Mom just weeks before Horace Carby-Samuels evicted the Plaintiff.

Replacement of Bed, Box Springs / Mattress and Chesterfield [$2,000.00] – The Plaintiff was forced to replace items given to the Plaintiff that he had been using for more than 20 years. As a result of the unlawful eviction of Horace Carby-Samuels. The said Defendant was unlawfully dispossessed the outlined items and suffered costs as a result.

Court File No:

ONTARIO SUPERIOR COURT OF JUSTICE

BETWEEN

RAYMOND CARBY-SAMUELS II

Plaintiff

–and -

HORACE R CARBY-SAMUELS

Defendant

STATEMENT OF CLAIM

TO THE DEFENDANT

A LEGAL PROCEEDING HAS BEEN COMMENCED AGAINST YOU by the plaintiff. The claim made against you is set out in the following pages.

IF YOU WISH TO DEFEND THIS PROCEEDING, you or an Ontario lawyer acting for you must prepare a statement of defence in Form 18A prescribed by the Rules of Civil Procedure, serve it on the plaintiff's lawyer or, where the plaintiff does not have a lawyer, serve it on the plaintiff, and file it, with proof of service in this court office, WITHIN TWENTY DAYS after this statement of claim is served on you, if you are served in Ontario.

If you are served in another province or territory of Canada or in the United States of America, the period for serving and filing your statement of defence is forty days. If you are served outside Canada and the United States of America, the period is sixty days.

Instead of serving and filing a statement of defence, you may serve

THIS ACTION IS BROUGHT AGAINST YOU UNDER THE SIMPLIFIED PROCEDURE PROVIDED IN RULE 76 OF THE RULES OF CIVIL PROCEDURE.

CLAIM

1. The plaintiff, Raymond Carby-Samuels II, claims as against the defendant, Horace R. Carby-Samuels:

   (a) an Order directing Horace Carby-Samuels to cease and desist intefering in the ability of Raymond Carby Samuels II and the Plaintiff's disabled and sick Mom, Dezrin Carby-Samuels to see each other; and to immediately enable access to each other, without further delay, at a mutually convenient location for both the Plaintiff and the Plaintiff's mother that takes into consideration the disabilities of the Plaintiff's mother.

The Parties

1. Raymond Carby-Samuels II is the son of Horace R. Carby-Samuels.

The Facts

1. The Plaintiff and the Plaintiff's disabled and sick Mother have not been able to see each other since 12 June 2015.

1. The Defendant has saw fit to treat the Plaintiff's Mom not as a human being who can see who she likes that is a civil right affirmed by freedom of association pursuant to the Canadian Charter of Rights and Freedoms but as the Defendant's property illegally subject to forcible confinement.

1. No law empowers the Defendant to legally intefere in the ability of two law abiding citizens to see each other by subjecting one of those citizens to confinement against the will of that citizen as affirmed by both the Canadian Charter of Rights and Freedoms and the Canadian Criminal Code.

1. The Plaintiff's Mom has documented to the Plaintiff of being subject to abuse (Appendix 1) and seeks immediate access to the Plaintiff's Mother to determine her medical needs and whether she is being subjected to further neglect and abuse by the Defendant.

Court File No 15-667

ONTARIO

SUPERIOR COURT OF JUSTICE

BETWEEN

RAYMOND CARBY-SAMUELS II

Plaintiff

–and –

HORACE R CARBY-SAMUELS

Defendant

REQUISITION ~~FOR~~ to Note in DEFAULT ~~JUDGMENT~~

TO THE LOCAL REGISTRAR AT 161 ELGIN STREET IN OTTAWA, ONTARIO

I, note defendant in Default for failure to file a

~~Where the defendant has not been noted in default, begin with: I REQUIRE you to note the defendant HORACE R. CARBY-SAMUELS in default in this action on the ground that he did not file a Statement of Defence in the time alloted by the Ontario Rules of Civil Procedure.~~

Statement of defense in the time prescribed

I REQUIRE default judgment to be signed against the defendant HORACE R CARBY-SAMUELS.

Default judgement may properly be signed in this action ~~because the claim is for:~~ by Rule 18 Ontario Rule of Civil Procedure.

[ ] Immediate and permanent access to seeing my Mother unhibited by the Defendant and/or his agents

[ ] a debt or liquidated demand in money c/s

[ ] recovery of possession of land

[ ] recovery of possession of personal property

Court File No: 15-66772

ONTARIO SUPERIOR COURT OF JUSTICE

BETWEEN

RAYMOND CARBY-SAMUELS II

Plaintiff

-and-

HORACE R CARBY-SAMUELS

Defendant

JUDGEMENT

On reading the Statement of Claim in this action and the proof of service on the Statement of Claim on the Defendant, Horace R Carby-Samuels, having been noted in default,

1. IT IS ORDERED AND ADJUDGED that the defendant, Horace R. Carby-Samuels pay to the plaintiff the sum of $25,000 and the sum of $532.00 for the costs of this action.

2. IT IS ORDERED AND ADJUDGED that the defendant, Horace R. Carby-Samuels also immediately facilitate on-going and permanent access by

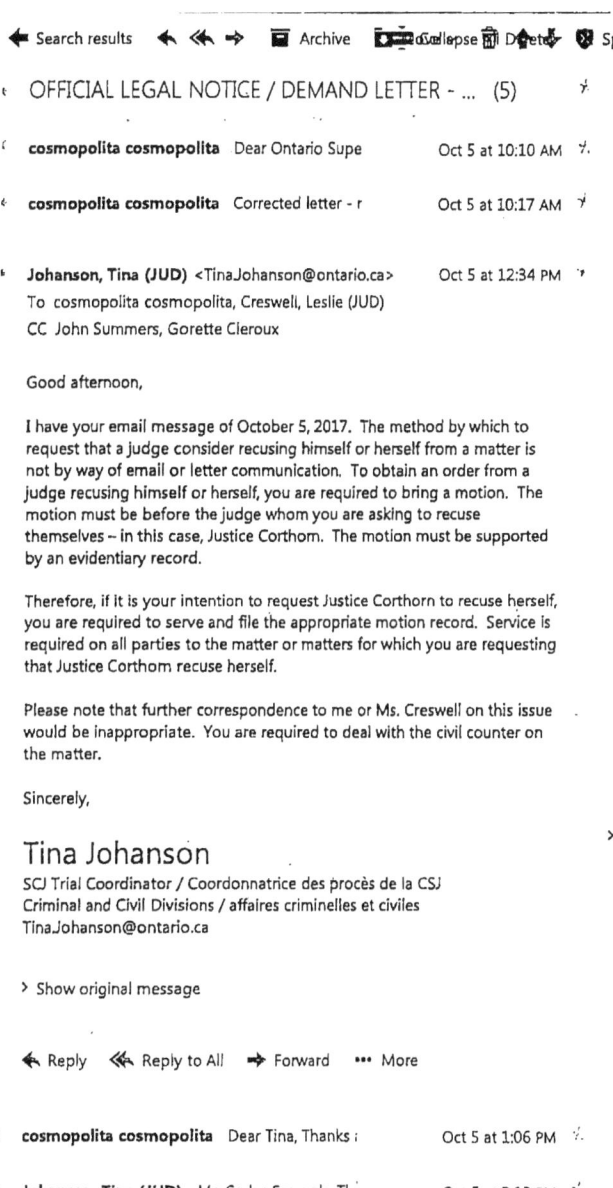

OFFICIAL LEGAL NOTICE / DEMAND LETTER - ... (5)

cosmopolita cosmopolita Dear Ontario Supe   Oct 5 at 10:10 AM

cosmopolita cosmopolita Corrected letter - r   Oct 5 at 10:17 AM

Johanson, Tina (JUD) <TinaJohanson@ontario.ca>   Oct 5 at 12:34 PM
To cosmopolita cosmopolita, Creswell, Leslie (JUD)
CC John Summers, Gorette Cieroux

Good afternoon,

I have your email message of October 5, 2017. The method by which to request that a judge consider recusing himself or herself from a matter is not by way of email or letter communication. To obtain an order from a judge recusing himself or herself, you are required to bring a motion. The motion must be before the judge whom you are asking to recuse themselves -- in this case, Justice Corthorn. The motion must be supported by an evidentiary record.

Therefore, if it is your intention to request Justice Corthorn to recuse herself, you are required to serve and file the appropriate motion record. Service is required on all parties to the matter or matters for which you are requesting that Justice Corthorn recuse herself.

Please note that further correspondence to me or Ms. Creswell on this issue would be inappropriate. You are required to deal with the civil counter on the matter.

Sincerely,

Tina Johanson

SCJ Trial Coordinator / Coordonnatrice des procès de la CSJ
Criminal and Civil Divisions / affaires criminelles et civiles
TinaJohanson@ontario.ca

> Show original message

← Reply   ← Reply to All   → Forward   ••• More

cosmopolita cosmopolita Dear Tina, Thanks   Oct 5 at 1:06 PM

Johanson, Tina (JUD) Mr. Carby-Samuels, Th   Oct 5 at 2:12 PM

Click to Reply, Reply All or Forward

FILE NUMBER: 15-6677

ONTARIO
SUPERIOR COURT OF JUSTICE

BETWEEN

RAYMOND CARBY-SAMUELS

Plaintiff

– and –

HORACE R CARBY-SAMUELS

Defendant

AFFIDAVIT OF RAYMOND CARBY-SAMUELS

I, of the City of Ottawa in the Province of Ontario, MAKE OATH AND SAY (or AFFIRM):

1. I, Raymond Carby-Samuels, confirm and attest to the fact that I have a reasonable apprehension of bias regarding the expressed ability of Justice Sylvia Corthorn to preside over the fair and impartial administration of justice as outlined by the Canadian Judicial Council's Code of Ethics.
2. I submit this Motion seeking the immediate and if possible retroactive recusal of Justice Sylvia Corthorn on all matters related to the Defence Counsel's Motions for Summary Judgement and Vexatious Litigant, and any

other matter related to Court File 15-66772 based upon the legal advisement of Tina Johanson, SCJ Trial Coordinator, Criminal and Civil Divisions of the Superior Court of Justice in Ottawa. [Exhibit 1]

3. I made a complaint to the Canadian Judicial Council dated 6 October 2017 outlining grounds for Justice Sylvia Corthorn's immediate recusal from Court File 15-66772. [Exhibit 2]

4. DISCRIMINATION - Justice Corthorn subjected me to *prima facie* discrimination involving differential treatment as defined by the *Ontario Human Rights Code* by fabricating a "Leave for Urgent Motion" process that is not authorized by the *Ontario Rules of Civil Procedure*; has no apparent legal precedent in common law and gave the appearance of handicapping my efforts pursue my Motion as a self-represented litigant.

5. INSTITUTIONALIZED RACISM / DISCRIMNATION – Whereas Justice Macloed on 24 March 2017 sought to endorse his sought independent verification of my Mom's well-being to ensure that my Mom has not been held "prisoner" to borrow his words, Justice Corthorn expressed no such interest in verifying the safety and security of my Mom, as a black woman, pursuant to the *Canadian Charter of Rights and Freedoms* and have the appearance of racism. Justice Corthorn apparent lack of demonstrated concern for the factual verification of my Mom's well-being and desires that is incumbent of any Judge that seeks to uphold our Constitution requires her immediate recusal. Furthermore, Justice Corthorn gave no regard to the physical disabilities of my Mom in being able to present herself in the Courtroom in violation of Equality Rights stipulated in Section 15(1) of the *Canadian Charter of Rights and Freedoms* while ignoring my presented written evidence of my Mom's desires in lieu of her attendance.

6. APPARENT PREJUDICE IN FAVOUR OF DEFENCE. Justice Sylvia Corthorn on multiple occasions demonstrated apparent bias. This included allowing the Defence to submit documents late in respect of the *Ontario Rules of Civil Procedure* which is based upon supporting a fair litigation process. While Justice Corthorn allowed Defence Counsel to submit late documents, in Justice Corthorn's ruling on the Leave for Urgent Motion, she scolded the Plaintiff who is a self-represented litigant for having made a late submission as a result of the tardiness of the Plaintiff's lawyer who he had no control over. Justice Corthorn also accepted the veracity of claims made by

Defence Counsel regarding the wishes of the Plaintiff's Mom as being the same as the Defendant when she referred to "my parents" in No 11 of her so-called Leave for Urgent Motion ruling even though the Defence Counsel had refused to independently verify the well-being and desires of my Mom. Justice Corthorn therefore has demonstrated a penchant to rule in favour of Defence Counsel without any basis of facts / evidence while disregarding my evidence regarding the stated desires of my Mom.

7. ACCEPTANCE OF APPARENT FAKE SIGNATURE – I have observed by meticulous consistence of my father's signature over the years. Justice Corthorn accepted an affidavit during the Leave for Urgent Motion which was not only late; and contained false information but also contained a signature which in no way resembled signatures by the Defendant that have been consistent in previous Affidavits of the Defendant.

8. KNOWINGLY ACCEPTING FRAUDULENT REPRESENTATION IN AN AFFIDAVIT – Justice Corthon has accepted affidavits knowingly with false information proving a willingness to use this false information to support an Endorsement that has been subjected to prejudice. Examples of Justice Corthorn knowingly accepting Defence Counsel's false information to prejudice the Plaintiff include the Defence Affidavits references to "my parents" not wanting to see or have contact with me when she knew that the Defendant rejected Judge Macloed's sought independent verification; and the Defendant's Affidavit fraudulently alleging that I had been "blacklisted" by Ottawa Ambulance Services even though I presented official correspondence from Ottawa Ambulance Services denying such a "blacklisting". Furthermore, even though Defence Counsel has claimed that the Defendant wants to have no contact with the Plaintiff, Justice Corthorn ignored evidence presented by the Plaintiff that the Defendant actually called the Plaintiff on 21 August 2017 and talked for over two minutes. This is clear proof that Defence Counsel's representation concerning the alleged desire of the Defendant not to have contact as being fraudulent. [Exhibit 2]

9. THE ACCEPTANCE OF INADMISSIBLE AFFIDAVITS submitted by Defence Counsel in support of their Motions for Summary Judgement and Vexatious Litigation. Justice Corthorn has shown a lack of respect for me as a self-represented litigant pursuant to Section 24 of the *Canadian Charter of Rights and Freedoms* by allowing Defence Council to run amok of

established practices of proper Affidavits in relation to the *Ontario Rules of Civil Procedure*. This includes Justice Corthorn allowing Defence Counsel to submit an affidavit by Gorette Cleroux who works for John Summers whose testimony is based upon heresay she skimmed online. At the same time, Justice Corthorn has allowed Defence Council to unilaterally block my own *bona fide* affidavit submissions.

10. DENIAL OF MY RIGHT TO LEGAL REPRESENTATION – My lawyer had sought to seek an adjournment of the Motions for Summary Judgement of Vexatious Litigation to allow him time to prepare since he had take so much time to prepare the Urgent Motion. Justice Corthorn denied my lawyer's request and then forced me to defend myself against Motions for Summary Judgement and Vexatious Litigation against a lawyer who apparently was accepted to the Bar in 1999.

Affirmed before me at the City of Ottawa in the Province of Ontario on _____ OCT 1 0 2017 _____

Commissioner for Taking Affidavits

(Signature of deponent)

OFFICIAL LEGAL NOTICE / DEMAND LETTER - ... (5)

cosmopolita cosmopolita	Dear Ontario Supe	Oct 5 at 10:10 AM
cosmopolita cosmopolita	Corrected letter - r	Oct 5 at 10:17 AM

Johanson, Tina (JUD) <TinaJohanson@ontario.ca>   Oct 5 at 12:34 PM
To cosmopolita cosmopolita, Creswell, Leslie (JUD)
CC John Summers, Gorette Cleroux

Good afternoon,

I have your email message of October 5, 2017. The method by which to request that a judge consider recusing himself or herself from a matter is not by way of email or letter communication. To obtain an order from a judge recusing himself or herself, you are required to bring a motion. The motion must be before the judge whom you are asking to recuse themselves – in this case, Justice Corthorn. The motion must be supported by an evidentiary record.

Therefore, if it is your intention to request Justice Corthorn to recuse herself, you are required to serve and file the appropriate motion record. Service is required on all parties to the matter or matters for which you are requesting that Justice Corthorn recuse herself.

Please note that further correspondence to me or Ms. Creswell on this issue would be inappropriate. You are required to deal with the civil counter on the matter.

Sincerely,

Tina Johanson

SCJ Trial Coordinator / Coordonnatrice des procès de la CSJ
Criminal and Civil Divisions / affaires criminelles et civiles
TinaJohanson@ontario.ca

> Show original message

← Reply   ← Reply to All   → Forward   ••• More

cosmopolita cosmopolita	Dear Tina, Thanks	Oct 5 at 1:06 PM
Johanson, Tina (JUD)	Mr. Carby-Samuels, Th	Oct 5 at 2:12 PM

Court File: 15-66772

B.P 24191 – 300 Eagleson Rd
Kanata, Ontario K2M 2C3

6 October 2017

Canadian Judicial Council,
Ottawa, Ontario, K1A 0W8

Complaint Against Justice Sylvia Corthorn

Dear Canadian Judicial Council representative,

I very respectfully submit a complaint to your Office regarding apparent judicial misconduct and breaches in violation of the *Canadian Judicial Council's Code of Ethics*.

I'm requesting a full investigation of Justice Corthon's treatment of my Court Claim since Her Honour had seized my Claim without my voluntary consent.

I'm hoping that Justice Sylvia Corthorn will voluntarily recuse herself from presiding any further on my Court File 15-66772 on the Ontario Superior Court of Justice in matters specifically relating to my sought Urgent Motion to visit my elderly and sick mother and in general matters related prevailing Defence Motions.

Justice Sylvia Corthorn has totally disregarded the prior endorsement of Justice Macloed who sought independent verification to borrow His Honour's words that my Mother "is not being held prisoner" by my father. [Exhibit 1 – attached]

In doing so, Justice Corthorn to-date has acted in callous disregard of my Mom's life, and in general, the rights of the physically disabled and the plight of women suffering from spousal abuse and human decency along with my own civil rights.

Justice Corthorn for months has perpetuated the abuse of my Mom that she has been subjected to by my father in addition to the subversion of my own rights.

Evidence that I submitted to Justice Corthorn regarding abuse and neglect involving enforced social isolation and deprivation of access to medical care by the Defendant that my Mom had sought to protect her health have been of no apparent concern to this Judge. This blocking of access to medical care has involved the depriving of speech therapy which resulted in my Mom losing the ability to talk.

Justice Corthorn has denied my Mom her civil rights prescribed in Section 7 regarding "Life, liberty and the security of person" by showing total disregard to my Mom's complaints of abuse and my efforts to establish contact with my Mom, which Her Honour has no basis in law to frustrate, in violation of my freedom of conscience and religion as affirmed in the *Canadian Charter of Rights and Freedoms*.

In Justice Corthon's decision [no 11], she referred to what "my parents" want in relationship to my Mother when she has no basis of fact to be making this reference.

The Defendant denied Justice's MacLoed stated endorsement in the transcript attached of my 24 March 2017 Motion to support a process of independent verification to ensure to borrow His Honour's words that my Mom is "not being held prisoner".

It is therefore a categorical demonstration of prejudice and bias for Justice Corthorn to then make a claim of what "my parents" [i.e. cited in no 11 of her Ruling – Exhibit 2] want solely based on the veracity of Defendant's heresay claims in his affidavit that he has sought to block independent verification.

Justice Corthon has shown in Her Honour's ruling that unlike Justice Macloed, she will not be guided by evidence and facts. Instead, Justice Corthorn has shown a prejudicial bias in support of / in favour of any and all claims of the Defendant irrespective of any evidence to the contrary.

I have presented evidence to Justice Corthorn that my Mom has maintained a desire to see me. But instead, Justice Corthorn has made misleading statements regarding the desires of my Mom without any basis of fact or evidence.

There is no greater responsibility entrusted to Judges across Canada under our *Canadian Charter of Rights and Freedoms* that the protection of life.

The Supreme Court of Canada has affirmed that judges are required to use their inherent jurisdiction to affirm the protection of life and especially in matters regarding children and the physically disabled like my Mom; and Justice Corthorn has failed miserably in her Oath to Her Majesty which is implicitly based on this axiom.

Furthermore, Justice Corthorn elected to base her decision on an Affidavit submitted by Defence Counsel that was late in violation of the *Ontario Rules of Civil Procedure*, contained verifiable slander alleging that I had been "blacklisted" by the Ottawa Ambulance Services" [Exhibit 4] and according to my Handwriting experts, the signed Affidavit was subject to forgery. [Exhibit 3].

In her ruling, Justice Corthorn sought to chastise the lateness of my lawyer who had been preparing the Urgent Motion but failed to similar chastise the repeated lateness of Defence Counsel in violation of Civil Procedure which further shows bias.

I would also add that Justice Corthorn has subjected me to differential treatment in violation of the Ontario Human Rights Code by requiring that my Urgent Motion be submitted first through a "Leave of Urgent Motion" to Her Honour. There's no such thing in the Ontario Rules of Civil Procedure as a "Leave of Urgent Motion" which she contrived in violation of my civil rights and supports a reasonable apprehension of bias

I hope that Justice Corthorn will do the Honorable thing and immediately recuse hersel from having subjected me to bias and prejudice in her Courtroom and for having perpetuated the abuse of my Mother which had resulted in my reasonable apprehensic of bias against her ability to treat my file based upon actual evidence and facts, and to affirm my desire for equity pursuant to Section 96 of the Courts of Justice Act

Thanks for your consideration.

Kind regards,

Raymond Carby-Samuels

cc. Office of Justice Corthorn

Offices of MacNamara, JS

EXPERT AFFIDAVIT OF GRACIE CARR

STATE OF NEW YORK

COUNTY OF BROOME

BE IT KNOWN, that on this 10th day of September 2017.

BEFORE ME, a duly sworn and competent authority in and for the County of Broome, NOTARY PUBLIC, and the undersigned affiant and competent witness appearing herein below,

DID PERSONALLY APPEAR: GRACE CARR, a person of fully age of Majority, residing and domiciled in the State of New York, County of Broome.

WHO AFTER BEEN DULY SWORN BY ME, did depose and state:

(1) My name is Dr Grace Carr and I have personal knowledge of the matters contained in this Affidavit. I am a licensed and practicing Forensic Expert in detecting forged signature in the State of New York. I have been practicing as a Forensic Expert for 10 years. I am over the age of eighteen years, am of sound mind, having never been convicted of a felony or a crime of moral turpitude; I am competent in all respect to make this declaration. I have personal knowledge of the matters herein.

(2) I have studied, trained and hold a certification in the examination, comparison, analysis and identification of Signatures from The International School of Forensic Document Examination. I have served as an expert within pending litigation matters.

(3) I was asked to compare the signature on Exhibit A, Exhibit B and Exhibit C. After carefully examining and analyzing the signature in Exhibit A, Exhibit B and Exhibit C. It is my opinion that the signatures of Mr. Horace Carby-Samuels in three different documentation are resulted from three different timelines.

(4) In the first documentation is Court File no. 1771624 which seems to hold the original signature of Mr. Horace Carby-Samuels (exhibit A) Similarly in the second documentation, Court File no.15-66772 (exhibit B) which has the alleged false signature along with the third documentation with the same Court File no. 15-66772(exhibit C) which has been used as preference for additional clarity.

(5) From the basic analysis, the first and third documents are signed by the same individual however; it seems to be clear that the second documentation has a forged signature .According to the formal analysis this type of forgery of signature would be classified as the simulated signature, or "free hand forgery" as it is sometime known. This forgery is constructed by using a genuine signature as a model. The forger generates an artistic reproduction of this model. Depending on his skill and amount of practice, the simulation may be quite good and bear remarkable pictorial similarity to the genuine signature.

(6) Many simulations created with a model at hand will contain at least some of the general indicators of forgery, such as tremor, hesitation, pen lifts, blunt starts and stops, patching, and static pressure. They will have a slow "drawn" appearance. The practiced simulation is most often a higher quality creation in that the model signature has been memorized and some of the movements used to produce it have become semi-automatic. This simulation can be written with a more natural fluid manner. There can be tapered starts and stops, changes in pen pressure, and much less tremor in the moving line. Speed lends fluidity to writing. The more rapidly the pen moves while creating the genuine writing or signature, the more difficult the genuine writing is to imitate. Rapidly formed movements are scrutinized more closely than slower counterparts. A slowly written signature is not only easier for the forger to duplicate with some fashionable degree of pictorial similarity; the product will also display indications of non-genuineness than the forgery of a rapid and fluidly executed signature. The writer of a simulation must, of necessity, pay more attention to the form of a letter than the speed of his pen.

(7) Both practiced and non-practiced simulations will still have notable shortcomings. The forger naturally puts his greatest effort into those parts of the name that he expects to fall under the greatest scrutiny. Although letter forms (especially the more prominent, large or beginning letters) may almost duplicate the genuine letters, proportions and height ratios will seldom be correct. Internal portions of the names (smaller, less prominent letters and pen movements) will usually display the greatest divergence from the correct form and movements found in the genuine signature. During the creation of a simulated forgery, the author attempts to duplicate the writing style of another individual. By doing this, the forger leaves behind little, if any, of his own distinctive writing style. By doing an emulation of someone else's signature, he also produces one of the best of all possible disguises of his own handwriting. Infrequently, some of the forger's own individual characteristics may appear in the disputed writing. The limited quantity of these characteristics which appear on those occasions is such that identification of the author almost never occurs. If there are a sufficient number of significant differences between the questioned signature and the genuine signatures, and these same differences appear in the practiced simulations, there may be a basis to associate the forgery to the forger within some degree of probability. An absolute identification, nonetheless, even under these circumstances is infrequent.

(8) Closely related to this form of identification process is that of determining the number of different forgers from a quantity of simulations. On occasion there will be two or more forgers attempting to reproduce the same signature. It may be possible to group or associate simulations of the same name by the combinations of defects within the forgeries. By associating and grouping the similar defects (when compared to the genuine signature) it may be possible to conclude and illustrate that there are indeed, two or more different forgers.

(9) The second documentation (Exhibit 2) clearly projects the forged signature for the following reasoning

In the second document it can identified that the forger places the pen point in contact with the paper, and then starts writing. When he or she is finished with the name or some portion thereof, he or she stops the pen and lifts it from the surface. This has cause the emphasized blunt start and ending where the pen was placed in contact with the surface. At times this contact is held so long that the pen contains two fluid inks in the front letter of the signature, it has wet the paper and migrate outward from the contact point.

There may be unnecessary and extraneous marks caused by pen starts and stops. The writer may decided after putting his or her pen in contact with the paper, that it is in the wrong spot, picks it up and moves it to a position considered more correct. Normally a signature's starts and stops are much more dynamic which can be noticed in the other two documents. The pen is moving horizontally before it contacts the paper and is lifted at the end while still in flight. This leaves a tapered appearance at the beginnings and endings of names or letters.

In this situation it can occasioned that the pen stops at an unusual point in the writing; perhaps during radical change in direction is about to take a new letter formation is about to be started. This may take on the appearance of a larger gap in the written line where one is not expected, or an overlapping of two ink lines where there should be only one continuous line which clearly in the second document but not the other two, where it seems to be following the same pattern throughout the signature.

Because the creation of most forms of non-genuine signatures are little more than drawings, the pen is moving so slowly that small, sometimes microscopic changes in direction take place in what should be a fluid-looking line. The resultant line is not smooth, but reflects the "shaking" pen. It can be seen that the lines in the signature of the second documentation is much larger than the rest two and has microscopic shakes.

Again, because the pen is moving slowly rather than with the dynamic movement associated with most genuine writings, the ink line remains constant in thickness, resulting from the same constant pressure exerted on a slowly moving pen. There will be little, if any, tapering of internal lines. This is clearly evident in the second document's signature which constantly remains in the same thickness.

Sometimes when the genuine writer makes an error while writing our own signature, more commonly individuals may leave the signature alone, caring little about the mistake or imperfection, while others will simply "fix" the signature by correcting the offending portion. This might have been done in this situation to make the signature more readable, or because a defect in the pen or paper has affected what we perceive to be our "normal" signature, or for some other reason that may even be subconscious.

However by analyzing the previous signature that seems very unlikely. These "fixes" are patent, with no attempt made on the part of the writer to mask or otherwise hide the correction for which some letters are crossing the others out.

These signature corrections are quite different than the patching that is frequently found in non-genuine signatures. On these occasions, the writer is not attempting to make the signature more readable, but to make its appearance passable. He or she is fixing an obvious defect that he or she perceives as detectable, and might uncover his fraudulent product and foil his scheme. These usually take the form of a correction to a flaw in the writing line rather than in the form of a letter. Extensions to entry or terminal strokes, or to lower descending portions of letters, along with corrections to embellishments, are typical of non-genuine patching.

It is my professional opinion that the documentation in (exhibit B) has a forged signature of Mr. Horace R. Carby-Samuels and with intent of malicious actions.

Dated: September 10, 2017

I affirm the truth of this statement

GRACE CARR

STATE OF NEW YORK
COUNTY OF BROOME

I, the undersigned Notary Public, in and for the said State and County, hereby certify that Dr Grace Carr whose name is signed to the foregoing Affidavit, and who is known to me, acknowledged before me on this day that, being informed of said Affidavit, He executed same voluntarily on the day the same bears date.

Given under my hand and seal this 10th day of September, 2017

Kieran Ryan

Notary Public

To: The Ontario Supreme Court of Justice

From:

Date: September 16th 2017

Re: Horace R. Carby-Samuels v. Raymond Carby-Samuels, Court file no. 17-71624, Court file no. 1566772

ISSUE

Mr. Raymond Carby Samuels has brought forward the following documents in Exhibit A, Exhibit B and Exhibit C for investigation in the claims of forgery of the signatures of Mr. Horace R. Carby-Samuels.

From handwriting experts reports it has been analysed the signature of Mr. Horace Carby-Samuels in three different documentation are resulted from three different timelines.

In the first documentation is Court File no. 1771624 which seems to hold the original signature of Mr Horace Carby-Samuels (exhibit A)

Similarly in the second documentation, Court File no.15-66772 (exhibit B) which has the alleged false signature along with the third documentation with the same Court File no. 15-66772 (exhibit C) which has been used as preference for additional clarity.

From the basic analysis, the first and third documents are signed by the same individual however; it seems to be clear that the second documentation has a forged signature.

BRIEF ANSWER

According to the formal analysis this type of forgery of signature would be classified as the simulated signature, or "free hand forgery" as it is sometime known. This forgery is constructed by using a genuine signature as a model. The forger generates an artistic reproduction of this model. Depending on his skill and amount of practice, the simulation may be quite good and bear remarkable pictorial similarity to the genuine signature.

Many simulations created with a model at hand will contain at least some of the general indicators of forgery, such as tremor, hesitation, pen lifts, blunt starts and stops, patching, and static pressure. They will have a slow "drawn" appearance. The practiced simulation is most often a higher quality creation in that the model signature has been memorized and some of the movements used to produce it have become semi-automatic. This simulation can be written with a more natural fluid manner. There can be tapered starts and stops, changes in pen pressure, and much less tremor in the moving line. Speed lends fluidity to writing. The more rapidly the pen moves while creating the genuine writing or signature, the more difficult the genuine writing is to imitate. Rapidly formed movements are scrutinized more closely than slower counterparts. A slowly written signature is not only easier for the forger to duplicate with some fashionable degree of pictorial similarity; the product will also display indications of non-genuineness than the forgery of a rapid and fluidly executed signature. The writer of a simulation must, of necessity, pay more attention to the form of a letter than the speed of his pen.

Both' practiced and non-practiced simulations will still have notable shortcomings. The forger naturally puts his greatest effort into those parts of the name that he expects to fall under the greatest scrutiny. Although letter forms (especially the more prominent, large or beginning letters) may almost duplicate the genuine letters, proportions and height ratios will seldom be correct. Internal portions of the names (smaller, less prominent letters and pen movements) will usually display the greatest divergence from the correct form and movements found in the genuine signature.

During the creation of a simulated forgery, the author attempts to duplicate the writing style of another individual. By doing this, the forger leaves behind little, if any, of his own distinctive writing style. By doing an emulation of someone else's signature, he also produces one of the best of all possible disguises of his own handwriting. Infrequently, some of the forger's own individual characteristics may appear in the disputed writing. The limited quantity of these characteristics which appear on those occasions is such that identification of the author almost never occurs.

If there are a sufficient number of significant differences between the questioned signature and the genuine signatures, and these same differences appear in the practiced simulations, there may be a basis to associate the forgery to the forger within some degree of probability. An absolute identification, nonetheless, even under these circumstances is infrequent.

Closely related to this form of identification process is that of determining the number of different forgers from a quantity of simulations. On occasion there will be two or more forgers attempting to reproduce the same signature. It may be possible to group or associate simulations of the same name by the combinations of defects within the forgeries. By associating and grouping the similar defects (when compared to the genuine signature) it may be possible to conclude and illustrate that there are indeed, two or more different forgers.

REASONING OF FACTS

The second documentation (exhibit 2) clearly projects the forged signature for the following reasoning

1. **Blunt starts and stops**

    In the second document it can identified that the forger places the pen point in contact with the paper, and then starts writing. When he is finished with the name or some portion thereof, he stops the pen and lifts it from the surface. This has cause the emphasized blunt start and ending where the pen was placed in contact with the surface. At times this contact is held so long that the pen contains two fluid ink in the front letter of the signature, it has wet the paper and migrate outward from the contact point.

There may be unnecessary and extraneous marks caused by pen starts and stops. The writer may decided after putting his pen in contact with the paper, that it is in the wrong spot, picks it up and moves it to a position considered more correct. Normally a signature's starts and stops are much more dynamic which can be noticed in the other two documents. The pen is moving horizontally before it contacts the paper and is lifted at the end while still in flight. This leaves a tapered appearance at the beginnings and endings of names or letters.

2. **Pen lifts and hesitation**

In this situation it can occasioned that the pen stops at an unusual point in the writing; perhaps during radical change in direction is about to take a new letter formation is about to be started. This may take on the appearance of a larger gap in the written line where one is not expected, or an overlapping of two ink lines where there should be only one continuous line which clearly in the second document but not the other two, where it seems to be following the same pattern throughout the signature .

3. **Tremor- minor shaking**

Because the creation of most forms of non-genuine signatures are little more than drawings, the pen is moving so slowly that small, sometimes microscopic changes in direction take place in what should be a fluid-looking line. The resultant line is not smooth, but reflects the "shaking" pen. It can be seen that the lines in the signature of the second documentation is much larger than the rest two and has microscopic shakes.

4. **Speed and pressure**

Again, because the pen is moving slowly rather than with the dynamic movement associated with most genuine writings, the ink line remains constant in thickness, resulting from the same constant pressure exerted on a slowly moving pen. There will be little, if any, tapering of internal lines. This is clearly evident in the second document's signature which constantly remains in the same thickness.

5. **Patching**

Sometimes when the genuine writer makes an error while writing our own signature, more commonly individuals may leave the signature alone, caring little about the mistake or imperfection, while others will simply "fix" the signature by correcting the offending portion. This might have be done this situation to make the signature more readable, or because a defect in the pen or paper has affected what we perceive to be our "normal" signature, or for some other reason that may even be subconscious.

However by analysing the previous signature that seems very unlikely. These "fixes" are patent, with no attempt made on the part of the writer to mask or otherwise hide the correction for which some letters are crossing the others out.

These signature corrections are quite different than the patching that is frequently found in non-genuine signatures. On these occasions, the writer is not attempting to make the signature more readable, but to make its appearance passable. He is fixing an obvious defect that he perceives as detectable, and might uncover his fraudulent product and foil his scheme. These usually take the form of a correction to a flaw in the writing line rather than in the form of a letter. Extensions to entry or terminal strokes, or to lower descending portions of letters, along with corrections to embellishments, are typical of non-genuine patching.

DISCUSSION

Penalty for Counterfeiting and Forgery in Canada

Each and every case of fraud is different and may result in varied consequences, however in this current scenario it is extremely vivid that the documentation was created for malicious reasoning. Therefore an individual can expect extensive prison time, as well as fines and community service work, or restitution. Other social consequences follow such as a criminal record limiting the ability to travel, and the difficulty in finding employment.

The Criminal Code of Canada states:

368(1) Uttering forged document

368(1) Every one who, knowing that a document is forged,

(a) uses, deals with or acts on it, or

(b) causes or attempts to cause any person to use, deal with or act on it, as if the document were genuine, is guilty of an indictable offence and liable to imprisonment for a term not exceeding fourteen years.

368(2) Wherever forged

368(2) For the purposes of proceedings under this section, the place where a document was forged is not material.

R.S., 1985, c. C-46, s. 368; 1992, c. 1, s. 60(F).

369 Exchequer bill paper, public seals, etc.

369 Every one who, without lawful authority or excuse, the proof of which lies on him,

(a) makes, uses or knowingly has in his possession

(i) any exchequer bill paper, revenue paper or paper that is used to make bank-notes, or

(ii) any paper that is intended to resemble paper mentioned in subparagraph (i),

(b) makes, offers or disposes of or knowingly has in his possession any plate, die, machinery, instrument or other writing or material that is adapted and intended to be used to commit forgery, or

(c) makes, reproduces or uses a public seal of Canada or of a province, or the seal of a public body or authority in Canada, or of a court of law, is guilty of an indictable offence and liable to imprisonment for a term not exceeding fourteen years. R.S., c. C-34, s. 327.

370 Counterfeit proclamation, etc.

370 Every one who knowingly

(a) prints any proclamation, order, regulation or appointment, or notice thereof, and causes it falsely to purport to have been printed by the Queen's Printer for Canada or the Queen's Printer for a province, or

(b) tenders in evidence a copy of any proclamation, order, regulation or appointment that falsely purports to have been printed by the Queen's Printer for Canada or the Queen's Printer for a province, is guilty of an indictable offence and liable to imprisonment for a term not exceeding five years. R.S., c. C-34, s. 328.

Interpretation of the Offence

Actus Reus

The act of forging the signature would be applicable enough to be considered as Actus reus for committing the act of forgery. (R v JJV, 1994 CanLII 6514 (NB CA))

Mens Rea

The mens rea for forgery under s. 366(1) requires an "intent to deceive" which requires an intent that is more than mere "carelessness or negligence". The intent to deceive should generally "be coupled with an intent that the document be used to someone's prejudice, or that a person be induced to act in a certain way." Prejudice need not result as long as there was an intent for the document to be treated as genuine.(R v Benson (M.) et al., 2012 MBCA 94 (CanLII))

The Crown must show the "falsity of the endorsement the document has been shown to be a forged document and its use with knowledge is sufficient to show the commission of the offence." (R v Elkin (1978), 42 C.C.C. (2d) 185 (B.C.C.A.))

The accused must have known that "the document was false and intended for somebody to act upon it as if it was genuine.".(Sebo, [1988] A.J. No. 475 (C.A.))

It is not necessary that the accused "intended" to defraud anyone. (R v Atwal, [2015] O.J. No. 3748 (C.J.) R v G.T., 2016 CanLII 82183 (NL PC) at para 59 per Gorman PCJ)

From the situation it can be concluded that the documentation were falsely created with intent to harm the applicant

"False documents"

A fake or false item that was made as a "novelty" item cannot be a "false document" and the creation of which does not carry the requisite *mens rea* for the offence. (R v Sommani, 2007 BCCA 199 (CanLII))

The document cannot simply be "false" but it must be proven to be "false" in relation to the purpose for which it was created. (R v Benson, 2012 MBCA 94 (CanLII) ("it must be false in relation to the purpose for which it was created"))

"False document" and "forged document" are not interchangable terms. (R v Hawrish, [1986] S.J. No. 846 (C.A.))

Till the investigation now, it can be classified that the documentation was forged.

Uttering vs. Forgery

Uttering forged documents is distinct from making forged documents. The "forgery" is the making of the document, the "uttering" is the use of the document. (R v Wightman, [2003] A.J. No. 1453 (P.C.) ("Forgery deals with the making of the document; uttering deals with the use of the document."))

It could be said that the documentation was created for the misuse of it against the applicant.

CONCLUSION

It can be concluded that the documentation in (exhibit B) has a forged signature of Mr. Horace R. Carby-Samuels and with intent of malicious actions.

EXHIBIT A

me as well as my daughter. Marcella is in the process of completing a Ph.D and lives in Sweden. The Respondent is trying to ruin her reputation as well because he states that he wants to ensure that she will never be able to get a job or to have her name on any collegial research on which she co-operates; and he has made specious reports to her faculty in the process of promoting her expulsion from the Ph.D program. Attached as Exhibit "L" are copies of the numerous postings.

32. I truly believe that the Respondent will continue to bring frivolous actions and use the court system to continue his harassment.

33. I make this Affidavit in support of my Application to have the Respondent found to be a vexatious litigant and for no other or improper purpose.

SWORN BEFORE ME in the City Of Ottawa, in the Province of Ontario this 25th day of January 2017.

Horace R. Carby-Samuels

A Commissioner, etc.

Lauren Michelle Danaman, a Commissioner, etc., Province of Ontario, while Student-At-Law. Expires June 18, 2019.

EXHIBIT B

5. With respect to the email from Maxine Fielding, I should point out that she lives in New Jersey. I sent her an email on June 1st, 2017 to inquire about Maxine's knowledge of the procedure that I was about to have, given her prior work at hospitals in the United States. Maxine replied to both myself and my daughter on June 3rd, 2017. On June 6th, Marcella communicated the care plan to Maxine in order to assure Maxine that homecare had been arranged successfully for my wife.

6. As I have mentioned in previous Affidavits, I have arranged nursing and personal care by professionals for my wife. She is not being denied access to visitors. Her relatives, friends and neighbours visit regularly without any issues. It is because of Raymond's continued attacks on both myself and my wife and his abusive behaviour towards us that has caused us to not want to see him. As a further example of his attacks, Raymond would regularly call the ambulance services to attend our home suggesting that there was an emergency. I am advised by ambulance services that they have now placed a block on his calls.

7. This recent Motion is yet a further attempt on Raymond to continually attack and abuse us. My wife is well cared for and is mentally competent. We are just tired of the constant abuse by Raymond.

8. I make this Affidavit in support of Raymond's request for an urgent Motion and for no other or improper purpose.

SWORN BEFORE ME in the City
Of Ottawa, in the Province of Ontario
this 14 day of September 2017.

_____
A Commissioner, etc.

_____
Horace R. Carby-Samuels

Zorian Adam Maksymec, a Commissioner, etc.,
Province of Ontario, while Student-At-Law.
Expires March 27, 2020.

EXHIBIT C

22. I make this Affidavit in support of my Motion and for no other or improper purpose.

SWORN BEFORE ME in the City
Of Ottawa, in the Province of Ontario   )
this 23rd day of January 2017.   )
)   _____
)   Horace R. Carby-Samuels
)
)
_____   )
A Commissioner, etc.

Lauren Michelle Danemaa, a Commissioner, etc.,
Province of Ontario, while Student-At-Law.
Expires June 14, 2018.

5. With respect to the email from Maxine Fielding, I should point out that she lives in New Jersey. I sent her an email on June 1st, 2017 to inquire about Maxine's knowledge of the procedure that I was about to have, given her prior work at hospitals in the United States. Maxine replied to both myself and my daughter on June 3rd, 2017. On June 6th, Marcella communicated the care plan to Maxine in order to assure Maxine that homecare had been arranged successfully for my wife.

6. As I have mentioned in previous Affidavits, I have arranged nursing and personal care by professionals for my wife. She is not being denied access to visitors. Her relatives, friends and neighbours visit regularly without any issues. It is because of Raymond's continued attacks on both myself and my wife and his abusive behaviour towards us that has caused us to not want to see him. As a further example of his attacks, Raymond would regularly call the ambulance services to attend our home suggesting that there was an emergency. I am advised by ambulance services that they have now placed a block on his calls.

7. This recent Motion is yet a further attempt on Raymond to continually attack and abuse us. My wife is well cared for and is mentally competent. We are just tired of the constant abuse by Raymond.

8. I make this Affidavit in support of Raymond's request for an urgent Motion and for no other or improper purpose.

SWORN BEFORE ME in the City
Of Ottawa, in the Province of Ontario
this 14 day of September 2017.

_____
Horace R. Cathy Samuels

_____
A Commissioner, etc.

Zorlan Adam Maksymec, a Commissioner, etc.,
Province of Ontario, while Student-At-Law.
Expires March 27, 2020.

Example of apparent deception

Court File No: C64716

ONTARIO COURT OF APPEAL

BETWEEN

RAYMOND CARBY-SAMUELS II

Appellant
(Applicant in Appeal)

- and –

HORACE CARBY-SAMUELS

Respondent
(Respondent in Appeal)

APPELLANT'S FACTUM

DATE 9 MARCH 2018

RAYMOND CARBY-SAMUELS
B.P. 24191 – 300 Eagleson Rd
Kanata, Ontario K2M 2C3

(514) 712-7516

TO: Mr. John E Summers
Bell Baker LLP
#700-116 Lisgar Street
Ottawa, Ontario K2P OC2
Tel: (613) 237-3334
Email: Jsummers@bellbaker.com

Lawyer for the Respondent in the Appeal

Court File No: C64716

ONTARIO COURT OF APPEAL

BETWEEN

RAYMOND CARBY-SAMUELS II

Appellant
(Applicant in Appeal)

- and –

HORACE CARBY-SAMUELS

Respondent
(Respondent in Appeal)

APPELLANT'S FACTUM

PART I – Order Under Appeal

1) The appellant, Raymond Carby-Samuels appeals the Summary Judgement of the Superior Court of Justice issued by Justice Sylvia Corthorn and dated 16 November 2017 in its entirety and seeks for that judgement to be set-aside by the Ontario Court of Appeal.

2) The appellant, Raymond Carby-Samuels also seeks for an amendment to the Vexatious Litigant Order dated 23 November 2017 also be set-aside

3) The appellant furthermore seeks a restoration of Justice Patrick Smith's Order dated 11 February 2016.

PART II – SUMMARY OF THE FACTS

4) The Appellant affirms his civil right to prepare this Factum as an expression of his religious conscience affirmed in the *Canadian Charter of Rights and Freedoms* in the presentation of facts related to his Appeal.

5) The Appellant in this Factum documents matters as a child of humanity who is also from the Source. In the process, the Appellant affirms his right to express himself in this Factum based upon the freedom of religion; and conscience affirmed in; and pursuant to Section 2 (a) of the *Canadian Charter of Rights and Freedoms*

Book of Authorities - Tab 7: *Syndicat Northcrest v Amselem* **(Book of Authorities)**

1) The Appellant affirms his civil right to prepare this Factum as an expression of his religious conscience affirmed in the *Canadian Charter of Rights and Freedoms* in the presentation of facts related to his Appeal.

2) The Appellant in this Factum documents matters as a child of humanity who is also from the Source. In the process, the Appellant affirms his right to express himself in this Factum based upon the freedom of religion; and conscience

affirmed in; and pursuant to Section 2 (a) of the *Canadian Charter of Rights and Freedoms*

3) Since January 2015 an apparent cabal reminiscent of the "fallen angels" have sought to subject the Appellant to persecution for the expression of his religious conscience which have been followed by a sought retribution and retaliation by these operatives.

4) On 8 January 2015, Horace Carby-Samuels, the Defendant and Marcella Carby-Samuels, his daughter began a series of mischievous telephone calls to the Ottawa Police Services (OPS) based upon the fraudulent allegations that the Appellant "suffers from mental illness" which led to the Appellant's eviction in late April 2015; and the Defendant's direction to the OPS to evict the Appellant was made without the support and consent of the Appellant's Mother, Dezrin Carby-Samuels who had sought to document in writing her lack of approval for what she described as the false allegations which were being made by both Horace and Marcella Carby-Samuels in relation to their calls to the OPS.

5) These activities supported with fraudulent allegations subjected the Appellant to emotion distress. The ignoring of these substantive representations regarding the apparent public mischief of the Defendant / Respondent which violates the Canadian Criminal Code which was totally omitted in Corthorn J's ruling supports the contention by the Appellant that he was subjected to a "reasonable apprehension of bias" in Summary Judgement proceedings.

6) Horace and Marcella Carby-Samuels' spreading of slander against the Defendant resulted in harassment by the OPS against the Appellant; and

operatives of the OPS then used these allegations to then direct the Nepean, Rideau and Community Resource Centre to take action against the Appellant on 15 June 2015 which sought to breach an Agreement reached between the Appellant and the Nepean, Rideau and Osgoode Community Centre.

7) On 12 June 2015 this Centre conveyed an intent to facilitate further access between the Appellant and his Mother and to act as witness against the Defendant for his role in perpetrating abuse and neglect which Centre staff observed taking place against the Appellant's Mom.

8) Notably also absent in Corthorn J's ruling was the Legal Demand letter issued by Todd Ji, the appellant's lawyer to enable the Appellant to have access to his personal and professional belongings which was apparently being subjected to the tort of conversion of property.

9) Corthorn J also failed to redress the legality of the eviction itself against the Appellant and demonstrated a tendency to "buy into" all arguments of Defence Counsel which were unsubstantiated through any evidence.

10) On 14 August 2017, Corthorn J denied the adjournment request of Mr. Gurbir Singh who is a Toronto lawyer who travelled all the way from Brampton to Ottawa to ask the court for an adjournment to enable to Mr Singh or another lawyer to prepare a defence against Motions for Summary Judgement and Vexatious Litigant. By rejecting Mr Singh's request that the Appellant be granted an adjournment, Corthon J denied the Appellant legal representation for the Vexatious Litigant and Summary Judgement proceedings which violated Section 24(1) of the *Canadian Charter of Rights and Freedoms*.

Canadian Criminal Code

- **140** (1) Every one commits public mischief who, with intent to mislead, causes a peace officer to enter on or continue an investigation by

  - (a) making a false statement that accuses some other person of having committed an offence;
  - (b) doing anything intended to cause some other person to be suspected of having committed an offence that the other person has not committed, or to divert suspicion from himself;
  - (c) reporting that an offence has been committed when it has not been committed; or
  - (d) reporting or in any other way making it known or causing it to be made known that he or some other person has died when he or that other person has not died.

11) On 14 August 2017, having acknowledged that the Defendant through affidavit "cannot speak for Appelllant's Mom", and having acknowledged that the Defendant failed to facilitate the "independent verification" sought by Justice Macloed on 24 March 2017, Corthon J appeared use the lie that the Defendant and the Appellant's Mom "speak as one" and both against the Appellant.

Tab 26 – Compendium of Evidence

Tab 20 – Compendium of Evidence – Independent Verification

12) Corthorn, J made her decision in the midst of a Recusal Motion that was being scheduled with the approval of Beaudoin J at the Ontario Superior Court of Justice in Ottawa. As a result, this Judge's decision had the appearance of being retaliation against the Appellant for having scheduled the Recusal Motion.

Exhibit Book – Tab 6

13) In Corthorn, J's, Summary Judgment against the Appellant, this Judge's ruling was the culmination of the same kind of apparent indiscretions which had provided Beaudoin, J with the impetus to approve the Appellant's effort to proceed with a Recusal Motion against Corthorn J.

Exhibit Book – Tab 6

Book of Authorities, *R v Brown* – Tab 8: Reasonable Apprehension of Bias

14) On 29 January 2013, the Appellant was subjected to bodily assault by the Defendant. This occurred at 30 Jarlan Terrace in Kanata, Ontario [the home of the Appellant's parents after the Appellant had expressed concern to the Defendant about him having subjected his Mother to abusive attacks which caused her to cry, shake and tremble.

Canadian Criminal Code

Unlawfully causing bodily harm

269 Every one who unlawfully causes bodily harm to any person is guilty of

- (a) an indictable offence and liable to imprisonment for a term not exceeding ten years; or
- (b) an offence punishable on summary conviction and liable to imprisonment for a term not exceeding eighteen months.

15) Corthorn J failed to consider any mitigating circumstances regarding the time lapse associated with bodily assault and police report which related to the Appellant living at his parents' house and being concerned how making a police report while living with the Defendant could further jeopardize his safety, and this lack of consideration furthermore substantiates a claim of a reasonable apprehension of bias by the trial judge.

16) The Statement of Claim launched by the Appellant in December 2014 was only made after a long waiting period after a legal demand letter from the Daniels Law Form which had been issued to the Defendant in early July 2017.

17) The appellant added other claims against the Defendant / Respondent which had formed the basis of a $25,000 judgement in damages against the Defendant which was made in Justice Patrick Smith's ordered rendered 11 February 2016.

Exhibit Book – Tab 12

18) The appellant acted in good faith as a self-represented litigant and actively sought the direction of counsel on several occasions and when he could afford it.

Reasonable Apprehension of Bias

19) On 10 October 2017, the Appellant affirmed an Affidavit to the Court in support of a Recusal Motion against Justice Sylvia Corthorn.

Exhibit Book – Tab 6

20) Justice Beaudoin accepted the Recusal Motion further to correspondence from Tina who had advised by email of the necessity of making a Recusal Motion against Justice Sylvia Corthon.

21) Court administrators under the authority of Justice Beaudoin were in the process of scheduling the recusal motion when Justice Sylvia Corthorn in violation of the customs and convention of the court pre-empted the Recusal Motion by expediting a decision of Summary Judgement against the Appellant.

22) Justice Sylvia Corthorn's declaration against the Appellant has the appearance of being a retaliation against the Appellant for acting within his rights to seek the recusal of Justice Sylvia Corthorn.

23) Indeed, while on the surface Justice Sylvia Corthorn's Order to declare Summary Judgement appears to be very "detailed", it is apparent that this Judge's "reasons" have been substantively plagiarized from Defence Counsel's unsubstantiated allegations;

24) Corthorn J begins her Summary Judgement by mischaracterizing and ignoring the breadth of the Appellant's Claim; and then in her point [19] attempts a *prima facie* "whitewashing" against the Plaintiff's evidence which she ignores and broadly characterizes as "limited".

Book of Authorities: Tab 2: *Murray v Toth*

25) Corthorn J's notable oversights are self-evident in her ignoring of the damages awarded by Justice Patrick Smith's ruling which related to depriving the Appellant of his belongings; unlawful eviction; and the enabling of visitation access of the Appellant and his Mom to each other which Corthorn J totally disregarded so she could mis-claim that the relief the Appellant sought were "not within the jurisdiction of the Court".

Reasonable Apprehension of Bias

26) On 10 October 2017, the Appellant affirmed an Affidavit to the Court in support of a Recusal Motion against Justice Sylvia Corthorn.

27) Justice Beaudoin accepted the Recusal Motion further to correspondence from Tina who had advised by email of the necessity of making a Recusal Motion against Justice Sylvia Corthon.

Book of Authorities, *R v Brown* **– Tab 8: Reasonable Apprehension of Bias**

28) Court administrators under the authority of Justice Beaudoin were in the process of scheduling the recusal motion when Justice Sylvia Corthorn in violation of the customs and convention of the court pre-empted the Recusal Motion by expediting a decision of "Summary Judgement".

29) Justice Sylvia Corthorn's declaration of Summary Judgement against the Appellant has the appearance of being a retaliation against the Appellant for acting within his rights to seek the recusal of Justice Sylvia Corthorn.

PART III – SPECIFIC QUESTIONS, FACTIONS AND LEGALITY

1. Was McNamara J.S. correct in setting aside the original Default Judgement o Patrick Smith J rendered on 11 February 206?

2. Was the Appellant subjected to procedural unfairness by Corthon J associated with a "reasonable apprehension of bias" by the following actions?

   Book of Authorities, *R v Brown* – Tab 8: Reasonable Apprehension of Bias

   A – Ignoring the sincerity of the Appellant who had sought an adjournment with Counsel present who had travelled from Toronto and Ottawa under conditions of sleep deprivation;

Book of Authorities, *Nadia Chiki v Canada* **– Tab 4**

B – Denying Legal Representation to the Appellant which required adjournment, and especially after Justices Roger and McNamara had advised that it would be in the interest of the Appellant to seek Counsel

Book of Authorities, *R v Lichtenwald* **– Tab 6**
Ontario Courts of Justice Act, s 96

C – Did the Court show a lack of equity to the Appellant as a self-represented litigant to be able to defend himself in complex legal proceedings that his was unfamiliar with which denied his ability to participate in a meaningful way?

Book of Authorities, *Nadia Chiki v Canada* **– Tab 4**

D – Did the Court subvert the Appellant constitutional rights pursuant to Section 24(1) of the *Canadian Charter of Rights and Freedoms?*

Canadian Judicial Council: Ethics Guidelines

E – Did the same Judge who seizing both Motions on Vexatious Litigant and Summary Judgement prejudice separate treatment of the both matters without being affected by a pre-disposition in one case relative to another?

Was Corthorn J obliged to wait for the scheduled recusal motion which had clearly been submitted to the Court and supported by an Affidavit before making a ruling on Summary Judgement?

3. Did Beaudoin J's approval on the recusal Motion process suggest that the appearance of the integrity of her decision to declare the Appellant a "Vexatious Litigant" may have been adversely affected by a "reasonable apprehension of bias" which prejudiced the Appellant?

4. Did Defence Counsel put their best evidentiary foot forward as required by case law on Summary Judgement by ignoring the breadth of damaged asserted by the Plaintiff throughout proceedings in light of the fact that the Plaintiff was a self-represented litigant?

Book of Authorities – Tab 5: Legal Comments on the *Sanzone* case

5. Did Corthon J prejudice the rights of the Appellant as a self-represented litigant by constructing a "two step" urgent motion process which she admitted to be unusual and inconsistent with established court procedure?

6. Was Corthorn J obliged to adjourn proceedings to enable the Appellant time as a self-represented litigant to pursue an examination of the authenticity of

the Defendant's signature used for Defence Counsel's affidavit submission on 18 September 2018 in relation to Corthorn J's "Leave for Urgent Motion" process?

- A) The Appellant contends that Justice Sylvia Corthorn was obliged to suspend any decision on Defence Motions for Summary Judgement and Vexatious Litigant in light of the scheduling of a recusal Motion under the auspices of Justice Beaudoin in the Superior Court, and by not doing so, the Court gave the appearance of supporting the Defence Motions as an act of retaliation against the Appellant and a corresponding lack of due process which the Appellant was entitled to receive.
- B) By Justice Corthorn rendering decisions including that of Summary Judgement on 16 November 2017 which didn't respect due process and the customs and conventions of the Court regarding such a recusal process, these decisions are without constitutional merit and therefore have no ethical force or effect in law.
- C) Justice Beaudoin would have only have endorsed the recusal motion if it had substantive grounds and that flies in the face of Justice Corthorn's decision to declare the Appellant a "Vexatious Litigant" and Order for Summary Judgement.
- D) Justice Sylvia Corthorn was obliged to ensure that the very detailed Affidavit-supported evidence presented by the Appellant on the reported criminal forgery perpetrated by Defence Counsel in their Affidavit of 18 September 2017 was thoroughly examined and by not doing so the Court enabled Defence Counsel to

rely on a prospective or apparent criminal act; and not allowing for such examination the lower Court's erred in its decision to support Defence Motions for Summary Judgement and Vexatious Litigant prejudices the rights of the Appellant to have received a fair and impartially conducted process;

Compendium of Evidence – Tab 28

- E) Justice Sylvia Corthorn ought to have respected the request by the Appellant's lawyer, Mr. Gurbir Singh who in acting as an officer of the Court in late August 2017, had sought an adjournment to provide the necessary time to prepare against the Defence Motions for Summary Judgement and Vexatious Litigant and by not doing so, Justice Sylvia Corthorn violated the rights of the Appellant as a self-represented litigant needing the very legal advice that Justices Roger and James McNamara had advised the Appellant to obtain which is especially the case in the complex proceedings of Vexatious Litigant (and Summary Judgement) based upon the legal advice the Appellant obtained from lawyers;
- F) Justice Sylvia Corthorn erred by expressly and baselessly supporting Defence Motions on Summary Judgement and Vexatious Litigant that prejudicially bought into Defence Counsel's convenient allegation that the Appellant's Mother doesn't want to see the Appellant when in fact the Defendant / Respondent had refused the independent verification previously sought by Justice Macloed on 24 March 2017 that the Appellant's Mom has not been held 'prisoner' to quote this honourable Justice.

- G) Justice Sylvia Corthorn erred by claiming in her rulings that the court has no power to provide the unimpeded access sought by the Appellant when in fact the Court under the honourable Justice Patrick Smith already had demonstrated the Court's inherent jurisdiction by enabling success access on 11 February 2016.

Exhibit Book – Tab 12

- H) Justice Sylvia Corthorn further erred by forcing the Appellant to submit to a "Leave of Urgent Motion" process which lawyers advised they could not assist with because such a process was apparently fictitious and has **no basis in law.**
- I) Justice Corthorn furthered erred by failing to give leeway to the Appellant as a self-represented litigant in the presentation of torts presented before Justice Patrick Smith in which the Appellant made a *de facto* amendment to his Claim which included compensation for having been illegally evicted; deprived of access to personal and professional belongings and for having been subjected to bodily assault by the Respondent wielding a knife on 29 January 2013; and this failure contravened the Ontario Court of Appeal's stated desire to give *leeway* to self-represented litigants who are not familiar with formal amendment and other court procedures in the apparent Court's desire to avoid self-represented litigant's rights being deprived *for simply not being lawyers.*

Book of Authorities – Tab 3 – Sanzone v Schecheter et al.

- J) Justice Sylvia Corthorn further erred by disregarding the fact that based upon timing, she was obliged to endorse matters to be sent to Mandatory Mediation pursuant to Rule 24.1 of the *Ontario Rules of Civil Procedure* and that such a request had been formally made by a lawyer acting in support of the Appellant in the winter of 2017; and that the filing of Defence Motions about one year after the filing of their Statement of Defence was an abuse of court procedure.

Ontario Rules of Civil Procedure

RULE 24.1 MANDATORY MEDIATION

PURPOSE

24.1.01 This Rule provides for mandatory mediation in specified actions, in order to reduce cost and delay in litigation and facilitate the early and fair resolution of disputes. O. Reg. 453/98, s. 1; O. Reg. 198/05, s. 2; O. Reg. 438/08, s. 15.

NATURE OF MEDIATION

24.1.02 In mediation, a neutral third party facilitates communication among the parties to a dispute, to assist them in reaching a mutually acceptable resolution. O. Reg. 453/98, s. 1.

24.1.04 (1) This Rule applies to the following actions:

1. Actions that were governed by this Rule immediately before January 1, 2010.

2. Actions that are commenced in one of the following counties on or after January 1, 2010:

i. The City of Ottawa.

- K) A letter from Defence Counsel for the Respondent dated 25 January 2015 confirms that a formal request for **mandatory** mediation was made before the Defence Counsel had filed their Motions for Summary Judgement and Vexatious Litigant.
- L) Furthermore, Justice Sylvia Corthorn erred in disregarding the *Ontario Rules of Evidence* by allowing Defence Counsel's secretary to submit an affidavit based upon non substantiated claims of the Defendant..
- N) Justice Beaudoin specifically had stated that the Appellant / Plaintiff had an "arguable case" which further puts the Court's decision on Summary Judgement (and Vexatious Litigant) into disrepute.
- O) The Respondent's expressed *bad faith* which made him ineligible to seek the equitable relief of the Court through a declaration of Summary Judgement include but are not limited to (a) his slander to the Ottawa Police Services that the Plaintiff "suffers from mental illness" on multiple police reports; (b) a pattern of evidence that both the Appellant and his mother suffered abuse at the hands of the Respondent which included a police report that the Respondent specifically directed bodily assault against the Appellant on 29 January 2013; (c) the Respondent showing a lack of any effort to inform the Appellant of the condition of his Mother resulting in pain and mental anguish by the Appellant; and the fact that the Appellant had to hire a lawyer in June 2015 to issue a Demand Letter to the Respondent to enable the Appellant and his Mother to see

each other which after social workers had confirmed that the Appellant's Mother did in fact want to see her son; and (d) the fact that the Respondent furthermore only released the belongings of the Appellant to his after this Demand Letter; and furthermore based upon the fact that Defence Counsel has sought to rely on a claim that the Appellant's Mother doesn't want to see him after the Defendant refused to enable the independent verification that would have confirmed the Appellant's Mother's desire and the fact that this was not allowed by the Defendant / Respondent suggests a desire to repress the Appellant's free will which this Court recognizes.

- P) Therefore, the Respondent / Defendant did not come to Court with the necessary 'clean hands' pursuant to the customs and conventions of constitutional law in general and legal-historically applied "Laws of Equity" which are precepts associated with Section 96 of the *Ontario Courts of Justice Act*.

-

PART IV – ISSUES

1. The Appellant's Claim is far more complex that what Corthorn J's ruling who subjected the Appellant to a "reasonable apprehension of bias"; and the ruling sought to evade the Appellant's Affidavit dated 10 October 2017 regarding a sought of Recusal Corthorn J;

6. The lower court then further compounded its error by failing to respect the **Mandatory Mediation** programme pursuant to rule 24.1 of the *Ontario Rules of Civil Procedure* sought by the Appellant and then further prejudicing the rights of the Appellant to provide the Respondent even more time to file its Motions for Vexatious Litigant and Summary Judgement beyond the time allowed by the court based upon its customs and conventions and after there had already had been a substantive amount of filings by both sides as stated by Beaudoin, J;

7. McNamara J.S. decision to set aside the Default Judgement of the Appellant is consistent with a reasonable apprehension of bias.

8. Indeed, Justice Beaudoin had already stated in response to an application by the Respondent pursuant to 2.1 of the *Ontario Rules of Civil Procedure* that the Appellant had an "arguable case" as a direct quote from this honourable Justice's ruling; and, as a result, by that pre-existent declaration, Corthorn, J, erred by then granting Vexatious Litigant [and Summary Judgement] as if the Appellant did not have an arguable case.

9. Such further and other relief as this Honourable Court may deem just.

PART V – ORDER

The Appellant asks that the Court set aside the Summary Judgement Order.

THIS APPEAL IS FOR -

1. Setting-aside the Judgement of McNamara JS which was before the Ontario Superior Court on 7 June 2016 re: Claim 15-66772 which disregarded the Default Judgement Order of Justice Patrick Smith on 11 February 2016
2. Setting aside of the Summary Judgement Declaration by Corthorn 6, of 16 November 2017 that was amended on 23 November 2017;
3. The restoration Justice Patrick's Smith's Order of 11 February 2016 inclusive of $25,000 in damages, based upon the affirmation that the Defendant was an experienced self-represented litigant who had successfully prepared his own affidavits to the Federal Court of Appeal; was aware of his obligations to file a reply to the original statement of claim; and having not done so has not reasonable excuse; and the setting aside of that Default was prejudicial to the Plaintiff who was also representing himself without a lawyer.

This Judgement bears interest at the rate of 2.00 percent per Year from this date/

Date: _____   Signed by _____

                                            Ontario Court of Appeal

                                            Toronto, Ontario

Schedule A

1   **Overall: Miscellaneous Case Law on Setting Aside**

2   ***Murray v Toth, 2012 ONSC 5815*** (Orchestrated Eviction / Distress)

3   ***Sanzone v Schechter et al*** *(Leeway to Self-Rep Litigant / Lawyering)*

4   ***Nadia Chiki v Canada, 2016*** *(Procedural Fairness Requires Lawyer)*

5   ***Sanzone Case Analysis*** *(Best Evidentiary Foot Forward)*

6   ***R. v Litchenwald 2017*** *(Legal Representation as Charter Right)*

        Section 24 (1) of the Canadian Charter of Rights and Freedoms

7   ***Amselem et al v Northcrest et al*** (religious conscience rights)

8   ***R. v. Brown,*** 2003 CanLII 52142 (ON CA)

- (Reasonable apprehension of bias)

Schedule B

Courts of Justice Act, R.S.O. 1990, c. C.43

Common Law and Equity

Rules of law and equity

96 (1) Courts shall administer concurrently all rules of equity and the common law. R.S.O. 1990, c. C.43, s. 96 (1); 1993, c. 27, Sched.

Rules of equity to prevail

(2) Where a rule of equity conflicts with a rule of the common law, the rule of equity prevails. R.S.O. 1990, c. C.43, s. 96 (2); 1993, c. 27, Sched.

Jurisdiction for equitable relief

(3) Only the Court of Appeal and the Superior Court of Justice, exclusive of the Small Claims Court, may grant equitable relief, unless otherwise provided. 1994, c. 12, s. 38; 1996, c. 25, s. 9 (17).

Family Law Act, R.S.O. 1990, c. F.3

Obligation of child to support parent

32 Every child who is not a minor has an obligation to provide support, in accordance with need, for his or her parent who has cared for or provided support for the child, to the extent that the child is capable of doing so. R.S.O. 1990, c. F.3, s. 32.

Criminal Code (R.S.C., 1985, c. C-46)

Unlawfully causing bodily harm

269 Every one who unlawfully causes bodily harm to any person is guilty of

(a) an indictable offence and liable to imprisonment for a term not exceeding ten years; or

- (b) an offence punishable on summary conviction and liable to imprisonment for a term not exceeding eighteen months.

- R.S., 1985, c. C-46, s. 269;
- 1994, c. 44, s. 18.

Theft

- 322 (1) Every one commits theft who fraudulently and without colour of right takes, or fraudulently and without colour of right converts to his use or to the use of another person, anything, whether animate or inanimate, with intent
  - (a) to deprive, temporarily or absolutely, the owner of it, or a person who has a special property or interest in it, of the thing or of his property or interest in it;

Public mischief

- 140 (1) Every one commits public mischief who, with intent to mislead, causes a peace officer to enter on or continue an investigation by

- (a) making a false statement that accuses some other person of having committed an offence;
- (b) doing anything intended to cause some other person to be suspected of having committed an offence that the other person has not committed, or to divert suspicion from himself;
- (c) reporting that an offence has been committed when it has not been committed;

Forgery

- **366** (1) Every one commits forgery who makes a false document, knowing it to be false, with intent
  - (a) that it should in any way be used or acted on as genuine, to the prejudice of any one whether within Canada or not; or
  - (b) that a person should be induced, by the belief that it is genuine, to do or to refrain from doing anything, whether within Canada or not.

- **Sought Court Intervention regarding Religious Conscience**

Necessities of Life

- **215** (1) Every one is under a legal duty
  - (b) to provide necessaries of life to their spouse or common-law partner; and
  - (c) to provide necessaries of life to a person under his charge if that person

- (i) is unable, by reason of detention, age, illness, mental disorder or other cause, to withdraw himself from that charge, and
- (ii) is unable to provide himself with necessaries of life.

- *Offence*

(2) Every one commits an offence who, being under a legal duty within the meaning of subsection (1), fails without lawful excuse, the proof of which lies on him, to perform that duty, if

- (a) with respect to a duty imposed by paragraph (1)(a) or (b),
    - (i) the person to whom the duty is owed is in destitute or necessitous circumstances, or
    - (ii) the failure to perform the duty endangers the life of the person to whom the duty is owed, or causes or is likely to cause the health of that person to be endangered permanently; or
- (b) with respect to a duty imposed by paragraph (1)(c), the failure to perform the duty endangers the life of the person to whom the duty is owed or causes or is likely to cause the health of that person to be injured permanently.

- *Punishment*

(3) Every one who commits an offence under subsection (2)

- (a) is guilty of an indictable offence and liable to imprisonment for a term not exceeding five years; or

- (b) is guilty of an offence punishable on summary conviction and liable to imprisonment for a term not exceeding eighteen months.

Assault

- **265** (1) A person commits an assault when
    - (a) without the consent of another person, he applies force intentionally to that other person, directly or indirectly;
    - (b) he attempts or threatens, by an act or a gesture, to apply force to another person, if he has, or causes that other person to believe on reasonable grounds that he has, present ability to effect his purpose;

Forcible Confinement

279 (1) Every person commits an offence who kidnaps a person with intent

(2) Every one who, without lawful authority, confines, imprisons or forcibly seizes another person is guilty of

- (a) an indictable offence and liable to imprisonment for a term not exceeding ten years; or

Raymond Carby-Samuels (Apellant) v
Horace Carby-Samuels (Respondent)

C64716

Perfection of Appeal – Vexatious Litigant

COURT OF APPEAL FOR ONTARIO

PROCEEDING COMMENCED AT TORONTO

FACTUM

RAYMOND CARBY-SAMUELS – BP 24191 –

300 Eagleson Rd, Kanata, ON K2M 2C3

RCP-E 4C (November 1, 2005)

Court File No: 15-66772

ONTARIO SUPERIOR COURT OF JUSTICE

BETWEEN

RAYMOND CARBY-SAMUELS II

Plaintiff

-and-

HORACE R CARBY-SAMUELS

Defendant

AFFIDAVIT OF RAYMOND CARBY-SAMUELS ON THE TORTS OF HORACE CARBY-SAMUELS

Regarding Defendant's Vexatious Motion for Summary Judgement

I, Raymond Carby-Samuels II of the City of Ottawa in the Province of Ontario, Canada AFFIRMS:

1 – On 29 January 2013, Horace Carby-Samuels leaped from the kitchen table, took out a sharp kitchen knife and held it to my stomach as if he was about to stab me there, in response to my concerns about the distress and profound psychological trauma he had been causing my Mom that was making her shake and cry. [ASSAULT]

2 – I grabbed the kitchen knife with my left hand as he continued to push it toward my stomach which resulted in him almost completely severing my small finger in my left hand. [BODILY ASSAULT]

3 - My Mom was too shaken to call the ambulance and the Defendant simply ignored

me as I was forced to call 911 with my right hand as I bled profusely. [INTENTIONAL INFLICTION OF EMOTIONAL DISTRESS]. (Police Report Attached – Exhibit 1)

4 - The Defendant caused me to go into emergency restronstructive sugery under the supervision of Dr Nicolas Guay who said I would require many months of rehabilitation in which I would not be able to work. (Exhibit 1A)

5 – The Defendant, as a result, casued me a significant economic loss from having to take time-off from work as a result of the stabbing attack that he perpetrated. [ECONOMIC LOSS]

6 – After having subjected me to bodily assault, the Defendant's verbal abuse against me and my Mom worsened. This coincided with a pattern of shocking lapses in driving attentiveness which culminated in 2015 when I witnessed the Defendant driving through red lights, stop signs, and becoming disoriented where he was, which also involved swerving and nearly getting hit by vechicles on the Queensway and elsewhere.

7 - My Mom used to like to accompany my father during drives in the night because she feared that he may collide into other vehicles because of also worsening eyesight related problems. My Mom and I both suffered verbal abuse in our efforts to call his attention to other vehicles on the road.

8 – The Defendant suffers from Type 2 Diabetes, eye problems which had been medically examined and chronic high blood pressure.

9 – Type 2 Diabetes that the Defendant suffers from has been linked to symptoms displayed by the Defendant that has caused him to prevent my access to seeing my Mother and accompanying manifestations of violence. (Exhibit 2)

10 - The Defendant's daughter, Marcella Carby-Samuels who knows that the Defendant has Type 2 Diabetes, and his lawyer, John Summers appears to have exploited / manipulated adverse mental state brought on by the Defendant's Type 2 Diabetes Condition for sought financial and/or other gain.

11 - The Mental Health Assessment which was done on the Defendant at an Ottawa Hospitalthat's cited in the Defendant's court materials was conducted by the police based upon corroborating testimony supplied by a neighbour – Ms. Anne Walker, who has visited my Mom and observed the distress that she was being subjected to under conditions which was being enforced by the Defendant.

12 - Ms. Anne Walker had told me that she had observed that my Mother was half-naked in the family room and that the house seemed to be out of food that she offered to get for

the Defendant who refused her assistance Ms. Walker told me.

13 - Ms. Walker also commented to me on the unsanitary / filthy conditions of the House under the apparent dysfunctional control of the Defendant.

14 - I hold the Defendant legally responsible for subjecting my Mom to abusive and neglectful conditions which resulted in the decline of her health alongside forcible a unlawful separation which deprived me of my Mother as a prime source for spirtual guidance and wisdom in my personal and professional life.

15 - The conditions associated with the Mental Health Assessment was subjected to apparent police intimidation tactics / threats by Detective Robert J Griffin who also threatened me multiple times in front of witnesses as he sought to also apparently threaten the Nepean Rideau and Osgoode Resource Centre on 15 June 2015 to stop enabling access to my continued seeing of my Mother that the Centre had sought to facilitate.

16 - I didn't sign a declaration that the Defendant was "insane" and the assertion wit his submission to the Court is unsubstantiated (no 7 of the Factum of the Defendant)

17 – Dectecive Robert Griffin accosted and threatened me at my new residence in Kanata while he was in plain clothes, unshaven and in an unmarked police car, the v same day that the cited test was done and suggested to me that he ensured that the te results would come out favourably for the Defendant, and then proceeded to threater in violation of my human rights.

18 – The Nepean, Rideau, and Osgoode Community Resource Centre had pledged to help secure my continued access to seeing my Mom and 12 June 2015, and even told they would testify in court if I called upon them.

19 – Ms Alison Timons of the Centre indicated that she and her assistant would testif court that the Defendant had blocked vital access to helping my Mother. However th were intimidated by Dectective Robert J. Griffin to cease and desist further contact w me when he visited them on 15 June 2015 under the urging of the Defendant, and Marcella Carby-Samuels, the Defendant's daughter who "hired" this Detective to the harass me under the fradulent imputation that I suffered from "mental illness".

20 - My Mother and a family relation suggested to me that Marcella, my sister, was pursuing a manipulative campaign to get the police to arrest me based upon phony phone calls to the police that she coordinated with the Defendant in her desire to obta total financial control of the Family Estate when my parents would eventually pass away.

21 - Indeed, it was Marcella Carby-Samuels who made the first phony phone call to the police in early January 2015 based upon a littany of lies she put in a police report.

22 – The Defendant did not have a close relationship with his Mother who had died when he was relatively young.

23 - In his Type 2 Diabetic condition, the Defendant became apparently violent and jealous of my close relationship to my Mother and began to subject me to harassment in my efforts to provide care giving to my Mom alongside his negligence in care-giving for my Mom who had been diagnosed with a medical condition which I sought to assist her in recovery and healing.

24 – In early January 2015, the Defendant began a campaign to call the Ottawa Police Services which continued into April 2015 when I was unlawfully evicted by the Defendant without any notice during very early morning hours.

25 - These specious and irrational complaints to the Police were notably based upon fraudulent claims that I was holding the Defendant and my Mom "hostage" and that I suffered from "mental illness". Such allegations subjected me to police harassment for many months . This claim was denied by my Mom when she could still write. (Exhibit 3) [PUBLIC MISCHIEF, DEFAMATION, INTENTIONAL INFLICTION OF EMOTIONAL DISTRESS]

26 – The Defendant got Detective Robert J Griffin to stalk, threaten me with violence not to inform my friends or relatives concerning my observations and experiences of abuse; and this was done in front of a witness. [HUMAN RIGHTS VIOLATION]

27 - In late April 2015, the Defendant evicted me from my parents' home without any notice and without the necessary joint approval of my Mom as the co-owner of the house. [UNLAWFUL EVICTION in common law]

28 - This eviction was done in the early morning (sometime around 2 am) that posed a threat to my safety. [INTENTIONAL INFLICTION OF EMOTIONAL DISTRESS]

29 – The Defendant sought to evict me to sever my relationship to my Mother and then made up cover stories against me in his Affidavit similar to the cover stories he made in his claims against the Government of Canada and his Public Sector Union during the 1990's which was judged by his supervisor and later by Federal Court of Canada to be baseless. (Exhibit 3a)

30 - From much of late April 2015 to mid-June 2015, the Defendant blocked access to

my use of most of my personal and professional belongings. This included my bed, clothes, academic books and many other items. This resulted in me having to purchase thousands of dollars worth of furnishings / replacement items and losing contracts as a result of not having access to professional materials. [ECONOMIC LOSS]. This was noted in a letter issued by a lawyer (Exhibit 4)

31 - The Defendant evicted me after I had spent considerable time and money publishing his over 500 pp book entitled "Work, the Economy and Human Development" that no one else would publish over a more than 30 year period. [ECONOMIC LOSS]

32 - Previous to my father forcibly servering my relationship to my Mother as a result of is apparent criminal interference, I had not been out of contact with my Mother for more than three or four days. The Defendant has subjected me to the intentional infliction of emotional distress by forcing me to be out of contact from my Mother since 12 June 2015 when she has needed and sought my assistance. This intentional infliction of emotional distress has also involved my witnessing him assault my Mom; and cause her profound psychological trauma.

33 - Todd Ji, an Ottawa Lawyer pressured the Defendant (Exhibit 4) to enable me to get access to my personal and professional belogings by shipping them all out to U-Haul Storage without my consent. I hold the defendant responsible for all storage expenses that I have incurred as a result of him evicting me without the necessary joint permission of my Mother as a co-owner of the property under the laws of joint marital ownership. [U- Haul Expneses Attached – Exhbit 5]

34 - The Defendant never returned by 12 speed customized bicycle that I want back. [THEFT BY CONVERSION – ILLEGAL MIS-APPROPRIATION OF PROPERTY]

35 - The Defendant has refused to provide sought independent verification that my Mom is not being held "prisoner" by the Defendant to borrow the Court's used word. The Defendant asserts that he has sought to respect my Mom's continued mental competence while refusing to allow my Mom to meet with who she wants; and that was confirmed by the Defendant refusing to allow the independent verfication sought of the Court. [THE DEFENDANT HAS ACTED IN BAD FAITH]

36 - The Defendant has caused me considerable expenses at trying to re establish contact with my Mom under the spectre of the Defendant's apparent criminal interference.

37 – The Defandant made me incur other expenses including process server and lawyer costs. (Exhibit 6)

38 – I seek monetary damages for the torts described herein and for the Defendant to

cease and desist his apparent criminal inteference against my Mother and I being able to both see and meet each other, which was further subverted by the Defendant when he had used Detective Robert J. Griffin to threaten the Nepean, Rideau and Osgoode Community Resource Centre on 15 June 2015.

39 – I have not been able to see my Mom since 12 June 2015 because the Defendant has taken advantage of the physical disabilities of my Mom, and subjected her to threats, intimidation and imposed social isolation which was further demonstrated in the Defendant's blocking to the Court supported independent verification. (Exhibit 7)

40 – I have retained video of my last conversation with my Mom on 12 June 2015 in which I asked her if she wanted me to help her in recovery and she nodded 'yes'.

41 - I had bought a tread mill [████████████████] for my Mom so that she could exercise, but the Defendant blocked my Mom and I from using it. I hold the Defendant responsible for over $1000.00 that I had wasted buying that tread mill.

42 – In my view, the Defendant has refused Court-sought independent verification because he fears that my Mom wanting to see me would expose both the Defendant and his daughter to the loss of this case and possible criminal prosecution at the conditions of forcible confinement, abuse and trauma that he has subjected my Mom.

AFFIRMED BEFORE ME
At the City of Ottawa
In the Province of Ontario
The 9th day of May, 2017;

Commissioner

Raymond Carby-Samuels

Related Attachment - CIVILIAN WITNESS STATEMENT
Attachment Description: **HORACE RAYMOND CARBY-SAMUELS**

OTTAWA POLICE SERVICE — STATEMENTS / DÉCLARATION — PAGE _1_ OF _1_
OCC ✗ YEAR 15 CASE #: 103702

SURNAME: Carby-Samuels   G1: H.   G2: Raymond

SUBMITTED BY: GARDINER   CADRE #: 2224   DATE SUBMITTED: 2015/04/26

STATUS: ☐ FINAL ☐ OPEN

LOCATION STATEMENT TAKEN: 700 Eagleson Rd

In January 2013, while my [?] I expressed concerns to my father in the kitchen at 30 Jocelyn Terrace while he was sitting at the kitchen table. At the time, I was standing beside the fridge in the kitchen. Shortly afterwards, he became virulently angry. This was epitomized by shouting at me with a 'wild stare' that I had no right to say anything about how he treats my mom in "his house". He then proceeded to charge me from the desk while I continued to stand beside the fridge. He then quickly grasped a very sharp kitchen knife that he proceeded to point at the centre of my stomach in a threatening way as if he wanted to stab me. Fearing possible death from such a stab, I grabbed the knife. His hand was over the handle, so I ended up grasping the sharp edge of the knife, that resulted in my little finger almost severing off, and blood gushing all over. I asked my mom to call 911, but she was choking in shock. I used one hand (left) to precariously call 911 with one hand. Paramedics + police arrived shortly after.

SIGNATURE OF PERSON MAKING STATEMENT: *[signature]*

	OTTAWA POLICE SERVICE
	GENERAL OCCURRENCE HARDCOPY
GO# 2016-42733	INFORM

RELEASED TO PUBLIC
Purpose: **PUBLIC**
Date Released: Friday, 2016-Feb-19
Time Released: 11:59
Person: **CARBY-SAMUELS, RAYMOND**

GENERAL RELEASE INSTRUCTIONS
QUEENSVIEW LOBBY

OTTAWA POLICE SERVICE
GENERAL OCCURRENCE HARDCOPY

GO# 2016-42733   INFORMATION (G

General Occurrence Information

Main offence: **INFORMATION (GENERAL) - COMPLETED**
Operational status: **OPEN**
Location: **30 JARLAN TER, OTTAWA**
District: **12** Zone: **203** Atom: **120314**
Reported on: **Thursday, 2016-Feb-18 14:48**
Occurred on: **Thursday, 2016-Feb-18 14:48**
Submitted by: **2066 LAFOREST, PAUL J.**   Org unit: **WEST PLATOON D**

CCJS Information

CCJS Status: **NON-CRIMINAL-INACTIVE**
Offences committed: **INFORMATION (GENERAL) - COMPLETED**
Location type: **SINGLE HOME, HOUSE**
Study flag: **REPORT FROM MRE**

Related Person(s)

1. COMPLAINANT 1 - CARBY-SAMUELS, RAYMOND II

Sex: MALE, Born on: 1968-Feb-28
Residing at: 495 COLDWATER CRES, OTTAWA
ONTARIO, K2L3L5

Phone numbers

Type	Phone #	Ext.	
HOME	(514) 712-7516		(Primary)
CELLULAR	(514) 712-7516		(Primary)
BUSINESS	(514) 712-7516		(Primary)
BUSINESS	(514) 712-7156		
HOME	(613) 591-3528		
HOME	(613) 599-5344		

OTTAWA POLICE SERVICE
GENERAL OCCURRENCE HARDCOPY

GO# 2016-42733   INFORMATION (GE

Narrative: INVESTIGATIVE ACTION - 1
Author: 2066 LAFOREST, PAUL J.
Related date/time: Thursday, 2016-Feb-18 16:10

On 18 Feb 2016 at 1504 hrs Cst STAM and I, Cst LAFOREST were dispatche
30 Jarlan Terr reference a keep the peace call generated. Information
the call was provided by Raymond CARBY-SAMUELS(M:1968-02-28) as follow

COMPL IS O/S TO C HIS MOM - COMPL HAS A COURT ORDER 2C HIS MOM - FATHE
BLOCKING ACCESS - FATHER=HORACE CARBY-SAMUELS

When we arrived on scene I observed two males standing beside an Audi
, outside of the a/m residence waiting. A
exited the patrol vehicle one male exited the car and produced a video
camera and began filming the interaction immediately. I was approached
the complainant Raymond who advised he was here to see his mother. Raym
produced a Court Order dated 11 Feb 2016.

There were two stipulations outlined on the order.

1. That Horace pay Raymond $25,000 and $550.00 for legal fees.

2. That Raymond have access to his mother, Desrin
CARBY-SAMUELS in order to assess if she require nutrition
or care-giver assistance starting at 3PM each day.

Raymond informed me he had knocked on the door and asked his father for
entry showing him the court order. Raymond stated he had the same order
delivered to his father, so he was aware he would be showing up at 1500
hrs. Horace denied Raymond access and told him to leave. Therefore poli
were called.

On Raymond's behalf I conducted a door knock

I returned to the road to speak with Raymond, who's friend was still
filming the interaction. I informed Horace was not willing to speak with
police and was being uncooperative with the matter. Raymond demanded tha
arrest his father as he was committing a criminal offence. I informed
Horace I had no reason to force entry into Horace's residence to aid wit
the enforcement of a vague Court Order or arrest him for not abiding by

OTTAWA POLICE SERVICE
GENERAL OCCURRENCE HARDCOPY

GO# 2016-42733   INFORMATION (GENERA

that order.

[redacted]

I returned to Raymond and informed him to continue documenting his attempts to see his mother and pursue further legal advice and action.

[redacted]

END
Cst LAFOREST
2066

OTTAWA POLICE SERVICE
GENERAL OCCURRENCE HARDCOPY

GO# 2016-42733   INFORMATION

Narrative: CONCLUDING REPORT - 1
Author: 2066 LAFOREST, PAUL J.
Related date/time: Thursday, 2016-Feb-18 16:53

If the following statement applies, use the CCJS status of 'Z'-Non-Criminal-Inactive.

This General Occurrence is being cleared as Non-Criminal as it has no evidence or allegation of a Criminal Offence.

This report will be considered final unless new leads come to light.

Remarks:
[

Murray v. Toth, 2012 ONSC 5815 (CanLII)

Date: 2012-10-17
File: 11-28809SR
Number:
Citation: Murray v. Toth, 2012 ONSC 5815 (CanLII), <http://canlii.ca/t/ft8dl>, retrieved on 2018-02-20

CITATION: Murray v. Toth, 2012 ONSC 5815
COURT FILE NO.: 11-28809SR
DATE: 2012-10-17

ONTARIO
SUPERIOR COURT OF JUSTICE

BETWEEN:	)	
Tracey Murray	)	Ms. M. Birdsell, for the Plaintiff
	) Plaintiff	
- and -	)	
Richard Toth	)	No one appearing
	) Defendant	
	))	**HEARD:** 5 September 2012, and reserved for decision

CRANE J.

Facts

[1]   Tracy Murray is a 45 year-old single mother, suffering from diabetes, scoliosis and Scheuermann's disease. She has been unable to work for the last 25 years and her income consists

of Ontario Disability and Canadian Pension Plan payments.

[2] In 2003 she was injured in a motor vehicle accident. She was engaged in litigation to recover damages from that accident when through a mutual friend she met the defendant, Richard Toth. At the time Ms. Murray was living on Manitoulin Island and Mr. Toth was living in Hamilton. Mr. Toth visited often, sometimes bringing gifts for Ms. Murray's two children. Before the litigation was complete, Mr. Toth suggested that Ms. Murray and her children live with him in Hamilton.

[3] Ms. Murray agreed to move to Hamilton; however, she initially resisted living with Mr. Toth. In July 2009, Ms. Murray and her children moved to an apartment in Hamilton. In September of 2009 Ms. Murray received approximately $70,000 in damages from the motor vehicle accident litigation. She retained a real estate agent and began looking to buy a house for herself and her children. She never did purchase a house. Toth had convinced her to move in to his house. Ms. Murray moved in on 24 September, 2009 with the expectation that she would pay for her children's expenses and Mr. Toth would pay for all other household expenses. Ms. Murray also believed that Mr. Toth intended to gift one half of the ownership of the house to her children.

[4] In October 2009, Mr. Toth proposed marriage. Ms. Murray accepted. No date was set.

[5] As soon as Ms. Murray moved into his house, Mr. Toth began borrowing large sums of money. After she moved in she learned that Mr. Toth was several months in arrears with his bills. She lent him money to pay his outstanding bills, and continued to pay many of his bills for their shared expenses. In addition, she paid for improvements and renovations of the house, on the belief that one day her children would benefit. She paid for all the expenses in the house, up to and including replacing the kitchen sink. She paid for the purchase of motorcycles and accessories for motorcycles. Mr. Toth told Ms. Murray that he planned to make money from selling motorcycles, and that with this money he would be able to pay her back. On one occasion Mr. Toth borrowed Ms. Murray's bank card (to make a $100 purchase). He then withdrew $1,200 from her account without her permission.

[6] During the short time they lived together Ms. Murray purchased a Ford truck and a Harley Davidson motorcycle for her own use. Ms. Murray registered these vehicles under Mr. Toth's name, on the basis that his insurance rates were superior to her own.

[7] She also purchased a bicycle for her son and a refrigerator to store her insulin. Both of these items disappeared from the house. Mr. Toth claimed to have no knowledge of their whereabouts.

[8] On July 9, 2010, without notice to her from Mr. Toth, the police supervised the eviction of Ms. Murray and her two children from the house. Ms. Murray believed she had two and one-half hours to pack and remove all of her furniture and belongings, and leave the property. Mr. Toth was not present at the eviction, though two of his friends showed up and offered "to help" Ms. Murray. With no alternatives, Ms. Murray relied on Mr. Toth's friends to move her furniture and store her truck (she could not drive the truck as the insurance had expired). In exchange, she sold Mr. Toth's friend her motorcycle for $10,000. She had only recently purchased this motorcycle for $15,000 and days earlier she had rejected his identical offer.

[9] I find on all the evidence upon inference that Mr. Toth orchestrated the eviction with his friends so as to control Ms. Murray and her remaining assets.

[10] Ms. Murray's life went steadily downhill after eviction. She felt forced, with no alternative

another of Mr. Toth's friends. During the move, much of her furniture was destroyed or failed to arrive. They had no beds, and alternated sleeping on the couch. She never saw her truck again. She was eventually paid the $10,000 for the motorcycle, but by that time she was told that she owed most of it to the bar owner for rent and bar meals.

[11] For the five weeks, while Ms. Murray and her children lived in deplorable conditions, Mr. Toth refused to forward her CPP and Disability payments. As a result she and her children incurred a large debt with the bar owner, buying the majority of their meals from his kitchen on credit. When Ms. Murray received payment for the motorcycle the bar owner claimed an excessive portion of it for rent and food.

[12] To make matters worse, the lives of Ms. Murray's children were threatened by Mr. Toth's friends. She sent them to live with her mother in Manitoulin Island and then soon followed. Ms. Murray was humiliated, shocked and drained by this ordeal.

Default Judgment

[13] Mr. Toth did not defend the action and was noted in default. Default proceeding are governed by Rule 19 of the *Rules of Civil Procedure*, R.R.O. 1990, Reg. 194. Under Rule 19.02 a defendant who has been noted in default is deemed to admit the truth of the allegations of fact made in the statement of claim. Under Rule 19.06 if the facts alleged establish that the plaintiff is entitled to judgment, the plaintiff will succeeded. Admissions of fact will not necessarily be sufficient to entitle a plaintiff to judgment on a motion for judgment or at trial. It is for the court to conduct an investigation of whether the evidence is sufficient to entitle the plaintiff to judgment. (See for instance, *Nikore v. Jarmain Investment Management Inc.*, 2009 CanLII 46655 (ON SC)).

Repayment of Loan

[14] In the Statement of Claim, the plaintiff claims $17,800 for repayment of loans (claimed under breach of contract). At the time of trial, Ms. Murray had recalculated the loans to $14,182. The specifics of the expenses are set out at Tabs 7 and 8 in the plaintiff's Document Brief. Ms. Murray testified that she and Mr. Toth agreed that he would repay the money when she asked. Prior to commencing this action Ms. Murray requested the loan be repaid. Mr. Toth refused.

[15] The facts are uncontested. There is no dispute that between September 2009 and July 2010, Ms. Murray provided cheques, cash and gifts totalling $14,182 to her then boyfriend, Mr. Toth. When the relationship broke down upon the eviction of Ms. Murray, she demanded repayment of the loan; Mr. Toth refused. The question is whether the transfer of money constituted loans or gifts of money.

[16] Where one person transfers money to another in circumstances where the person paying the money is not in debt to the person receiving the money, or where there is no presumption of advancement, then the burden falls on the person receiving the money to demonstrate that the money was a gift and not a loan. There is no presumption of advancement in this case.[1] Therefore, Mr. Toth must demonstrate that the money was a gift, not a loan. In order to do so, he must demonstrate:

1. An intention to donate;
2. A sufficient act of delivery; and
3. Acceptance of the gift.

COURT OF APPEAL FOR ONTARIO

CITATION: Sanzone v. Schechter, 2016 ONCA 566
DATE: 20160713
DOCKET: C60966

Strathy C.J.O., Brown and Huscroft JJ.A.

BETWEEN

Marie Sanzone

Plaintiff (Appellant)

and

Dr. Ira Schechter, Dr. Michael Schechter, and Schechter Dental

Defendants (Respondents)

Jamie Spotswood, for the appellant

Mario Delgado, for the respondents

Heard: June 30, 2016

On appeal from the judgment of Justice Suhail A.Q. Akhtar of the Superior Court of Justice, dated July 30, 2015.

Brown J.A.:

[1] The appellant, Marie Sanzone, commenced a malpractice action in 2011 seeking damages against the respondent dentists for dental surgery performed in 2009. The appellant has represented herself throughout most of the proceeding. The respondents moved for summary judgment, which the motion judge granted, dismissing the appellant's action. She appeals.

[2] In my respectful view, the motion judge erred in granting summary judgment because the moving party dentists failed to discharge their obligation to put their best evidentiary foot forward on their motion. I would grant the appeal and set aside the judgment.

PROCEDURAL HISTORY

[3] Although the appellant commenced her action by Notice of Action in September 2011, she delayed in delivering a statement of claim until March 2013, at which time she obtained a master's order extending the time to serve her claim. The master set a timetable for the respondents' motion for security for costs and other matters. The respondents sought security for costs because the appellant lives in New York State.

[4] A revised timetable was ordered in November 2013, which required the security for costs motion to be heard by the end of July 2014, and the appellant to set down her action for trial by the end of December 2014.

[5] In August 2014, Master Brott dismissed the respondents' security for costs motion, holding that the appellant had demonstrated impecuniosity. The respondents' appeal was dismissed in October 2014.

[6] In December 2014, respondents' counsel informed the appellant that unless she delivered an expert report to support her claim, a motion for summary judgment would be brought to dismiss it. In February 2015, the respondents

secured a date in Civil Practice Court for their motion. Following one adjournment requested by the appellant, the motion was heard in July 2015.

THE EVIDENCE BEFORE THE MOTION JUDGE

[7] The primary relief sought by the respondents in their notice of motion was summary judgment dismissing the action because the appellant had "not served any documentation in support of the allegations raised in the Statement of Claim or any qualified expert report establishing a breach of the standard of care provided by the Defendants or that such breach caused the Plaintiff's injuries." As alternative relief, the respondents sought "an Order dismissing the action for delay as the Plaintiff has not set the matter down for trial as required under the timetable endorsed" by the master.

[8] In support of their motion, the respondents filed an affidavit from one of their lawyers describing the procedural history of the action and stating the appellant had not delivered an expert report in support of her claim. Neither of the respondent dentists filed an affidavit, nor did they file an expert's report on the issue of the standard of care.

[9] The appellant first filed a responding affidavit in which she explained the difficulties she faced as a self-represented litigant without legal training. As well, she described certain medical and financial challenges she faced.

[10] In a supplementary affidavit filed a week before the motion hearing, the appellant deposed that she was looking to retain an expert and would comply with the *Rules of Civil Procedure* when she had retained one. The appellant also attached, as an exhibit, a July 27, 2014 one-page letter from a dentist, Dr. Stanley Shafer, in which he stated the respondent dentists had not met the standard of care in two respects. In her affidavit, the appellant deposed that the "letter is by no means complete, however."

[11] The respondents then filed a further affidavit stating that Dr. Shafer's status as a dentist was listed as "inactive" in New York State, and his licence in Pennsylvania had expired in 2013.

THE REASONS OF THE MOTION JUDGE

[12] The motion judge held that Dr. Shafer's 2014 letter was inadmissible as an expert's report because it was not an affidavit upon which the doctor could be cross-examined and did not comply with rule 53.03 governing expert reports. Even had he admitted the letter, the motion judge would not have given it any weight because it lacked specifics and any evidence of causation.

[13] The motion judge referred to case law which states that in the absence of a supporting expert opinion, a plaintiff has no hope of success in a medical malpractice action and the action must be dismissed. He granted summary judgment on the basis the appellant had failed to file an expert report to support

her allegation that the respondent dental surgeons had not met the standard of care when performing surgery on her.

ISSUES ON APPEAL

[14] The appellant submits the motion judge committed two errors in dismissing her action:

i. The motion judge erred in finding that Dr. Shafer's letter was not admissible as an expert report on a summary judgment motion; and

ii. The motion judge failed to accord the appellant, a self-represented litigant, an appropriate amount of leeway on procedural matters, with the result that the dismissal of her action was not a fair and just result in the circumstances.

ANALYSIS

First ground of appeal: The admissibility of Dr. Shafer's letter

[15] The appellant submits the motion judge erred in ruling that Dr. Shafer's letter was inadmissible on the summary judgment motion. I do not agree. The principles governing the admissibility of evidence on a summary judgment motion are the same as those that apply at trial, save for the limited exception of permitting an affidavit made on information and belief found in rule 20.02(1) of the *Rules of Civil Procedure*.

[16] As a general rule, when a party seeks to adduce expert evidence on a summary judgment motion, the evidence of the expert must comply with rule 53.03, unless the opinion evidence is based on the witness' observation of or participation in the events in issue, as explained in *Westerhof v. Gee Estate*, 2015 ONCA 206, 310 O.A.C. 335, at paras. 60-62. A party can file either an affidavit from the expert containing his or her opinion or an affidavit from the expert with the report attached: *Danos v. BMW Group Financial Services Canada, a division of BMW Canada Inc.*, 2014 ONSC 2060, [2014] O.J. No. 1802, at para. 29, aff'd 2014 ONCA 887.

[17] In the present case, Dr. Shafer was not a participant expert, and his letter of July 27, 2014 did not meet the requirements of rule 53.03: it lacked a proper statement of his qualifications; it did not set forth the reasons for his opinion in the depth required by rule 53.03(2.1)(6); nor was it accompanied by an acknowledgement of expert's duty.

[18] Moreover, on the motion the appellant did not purport to tender Dr. Shafer's letter as an expert report. As stated in her July 13, 2015 affidavit, she was still "looking to retain an expert." She attached Dr. Shafer's letter as one "from a qualified dentist [that] speaks to some issues involved in this claim. The letter is by no means complete, however."

[19] Accordingly, I see no error in the motion judge's ruling that Dr. Shafer's letter was inadmissible on the summary judgment motion as the report of an expert.

Second ground of appeal: Whether the dismissal of the appellant's action was fair and just in the circumstances

[20] The appellant submits the dismissal of her action was not a fair or just result given her circumstances as an impecunious, self-represented litigant. The appellant contends the motion judge should have afforded her some leeway on procedural matters by (i) dispensing, in various ways, with the requirements of rule 53.03, (ii) affording her more time to comply with rule 53.03, or (iii) considering an alternative to the dismissal of her action.

[21] Fairness requires a judge to accommodate a self-represented party's unfamiliarity with the litigation process to enable her to present her case to the best of her ability: *Davids v. Davids* (1999), 125 O.A.C. 375 (C.A.), at para. 36. It is apparent from the transcript of the June 20, 2014 adjournment hearing that the motion judge tried very hard to do exactly that.

[22] Of course, any accommodation made by a judge to a self-represented party must respect the rights of the other party: *Davids*, at para. 36. A defendant is entitled to expect that a claim of liability brought against it will be decided by

the same rules of evidence and substantive law whether the plaintiff is represented by counsel or self-represented.

[23] That said, when a represented party invokes the mechanisms available under the *Rules of Civil Procedure* to seek some relief against a self-represented party, the represented party must ensure it complies fully with its own obligations under the rules, and not use the rules to take unfair advantage of the self-represented litigant.

[24] Rule 20.01(3) requires a defendant to "move with supporting affidavit material or other evidence" on a summary judgment motion. The respondent dentists, as the moving parties, bore the burden of persuading the court, through evidence, that no genuine issue requiring a trial existed: *Dawson v. Rexcraft Storage and Warehouse Inc.* (1998), 111 O.A.C. 201 (C.A.), at para. 16; *Connerty v. Coles*, 2012 ONSC 5218, [2012] O.J. No. 4313, at para. 9. They were not entitled to rely merely on the allegations in their statement of defence; the respondents were required to put their best evidentiary foot forward.

[25] They did not do so. Instead, they submitted to the motion judge that the decision of this court in *Kurdina v. Dief*, 2010 ONCA 288, [2010] O.J. No. 1551, required the dismissal of the appellant's action because the absence of any expert evidence in support of her claim demonstrated that no genuine issue

requiring trial existed. The motion judge accepted that argument. In my respectful view, he erred in so doing in the circumstances of this case.

[26] *Kurdina* involved a negligence claim against two psychiatrists. They moved for summary judgment, which was granted. In dismissing the plaintiff's appeal, this court observed, at para. 3:

> The respondents provided the evidence of Dr. Sugar, a qualified expert witness who swore that the respondents had not fallen below the standard of care in their treatment of the appellant. To avoid summary judgment, the appellant was required to adduce some expert opinion evidence from a qualified psychiatrist supporting her claim that the care she received fell below the applicable standard of care.

[27] In contrast to the evidence on the merits put forward by the moving party psychiatrists in the *Kurdina* case, in the present case the moving party dentists did not file any evidence going to the merits of their defence. They did not file their own affidavits explaining the treatment they gave the appellant, nor did they file an affidavit or report from a qualified expert on the issue of the standard of care. Instead, they filed affidavits from two associates in their counsel's office: one recounting the procedural history of the action; the other providing information about Dr. Shafer's qualifications.

[28] The respondents submit two cases support their position that simply filing a lawyer's affidavit was sufficient in the circumstances. In *Claus v. Wolfman* (1999), 52 O.R. (3d) 673 (S.C.), aff'd (2000), 52 O.R. (3d) 680 (C.A.), defendant

physicians and a hospital moved for summary judgment in a medical malpractice action arguing the plaintiff had failed to produce a supporting expert report. In the course of his reasons granting summary judgment, the motion judge commented that "it would therefore be open to a court to grant summary judgment dismissing a claim of this nature even without the expert opinion of the defendants": at para. 12. That comment was *obiter* because, in fact, the moving party physicians had filed a report of their own expert on the motion. In dismissing the appeal, this court relied on that expert evidence, noting the defendant physicians "have demonstrated that there is no evidence that such force as was applied [during the delivery] fell below an acceptable standard of care." The *Claus* case therefore does not support the respondents' submission.

[29] The second case is *Cassibo v. Bacso*, 2010 ONSC 6435, [2010] O.J. No. 5150, in which a defendant dentist obtained summary judgment dismissing a professional negligence claim. The plaintiff, who was represented by counsel, had not delivered an expert report by the time discoveries had concluded and the motion was brought. The motion judge observed, at paras. 15 and 17, that some courts have held that in a limited class of cases a plaintiff's expert report is not necessary where an inference of a breach of care or causation can be made without the necessity of expert evidence. However, the motion judge rejected the plaintiff's submission that the moving party defendant was not entitled to

summary judgment because he had not filed an expert report. The motion judge stated, at para. 20:

> Such an argument if accepted would effectively reverse the evidentiary burden. It would also as a practical matter lead to a difficult situation for defendants who would be forced to obtain costly expert opinions to respond to a case which has not been fully articulated by the plaintiff.

[30] I would respectfully disagree with that conclusion. First, the evidentiary burden on a moving party defendant on a motion for summary judgment is that set out in rule 20.01(3) – "a defendant may... move with supporting affidavit material or other evidence." As explained in *Connerty,* at para. 9, only after the moving party defendant has discharged its evidentiary burden of proving there is no genuine issue requiring a trial for its resolution does the burden shift to the responding party to prove that its claim has a real chance of success.

[31] Second, the decision in *Cassibo* stands outside the overwhelming weight of the case law that when medical practitioners move for summary judgment to dismiss a malpractice action, they file evidence on the merits of their defence, including expert reports.[1] That general practice is consistent with the evidentiary obligation borne by moving parties on summary judgment motions.

---

[1] See, for example, the type of evidence filed by moving party medical practitioners on summary judgment motions in *Kay v. Credit Valley Hospital,* 2008 CanLII 431 (ON SC), at para. 7; *Farooq v. Miceli,* 2012 ONSC 558, at para. 16; *Suwary v. Women's College Hospital,* [2008] O.J. No. 883 (S.C.), at para. 7; *Markowa v. Adamson Cosmetic Facial Surgery Inc.,* 2012 ONSC 1012, [2012] O.J. No. 762, at para.62;

[32] In the present case, given the absence of evidence from the moving party dentists in support of their defence, the motion judge should have addressed the threshold question of whether the respondents had discharged their evidentiary obligation as moving parties under rule 20 to put their best foot forward by adducing evidence on the merits. In my respectful view, the motion judge erred in failing to address that question.

[33] If the respondent dentists had filed evidence dealing with the merits of their defence in support of their summary judgment motion, it would have been open to the motion judge to treat the appellant's failure to deliver a compliant expert's report as a basis to dismiss her action. In light of the respondents' failure to file any such evidence, it was not open to the motion judge to grant summary judgment. He erred in so doing.

[34] In my view, the respondent dentists attempted to use rule 20 as a means to unfairly accelerate the delivery of an expert's report by the appellant. Rule 53.03(1) requires a party who intends to call an expert witness at trial to serve a report "not less than 90 days before the pre-trial conference." In the present case, no pre-trial conference date had been set.

[35] Where no pre-trial conference date has been set, it is open to a party to accelerate the exchange of expert reports by requesting under rule 50.13(1) a

---

McNeil v. Easterbrook, [2004] O.J. No. 3976 (S.C.), at para. 7; *Samuel v. Ho*, [2009] O.J. No. 172 (S.C.), at para. 6.

case conference which can be scheduled "at any time." At a case conference, a judge may give directions for any procedural step, including setting a timeline for the exchange of expert reports: rules 50.13(5)-(6). In crafting those directions at a case conference where the parties can raise all outstanding procedural issues, the judge can fairly balance the interests of both parties and establish a procedural roadmap for the balance of the proceeding tailored to the circumstances of the case and the abilities of any self-represented party. Single-judge case management, which addresses all the steps in a proceeding, not just the preparation of a single motion, offers a powerful tool by which judges can discharge their duty to accommodate self-represented parties' unfamiliarity with the litigation process to enable them to present their case to the best of their abilities.

[36] Although the parties had attended two case conferences before masters prior to the respondents launching their summary judgment motion, no timetable had been set for the exchange of expert reports. The timetables set by the masters had focused on the respondents' motion for security for costs. Accordingly, when the respondents brought their summary judgment motion, the appellant was not in default of her obligations under the rules regarding the delivery of an expert's report. By resorting to rule 20 to compel the self-represented appellant to deliver an expert report, without meeting their own

evidentiary obligations as moving parties under the rule, the defendants used the rules in a procedurally inappropriate manner.

[37] In those circumstances, the motion judge should not have granted summary judgment but, instead, should have focused on the moving parties' alternative relief – the dismissal of the action because the appellant had not set it down for trial by December 31, 2014, as directed by a master. Had the motion judge done so, no doubt he would have concluded that this action had reached the point where case management by a single judge was required in order to address the legitimate desire of the respondents to see the action moved along, while accommodating, in a reasonable and practical manner, the self-represented appellant's unfamiliarity with the process to enable her to present her case to the best of her ability.

DISPOSITION

[38] For these reasons, I would grant the appeal, set aside the summary judgment dismissing the action, and award the appellant costs of the appeal fixed in the amount of $5,000, inclusive of disbursements and HST.

Released: "GRS" (July 13, 2016)

"David Brown J.A."
"I agree G.R. Strathy C.J.O."
"I agree Grant Huscroft J.A."

TDJ Law
224 Hunt Club Road, Ottawa ON
T: (613) 501-1588 F: (613) 482-5038
E: toddji.Law@gmail.com
www.tdjLaw.com

Demand for a Meeting with Dezrin Carby-Samuels and the Return of Personal Effects

JUNE 10, 2015.

DELIVERED BY EMAIL AND REGULAR MAIL

By mail to:	By email to:
30 Jarlan Terrace	horaceanddezrincs@gmail.com
Ottawa ON	marcellacs@gmail.com
K2L 3L5	

Attention:
Horace R. Carby-Samuels
Marcella Carby-Samuels

Dear Sir/Madam:

Re: Abuse of Dezrin Carby-Samuels

I am the lawyer for Raymond Carby-Samuels.

Raymond has advised me that he has witnessed ongoing abuse, neglect and violence by Horace R. Carby-Samuels towards his mother, Dezrin Carby-Samuels. Specifically, toward the end of April 2015, Horace R. Carby-Samuels abused Raymond's mother, and filed a series of police reports and inquiries on or around April 21, 2015. Written notes were taken although no charges were laid.

Raymond has made repeated attempts to visit Dezrin Carby-Samuels, as per her request, but was prevented from doing so against his mother's wishes. Horace R. Carby-Samuels had made a firm commitment to allow Raymond to meet with his mother and to recover his belongings. This Agreement was made in the presence of police officers. Moreover, since Raymond has been the primary caregiver for his mother, we demand that you arrange a meeting between Raymond and his mother so that he can verify her safety and well-being by **June 12, 2015 at 12:00pm**.

We also demand that Raymond's personal items, which have been left on the property at 30 Jarlan Terrace, be promptly returned to him. Please contact me directly to advise when we may arrange a visit for Raymond to see his mother and recover his personal effects.

Unless we receive an acknowledgement of our request and cooperation from you to arrange the meeting before the stipulated date, I have Raymond's permission to pursue a court order to compel you to return the personal items and arrange for a meeting between Raymond and his mother. If legal proceedings are required, I will seek my client's costs against you.

To save time and unnecessary expense, I ask that you cooperate with Raymond's reasonable requests for a meeting and the return of his belongings.

Yours very truly,

TDJ Law
224 Hunt Club Road, Ottawa ON
T: (613) 501-1588 F: (613) 482-5038
E: toddji.Law@gmail.com
www.tdjLaw.com

Todd Ji
Barrister & Solicitor

T: (613) 501-1588
E: toddji.law@gmail.com
A: 224 Huntclub Road, Ottawa ON, K1V 1C1
www.tdjlaw.com

P.Siryuyumusi Law Office

302 St Patrick Street
Ottawa, Ontario
K1N 5K5

Tel: (613) 241-2754
Fax: (613) 241-0173
E-mail: siryuyumusi@lawyer.com

Ottawa, May 15, 2017

<u>To whom it may Concern</u>

Re : Raymond Carby-Samuels II

I, Pacifique Siryuyumusi, hereby confirm that I have met Raymond Carby-Samuels II two times at my office for consultation regarding the matter opposing him to his father Horace R. Carby Samuels.

During our discussions, it came to my attention that a motion was to be heard on May 16, 2017. It appeared that Mr Carby-Samuels II had not responded to the motion. I strongly advised him to respond to it sincee he did not seem to be aware of the need to do so. I explained to him that I have no time to respond to the motion on such a short notice, and I also explained to him that I will not be able to represent him before the court on that day.

I offered him to find another lawyer who can work on the case expeditiously since he did not know any other lawyer who can work on this matter. Unfortunately, Mr Carby-Samuels II advised me that the lawyer (Max Kilongozi) was too expensive for him.

It is my understanding that despite his efforts to find a lawyer, he has not been successful to retain a lawyer who can assist him before the court.

Should you need more information about this letter, please do not hesitate to call this office.

Pacifique Siryuyumusi

PACIFIQUE SIRYUYUMUSI
BARRISTER - SOLICITOR - NOTARY
302 ST. PATRICK STREET
OTTAWA, ONTARIO K1N 5K5
TEL. (613) 241-2754 FAX: (613) 241-0173

Gurbir Singh, LL.B.

Barrister, Solicitor
2250 Bovaird Drive Suite 316, Brampton, Ontario, L6R 0W1
Tel: 905-902-1529; Fax: 289-804-1721

Dear Mr. John Summers
Bell Baker
Suite 700 – 116 Lisgar Street
Ottawa, Ontario K2P 0C2

Please be advised that I have been recently retained by Mr. Raymond Carby-Samuels. My client has brought to my attention that your client, Horace Carby-Samuels who is the father of my client has been blocking the ability of my client and his Mother, Dezrin Carby-Samuels to freely see each other of their own volition since 12 June 2015.

I note that Dezrin was only able to last see her son that she expressly communicated to the Nepean, Osgoode and Rideau Community Resource Centre that she wanted to see, after my client took the initiative to see a lawyer who had sent your client a Legal Demand letter back in June 2015.

In a transcript of a Motion Hearing dated 24 March 2017 (Ontario Superior Court Claim 15-66772), you had confirmed that Ms Carby-Samuels remains mentally capable.

Judge Macloed who presided over the Motion Hearing in his wisdom, implored your client to allow Rabbi Yoey and yourself to visit Ms Carby-Samuels to re-confirm that she still wants to see her son.

However, in an email dated 27 March 2017, you had written back to my client indicating that Mr. Horace Carby-Samuels would not allow such a verification of Ms Carby-Samuels' desire.

I regard such an apparent on-going blocking of visitation by your client has inappropriately taken advantage of Ms Carby-Samuels' physical disabilities which has disregarded her rights to be able to have the opportunity to see who she wants, as the mentally capable person you had recognized in that Motion Hearing, as constituting criminal interference against both my client and his Mother.

No person in Canada has the right to deprive the ability of two mentally capable and law-abiding adults to freely see each other by subjecting one of those adults to *de facto* incarceration which resembles a form of forcible confinement of kidnapping as defined in the Criminal Code.

This in itself is grounds for my client having a claim against your client who has subjected my client to the intentional infliction of emotional distress of the forcible separation from a relationship with his Mother that both he and his Mother have enjoyed for more than 40 years.

I also note that my client has evidence that your client has abused his Mother. This evidence includes a written note in her writing which stipulates that "Dad abuses me".

I respectfully demand that you inform my Office within 5 Business Days of receiving this Demand Letter of arrangements to enable both my client and Rabbi Yoey to see his mother for the purposes of establishing her desires without any further criminal interference, in the same manner that my client and his Mother were able to last see each other on 12 June 2015.

Feel free in contacting me for further information.

Yours Truly,

Gurbir Singh

kelly manthorp heaphy *

barristers, solicitors, notaries

January 24, 2017

BY E-MAIL (jsummers@bellbaker.com)

Bell Baker LLP
Barristers and Solicitors
700-116 Lisgar Street
Ottawa, ON
K2P 0C2

Attention: John E. Summers

Dear Mr. Summers:

Re: Raymond-Carby-Samuels – Court File No. 15-66772 and 16-69142

Please direct all future correspondence and communications to Mr. Carby-Samuels. I have not been appointed as the lawyer in respect of the litigation.

On behalf of Mr. Carby-Samuels, I am writing to seek your consent to the relief sought for the motion scheduled for February 14, 2017. Please confirm in writing to Mr. Carby-Samuels the following information:

1) Your available dates for mediation until the end of June. If you are not available, please provide your first available dates; and
2) Which mediators are acceptable to you.

I request this information by no later than January 31, 2017. Once this information is provided, Mr. Carby-Samuels will draft a consent Order for your review and approval. If

---

*a division of kelly manthorp heaphy professional corporation
2323 riverside drive, suite B0001, ottawa, ontario K1H 8L5
phone: (613) 733-3000   fax: (613) 523-2924
miriam vale peters e-mail: mvp@kellymanthorp.com

Mr. Carby-Samuels does not hear from you or an appearance is required other than a consent Order, please be advised that he will be seeking costs against your client at the motion.

Yours very truly,

Kelly Manthorp Heaphy
per:

[signature]

Miriam Vale Peters
MVP/ah
cc: client

MOTION

BEFORE THE HONOURABLE JUSTICE C. MACLEOD
on March 24, 2011, at OTTAWA, Ontario

APPEARANCES:

E. Carby-Samuels — Self Represented
J. Summers — Counsel for the Respondent

THE COURT: So the instructions you're getting are [illegible]

MR. SUMMERS: Yes.

THE COURT: But....

MR. SUMMERS: And I'll say this for the benefit of Mr. Carby-Samuels and his supporters that are here, [illegible] that he allow a visit at least with the rabbi and so that the rabbi, and I apologize for referring to him as rabbi but I don't know his name. So I apologize for that. But so that he can speak with Mr. Carby-Samuels' mother and see if she has any desire to see her son at all.

She's not mentally incompetent, my understanding is she's not verbal but she's completely mentally competent, there's no issue there.

THE COURT: Can she write?

MR. SUMMERS: As far as I'm aware, yes. So now I've never met Ms. Carby-Samuels, I've only dealt with Mr. Carby-Samuels because he's my client so I can't — I don't want to comment too much about her abilities.

THE COURT: So I mean I think it would be in everyone's best interests for there to be some independent verification that she's not being held prisoner.

MR. SUMMERS: Yes.

THE COURT: And that she either does or doesn't wish to see her son and how she would like to do that and where because you know, the problem we

have today is simply that it's not before the
court in a form that I can deal with.

MR. SUMMERS: Yes.

THE COURT: That doesn't mean there isn't an issue
there potentially.

MR. SUMMERS: Yes. And arrangements had been
previously made Your Honour. I mean the police
have been involved; the elder abuse section of the
police force has been involved.

Access had been arranged at the Nepean Community
Resource Centre, they terminated that relationship
because of their interactions with Mr. Carby-
Samuels.

So there has been efforts and I continue to make
efforts because I agree with Your Honour, this
forum is not the forum for this to occur. And so
if there's any way to reconcile the family that
would obviously be the best approach.

THE COURT: Right.

MR. SUMMERS: And I continue to speak to my client
in that respect.

THE COURT: The fundamental question and again
it's not properly before me in a way that I can
deal with it today, is you know is your client
blocking his wife's wish...

MR. SUMMERS: Yes.

THE COURT: ...to see her son? And if she does
want to see him, perhaps he's quite entitled not
to have him come to the house.

MR. SUMMERS: Yes.

Superior Court File: 16-69142

ONTARIO
SUPERIOR COURT OF JUSTICE

BETWEEN

RAYMOND CARBY-SAMUELS II

Plaintiff

– and –

HORACE CARBY-SAMUELS

Defendant

MOTION FOR LEAVE TO AMEND STATEMENT OF CLAIM

TO: Mr. John E Summers
Bell Baker LLP
#700-116 Lisgar Street
Ottawa, Ontario K2P 0C2
Tel: (613) 237-3334
Email: Jsummers@bellbaker.com
Lawyer for the Defendant

Court File Number: 16-69142

ONTARIO SUPERIOR COURT OF JUSTICE

H. RAYMOND CARBY-SAMUELS

Plaintiff

– and –

HORACE CARBY-SAMUELS

Defendant

STATEMENT OF CLAIM

TO THE DEFENDANT:

A LEGAL PROCEEDING HAS BEEN COMMENCED AGAINST YOU by the plaintiff. The claim made against you is set out in the following pages.

IF YOU WISH TO DEFEND THIS PROCEEDING, you or an Ontario lawyer acting for you must prepare a statement of defence in Form 18A prescribed by the Rules of Civil Procedure, serve it on the plaintiff's lawyer or, where the plaintiff does not have a lawyer, serve it on the plaintiff, and file it, with proof of service in this court office, WITHIN TWENTY DAYS after this statement of claim is served on you, if you are served in Ontario.

If you are served in another province or territory of Canada or in the United States of America, the period for serving and filing your statement of defence is forty days. If you are served outside Canada and the United States of America, the period is sixty days.

Instead of serving and filing a statement of defence, you may serve and file a notice of intent to defend in Form 18B prescribed by the Rules of Civil Procedure. This will entitle you to ten more days within which to serve and file your statement of defence.

IF YOU FAIL TO DEFEND THIS PROCEEDING, JUDGMENT MAY BE GIVEN AGAINST YOU IN YOUR ABSENCE AND WITHOUT FURTHER NOTICE TO YOU. IF YOU WISH TO DEFEND THIS PROCEEDING BUT ARE UNABLE TO

PAY LEGAL FEES, LEGAL AID MAY BE AVAILABLE TO YOU BY CONTACTING A LOCAL LEGAL AID OFFICE.

IF YOU PAY THE PLAINTIFF'S CLAIM, and $500 for costs, within the time for serving and filing your statement of defence you may move to have this proceeding dismissed by the court. If you believe the amount claimed for costs is excessive, you may pay the plaintiff's claim and $400 for costs and have the costs assessed by the court.

TAKE NOTICE: THIS ACTION WILL AUTOMATICALLY BE DISMISSED if it has not been set down for trial or terminated by any means within five years after the action was commenced unless otherwise ordered by the court.

Date .... JUN 29 2016 .... Issued by ....
Local registrar

Address of court office

161 Elgin Street
Ottawa, Ontario

TO: HORACE CARBY-SAMUELS

John E. Summers, Lawyer

BELL BAKER LLP
Barristers and Solicitors
#700-116 Lisgar Street
Ottawa, Ontario K2P 0C2

THIS ACTION IS BROUGHT AGAINST YOU UNDER THE SIMPLIFIED PROCEDURE PROVIDED IN RULE 76 OF THE RULES OF CIVIL PROCEDURE.

CLAIM

1. The Plaintiff claims against the Defendant the following:

a) General damages in the amount of $30,000 or such other amount as this Honourable Court deems appropriate;

b) Special damages in the sum of $10,000 or such other amount as this Honourable Court deems appropriate;

c) Punitive damages in the sum of $10,000 or such other amount as this Honourable Court deems appropriate;

d) Aggravated damages in the sum of $10,000 or such other amount as this Honourable Court deems appropriate;

e) Pre- and post judgement interest in accordance with the provisions of the *Courts of Justice Act*, R.S.O. 1990, c C43, as amended.

f) Such further and other relief as may been fair and just to this Honourable Court.

THE PARTIES

2. The Plaintiff resides in Ottawa, Ontario

3. The Defendant resides in Ottawa, Ontario

BACKGROUND FACTS AND CIRCUMSTANCES / FACTUM

4. Raymond Carby-Samuels had witnessed Horace Carby-Samuels, the Defendant, abusing his Mom who was diagnosed with a medical condition which requires

vigilant support to her nutritional, vitamin and other care-giving requirement that Horace Carby-Samuels had neglected.

5. Raymond Carby-Samuels sought to report his observations to the Ottawa Police after having been subjected to assault with a weapon a couple years before when the Plaintiff had previously sought to discuss the matter with the Defendant.

6. Horace Carby-Samuels made vexatious representations to the police that the Plaintiff suffers from mental illness which was used as the basis to deflect any investigation against the Defendant who used the Police to keep the Plaintiff from having any visitation access to his Mother for more than a year.

BACKGROUND

7. Horace Carby-Samuels as a parent betrayed Raymond Carby-Samuels by making vexatious allegations against him which manifested in unwarranted police investigations and surveillance which resulted in mental anguish and emotional distress that was used to perpetrate auxiliary torts by the Defendant.

8. The Ottawa Police Service relied on the accuracy of the Defendant's statement as a parent who has known and been living with the Plaintiff more than 45 years.

9. Horace Carby-Samuels has perpetrated an apparent campaign of malice and deceit once characterized by Dezrin Carby-Samuels as "wicked".

10. Horace Carby-Samuels is the "father" of Raymond Carby-Samuels;

11. Dezrin Carby-Samuels is the mother of Raymond Carby-Samuels

DAMAGES

12. As a result of Horace Carby-Samuels' public mischief, Raymond Carby-Samuels has suffered irreparable damages, including, but not limited to -

    (a) Raymond Carby-Samuels has suffered emotional trauma and loss of enjoyment of life

    (b) Raymond Carby-Samuels has been been intimidated, harassed/psychological distressed including *inter alia* anxiety, nervousness, humiliation, embarrassment, mental distress, sleep disturbance, fatigue; and various physical pains requiring medical treatment.

(c) Raymond Carby-Samuels has suffered irreparable damage to his reputation and credibility among the officers and agents of the Ottawa Police Services, family relations and friends; and also the public at large through warnings issued by the police to neighbours who relied on the representation of Horace Carby-Samuels that Raymond Carby-Samuels has been suffering from mental illness which made him prone to violent behaviour.

(d) Raymond Carby-Samuels been subject to ridicule and contempt, as a result of the ensuing action of the Ottawa Police Services which relied on the public mischief of Horace Carby-Samuels and as a result Raymond Carby-Samuels may face this prejudice for the rest of his life;

(e) Raymond Carby-Samuels has suffered other damages, as well as out of pocket expenses and other special damages, the particulars of which, will be provided before trial;

(f) The Plaintiff pleads and relies of Section 140 of the *Criminal Code of Canada*, the law of equity pursuant to Section 96 of the *Courts of Justice Act*, R.S.O. 1990, the court's inherent jurisdiction to grant relief; and also relevant common law

Court File Number: 16-69142

ONTARIO SUPERIOR COURT OF JUSTICE

H. RAYMOND CARBY-SAMUELS

Plaintiff

-- and --

HORACE CARBY-SAMUELS

Defendant

AMENDED STATEMENT OF CLAIM

TO THE DEFENDANT:

A LEGAL PROCEEDING HAS BEEN COMMENCED AGAINST YOU by the plaintiff. The claim made against you is set out in the following pages.

IF YOU WISH TO DEFEND THIS PROCEEDING, you or an Ontario lawyer acting for you must prepare a statement of defence in Form 18A prescribed by the Rules of Civil Procedure, serve it on the plaintiff's lawyer or, where the plaintiff does not have a lawyer, serve it on the plaintiff, and file it with proof of service in this court office, WITHIN TWENTY DAYS after this statement of claim is served on you, if you are served in Ontario.

If you are served in another province or territory of Canada or in the United States of America, the period for serving and filing your statement of defence is forty days. If you are served outside Canada and the United States of America, the period is sixty days.

Instead of serving and filing a statement of defence, you may serve and file a notice of intent to defend in Form 18B prescribed by the Rules of Civil Procedure. This will entitle you to ten more days within which to serve and file your statement of defence.

IF YOU FAIL TO DEFEND THIS PROCEEDING, JUDGMENT MAY BE GIVEN AGAINST YOU IN YOUR ABSENCE AND WITHOUT FURTHER NOTICE TO YOU. IF YOU WISH TO DEFEND THIS PROCEEDING BUT ARE UNABLE TO

'PAY LEGAL FEES, LEGAL AID MAY BE AVAILABLE TO YOU BY CONTACTING A LOCAL LEGAL AID OFFICE.

IF YOU PAY THE PLAINTIFF'S CLAIM, and $500 for costs, within the time for serving and filing your statement of defence you may move to have this proceeding dismissed by the court. If you believe the amount claimed for costs is excessive, you may pay the plaintiff's claim and $400 for costs and have the costs assessed by the court.

TAKE NOTICE: THIS ACTION WILL AUTOMATICALLY BE DISMISSED if it has not been set down for trial or terminated by any means within five years after the action was commenced unless otherwise ordered by the court.

Date: JUN 29 2016

Issued by

Address of court office

161 Elgin Street
Ottawa, Ontario

TO: HORACE CARBY-SAMUELS

THIS ACTION IS BROUGHT AGAINST YOU UNDER THE SIMPLIFIED PROCEDURE PROVIDED IN RULE 76 OF THE RULES OF CIVIL PROCEDURE.

CLAIM

1. The Plaintiff claims against the Defendant the following:

a) General damages in the amount of $30,000 [$20,000] or such other amount as this Honourable Court deems appropriate;

b) Special damages in the sum of $10,000 [$ To be determined by Court] or such other amount as this Honourable Court deems appropriate;

c) Punitive damages in the sum of $10,000 [To be determined by Court] or such other amount as this Honourable Court deems appropriate;

d) Aggravated damages in the sum of $10,000 [$ To be determined by Court] or such other amount as this Honourable Court deems appropriate;

e) Pre- and post-judgement interest in accordance with the provisions of the *Courts of Justice Act*, R.S.O. 1990, c.C43, as amended

f) Public Mischief to Police involving Fraudulent Misrepresentation / Slander regarding the Defendant's representation to Police that the Plaintiff suffered from mental illness which lead the Ottawa Police Services to evict Plaintiff.. Tort - $10,000

g) The Defendant's illegal seizure of the personal and professional belongings of the Plaintiff from the time of the Defendant's eviction of the Plaintiff in late April 2015 until mid-June 2015 when the Defendant incurred additional costs to obtain a Legal Demand Letter from Todd in mid-June 2015 which demanded the release of belongings. The Defendant blocked access to belongings under a trespassing threat

 Tort - Illegal Seizure of Property - $4,000
 Costs to obtain Demand Letter and Legal Services - $1,000

h) Eviction without notice from 30 Jarlan Terrance after having established residence since there since 1986 – Violation of common law - $5,000

i) Assault and battery by Defendant with a knife causing permanent physical damage. Assault required Emergency Surgery and over 6 months of rehabilitation.

Assault causing bodily damage - $5000.00
Economic loss – not able to work for 6 months - $10,000
Child abuse [$ To be determined by Court]
Intentional Infliction of Emotional Distress – [$To be determined by Court]

j) Conspiracy with Marcella Carby-Samuels, the Defendant's daughter, in the coordination of Public Mischief to the Ottawa Police Services involving slanderous claims that the Plaintiff held 'his parents' "hostage" and has been "suffering from mental illness: - claims denied in writing by the Plaintiff's Mom when she could still write. The Defendant also in a coordinated conspiracy with Marcella Carby-Samuels and Defence Counsel has also engaged in apparent slander against the Plaintiff family friends and relatives who have stopped further communications with the Plaintiff after a relative released information to the Plaintiff about certain conditions with threatened the well-being

k) The Defendant has also continued to "bear false witness by fraudulently claiming in one affidavit that Ottawa Ambulance Services had "blacklisted" the Plaintiff.

Conspiracy to make Public Mischief in violation of the Canadian Criminal Code and to perpetrate slander and defamation and perjury - $5,000

k) Exercise Machine - The Plaintiff bought an exercise machine that the Defendant locked the Plaintiff from using it - $1,000

l) The Defendant has continued to deny access to the Plaintiff's room furnishings including bed, mattress, chesterfield. Plaintiff had to buy replacements at Ikea and the Hudson's Bay Company. The Defendant has also continued to deny access to the Plaintiff's 12 speed bicycle - $4,000.

l) Such further and other relief as may been fair and just to this Honourable Court.

THE PARTIES

2. The Plaintiff resides in Ottawa, Ontario

3. The Defendant resides in Ottawa, Ontario

BACKGROUND FACTS AND CIRCUMSTANCES/ FACTUM

4. Horace Carby-Samuels has subjected Raymond Carby-Samuels to abuse since he was a child which eventually resulted in him being attacked with a knife by his father on 29 January 2013 resulting in the need for emergency medical treat and not being able to work many months during required physical therapy at Ottawa''s Riverside Hospital.

vigilant support to her nutritional, vitamin and other care-giving requirement that Horace Carby-Samuels had neglected.

6. Raymond Carby-Samuels sought to report his observations to the Ottawa Police after having been subjected to assault with a weapon a couple years before when the Plaintiff had previously sought to discuss the matter with the Defendant.

7. Horace Carby-Samuels made vexatious representations to the police that the Plaintiff suffers from mental illness which was used as the basis to deflect any investigation against the Defendant who used the Police to keep the Plaintiff from having any visitation access to his Mother for more than a year.

8. The fraudulent misrepresentation resulted in the Plaintiff being evicted without notice from his home since 1986.

9. The Defendant for weeks from late April 2015 to mid June 2015 seized much of the belongings of the Plaintiff and the Defendant only released much his personal belongings (and also allowed the Plaintiff and his Mother to see each other) after the Plaintiff obtained the paid services of Todd Ji, a lawyer who issued a Legal Demand Letter to the Defendant that was dated 10 June 2015. Some belongings have yet to be released.

BACKGROUND

10. Horace Carby-Samuels as a parent betrayed Raymond Carby-Samuels by making vexatious allegations against him which manifested in unwarranted police investigations and surveillance which resulted in mental anguish and emotional distress that was used to perpetrate auxiliary torts by the Defendant.

11. The Ottawa Police Service relied on the accuracy of the Defendant's statement as a parent who has known and been living with the Plaintiff more than 45 years.

12. Horace Carby-Samuels has perpetrated an apparent campaign of malice and deceit once characterized by Dezrin Carby-Samuels as "wicked".

13. Horace Carby-Samuels is the "father" of Raymond Carby-Samuels;

14. Dezrin Carby-Samuels is the mother of Raymond Carby-Samuels

DAMAGES

15. As a result of Horace Carby-Samuels' public mischief, Raymond Carby-Samuels has suffered irreparable damages, including, but not limited to –

(15.a) Raymond Carby-Samuels has suffered emotional trauma and loss of enjoyment of life

(15.b) Raymond Carby-Samuels has been been intimidated, harassed/psychological

Court File Number: 16-69142

ONTARIO SUPERIOR COURT OF JUSTICE

H. RAYMOND CARBY-SAMUELS

Plaintiff

– and –

HORACE CARBY-SAMUELS

Defendant

Schedule A

AMENDED STATEMENT OF CLAIM

TO THE DEFENDANT:

A LEGAL PROCEEDING HAS BEEN COMMENCED AGAINST YOU by the plaintiff. The claim made against you is set out in the following pages.

IF YOU WISH TO DEFEND THIS PROCEEDING, you or an Ontario lawyer acting for you must prepare a statement of defence in Form 18A prescribed by the Rules of Civil Procedure, serve it on the plaintiff's lawyer or, where the plaintiff does not have a lawyer, serve it on the plaintiff, and file it with proof of service in this court office, WITHIN TWENTY DAYS after this statement of claim is served on you, if you are served in Ontario.

If you are served in another province or territory of Canada or in the United States of America, the period for serving and filing your statement of defence is forty days. If you are served outside Canada and the United States of America, the period is sixty days.

Instead of serving and filing a statement of defence, you may serve and file a notice of intent to defend in Form 18B prescribed by the Rules of Civil Procedure. This will entitle you to ten more days within which to serve and file your statement of defence.

THIS ACTION IS BROUGHT AGAINST YOU UNDER THE SIMPLIFIED
PROCEDURE PROVIDED IN RULE 76 OF THE RULES OF CIVIL PROCEDURE.

CLAIM

1. The Plaintiff claims against the Defendant the following:

a) General damages in the amount of $30,000 [$20,000] or such other amount as this Honourable Court deems appropriate;

b) Special damages in the sum of $10,000 [$ To be determined by Court] or such other amount as this Honourable Court deems appropriate;

c) Punitive damages in the sum of $10,000 [To be determined by Court] or such other amount as this Honourable Court deems appropriate;

d) Aggravated damages in the sum of $10,000 [$ To be determined by Court] or such other amount as this Honourable Court deems appropriate;

e) Pre- and post-judgement interest in accordance with the provisions of the *Courts of Justice Act*, R.S.O. 1990, c C43, as amended

f) Public Mischief to Police Involving Fraudulent Misrepresentation / Slander regarding the Defendant's representation to Police that the Plaintiff suffered from mental illness which lead the Ottawa Police Services to evict Plaintiff. Tort - $10,000

g) The Defendant's illegal seizure of the personal and professional belongings of the Plaintiff from the time of the Defendant's eviction of the Plaintiff in late April 2015 until mid June 2015 when the Defendant incurred additional costs to obtain a Legal Demand Letter from Todd Ji in mid June 2015 which demanded the release of belongings. The Defendant blocked access to belongings under a trespassing threat

    Tort – Illegal Seizure of Property - $4,000
    Costs to obtain Demand Letter and Legal Services - $1,000

h) Eviction without notice from 30 Jarlan Terrance after having established residence since there since 1986 – Violation of common law - $5,000

i) Assault and battery by Defendant with a knife causing permanent physical damage. Assault required Emergency Surgery and over 6 months of rehabilitation.

    Assault causing bodily damage - $5000.00
    Economic loss – not able to work for 6 months - $10,000
    Child abuse [$ To be determined by Court]
    Intentional Infliction of Emotional Distress – [$To be determined by Court]

j) Conspiracy with Marcella Carby-Samuels, the Defendant's daughter, in the coordination of Public Mischief to the Ottawa Police Services involving slanderous claims that the Plaintiff held 'his parents' "hostage" and has been "suffering from mental illness: -

vigilant support to her nutritional, vitamin and other care-giving requirement that Horace Carby-Samuels had neglected.

6. Raymond Carby-Samuels sought to report his observations to the Ottawa Police after having been subjected to assault with a weapon a couple years before when the Plaintiff had previously sought to discuss the matter with the Defendant.

7. Horace Carby-Samuels made vexatious representations to the police that the Plaintiff suffers from mental illness which was used as the basis to deflect any investigation against the Defendant who used the Police to keep the Plaintiff from having any visitation access to his Mother for more than a year.

8. The fraudulent misrepresentation resulted in the Plaintiff being evicted without notice from his home since 1986.

9. The Defendant for weeks from late April 2015 to mid June 2015 seized much of the belongings of the Plaintiff and the Defendant only released much his personal belongings (and also allowed the Plaintiff and his Mother to see each other) after the Plaintiff obtained the paid services of Todd Ji, a lawyer who issued a Legal Demand Letter to the Defendant that was dated 10 June 2015. Some belongings have yet to be released.

BACKGROUND

10. Horace Carby-Samuels as a parent betrayed Raymond Carby-Samuels by making vexatious allegations against him which manifested in unwarranted police investigations and surveillance which resulted in mental anguish and emotional distress that was used to perpetrate auxiliary torts by the Defendant.

11. The Ottawa Police Service relied on the accuracy of the Defendant's statement as a parent who has known and been living with the Plaintiff more than 45 years.

12. Horace Carby-Samuels has perpetrated an apparent campaign of malice and deceit once characterized by Dezrin Carby-Samuels as "wicked".

13. Horace Carby-Samuels is the "father" of Raymond Carby-Samuels;

14. Dezrin Carby-Samuels is the mother of Raymond Carby-Samuels

DAMAGES

15. As a result of Horace Carby-Samuels' public mischief, Raymond Carby-Samuels has suffered irreparable damages, including, but not limited to -

(15.a) Raymond Carby-Samuels has suffered emotional trauma and loss of enjoyment of life

Current Section: **Duhaime.org** » **Legal Dictionary**

Duhaime's Law Dictionary

Clean Hands Definition:

A maxim of the law to the effect that any person, individual or corporate, that wishes to ask or petition a court for judicial action, must be in a position free of fraud or other unfair conduct.

Related Terms: Equity, Pari Delicto, Commodum Ex Injuria Sua Nemo Habere Debet, Ex Turpi Causa Non Oritur Actio Equitable Estoppel

In the doctrine of **equity**, this clean hands maxim applies:

```
He that hath committed iniquity shall not have equity."
```
[1]

The maxim is sometimes expressed as:

```
"He who seeks equity must do equity."
```
[2]

In **Precision Instrument Manufacturing Corporation** ., Justice Murphy of the Supreme Court of United States wrote:

Older domestic violence victims feel helpless in the face of long-term abuse

Ignorance of abuse among older couples means many women don't think they will be believed when they ask agencies for help

Diane Taylor
Friday 23 December 2011 19.13 GMT

The death of Mary Russell, 81, from a bleed to the brain after an alleged assault by her 88-year-old husband Albert, has highlighted the fact that domestic violence among older couples is far more common than is generally thought.

Their age often means police, social care and health professionals are not as aware of the problem as they should be. "The abuse, whether physical or psychological, is often very long-term, perhaps throughout a 40-year marriage. The abuser can often present as very frail: if the woman has a disability or is in failing health it can add to her vulnerability," said Mary Mason, director of Solace Women's Aid, a London domestic violence service that has Equality and Human Rights Commission funding to develop a project for older women.

"Many people have a stereotype in their head of a woman who experiences domestic or sexual violence," she said. "Older women often tell us that they don't think they will be believed when they go to agencies for help.

"The abuse they experience is often so normalised that it's hard to think about leaving. Women this age group may be reluctant to think about moving into a refuge to be safe but once there the can receive very specific support to help them find safety, begin their recovery and achieve independence."

She described a couple of cases her service has worked with. One involved a 72-year-old woman married to a man of 82 who had inflicted physical and emotional abuse on her for 51 years.

Police were called to their home in May 2010 after he hit her with his walking stick. He was not charged with any offence and remains in the marital home. She is currently living with her daughter. Solace is helping the woman to explore divorce proceedings and is trying to get th husband into sheltered accommodation so his wife can move back into the marital home.

Another Solace case concerns a 67-year-old woman who has suffered physical and psychologica abuse from her husband for 40 years. Both have moderate learning disabilities, live in a nursing home and want to remain together. A Solace worker is monitoring the situation and advising on the best way to keep the woman safe.

Bridget Penhale, reader in mental health of older people at the University of East Anglia, is one c the few people studying this hidden area. She is working on a new EU-funded, six-country proje examining the prevalence of domestic violence among older people.

"Very few of these cases go to court because of the age of those involved, so we are looking at police files to see how many callouts police have responded to involving older people and domestic violence," Penhale said. "We are picking up on a lot of cases of assault and serious assaults on older women by their partners. It may be the case that the man has cognitive impairment, the police investigate and the CPS say it's not worth prosecuting. We want to look a the police arresting perpetrators as part of their response to this problem.

"As a society we have become much more aware and attuned to the fact that violence affects younger women in their relationships but the situation as it relates to older women is nowhere near as recognised. Older women don't know where to go to get help. Services specifically for them are few and far between."

Penhale hopes that a European-wide awareness raising campaign will be launched to improve understanding of, and responses to, the problem. She is working with the police and criminal justice agencies to develop a training module for officers. "We hope to pilot this with at least one force during next summer so that it can then be fine-tuned and made ready for further dissemination."

Theresa, 62

I got married at the age of 25 and right from the start there were little hints of what was to come from my husband. I was put down all the time and made to feel worthless and inferior. At first I tried to put everything he did to me to the back of my mind. In the kind of society I was living in wasn't allowed to acknowledge these things and didn't talk to anyone about what was happenin to me. Over a period of years the verbal and psychological abuse I suffered from my husband completely eroded my confidence. I wanted to go to college to pick up my studies but my husband told me I wasn't capable of doing this. I believed him. He told me that my job was to look after the house and garden and to care for our daughter. What started as psychological violence escalated into physical violence after my daughter was born. My husband used to hold me against the wall by my throat and twist my arm. I didn't want to acknowledge that this was violence. After my daughter grew up and left home my husband became more physically violent towards me, although hitting me and bashing me against the wall rarely left marks that I could complain about to anyone even if I'd wanted to. I put up with this for 36 years and eventually walked out at the age of 60 and sought help. When I walked out I didn't know who I was. I genuinely believed what my husband kept telling me, that I was worthless and useless and wouldn't be able to cope with life without him. I left my home and my job and came to London with nothing. I spent 18 months in a refuge and gradually regained my self-esteem. I learnt to cope with life again. I'm now in my own home and at last I've resumed my studies."

. *Theresa's name has been changed to protect her identity*

. *Solace Women's Aid Advice line Freephone number 0808 802 5565 National Domestic Violence Helpline 0808 2000 247.*

Domestic violence in old age: recent shocking cases
Andrew Castle, 61, attempted to kill his wife Margaret, 61, in a homemade electric chair

Malcolm Beardon, 79, denied murder but admitted manslaughter of his wife Margaret, 78

Ronald Edwards, 65, killed his partner Sylvia Rowley Bailey after an argument

Kenneth Mann, 81, killed his wife Doreen, 80 with two knives and a hammer, then drowned himself

Leslie Parsons, 88, killed his wife Dorothy then tried but failed to shoot himself

Since you're here ...

... we have a small favour to ask. More people are reading the Guardian than ever but advertising revenues across the media are falling fast. And unlike many news organisations, we haven't put up a paywall - we want to keep our journalism as open as we can. So you can see why we need to ask for your help. The Guardian's independent, investigative journalism takes a lot of time, money and hard work to produce. But we do it because we believe our perspective matters - because it might well be your perspective, too.

I appreciate there not being a paywall: it is more democratic for the media to be available for all and not a commodity to be purchased by a few. I'm happy to make a contribution so others with less means still have access to information. *Thomasine F-R.*
If everyone who reads our reporting, who likes it, helps to support it, our future would be much more secure.

Become a supporter
Make a contribution

- Domestic violence
- Older people
- Equality and Human Rights Commission (EHRC)
- Crime
- Police
- news

Bell Baker LLP
Barristers & Solicitors / Avocats & Notaires

116 LISGAR STREET, SUITE 700, OTTAWA, ONTARIO K2P 0C2
Phone 613-237-3444
Fax 613-237-1413

John E. Summers
613-237-3448 ext. 340
jsummers@bellbaker.com

www.bellbaker.com

VIA REGULAR MAIL & EMAIL

January 25, 2017

Mr. Raymond Carby-Samuels II
B.P. 24191 - 300 Eagleson Road
Kanata, ON K2M 2C3

Dear Mr. Carby-Samuels II:

Re: Carby-Samuels II v. Carby-Samuels
      Court File No. 16-69142
      Our File No. 1609 2615

I am in receipt of a letter from Ms. Peters dated January 24th, 2017. In that letter she confirms that she is not your lawyer but, she was writing to request that I confirm my available dates for a Mediation and which Mediators are acceptable to me.

As I have previously indicated, we are in the process of scheduling a Motion for Summary Judgment wherein we are seeking for the Claim to be dismissed. Once that Motion has been heard, we can address the issue of Mediation. In the event that the Motion is unsuccessful, we will schedule a Mediation forthwith thereafter. I can advise that I would be requesting Rick Brooks as a Mediator.

Would you like to attend our offices to pick up the materials or would you prefer us to arrange for the documents to be served upon you? If you are coming to our office, kindly let me know so I can arrange to have the materials ready for you.

James R. McIninch	Geoffrey A. Howard	Martin D. Owens
Roger R. Mills	Helmut R. Brodmann	Cheryl L. Hess
Wade L. Smith	James D. Wilson	John E. Summers
James F. Leal	Mélanie H. Levesque	Katie L. Laframboise
Matthew D. Frye		Damien Fannon

Counsel: Paul A. Webber, Q.C.,
John C. Clarke, Q.C. (Ret'd), David C. Thompson, Q.C. (Ret'd)

I trust the above is satisfactory.

Yours truly,

BELL BAKER LLP

Per: *John E. Summers*

JES:gmc

cc: Ms. Miriam V. Peters (via email) &
Client (via email)

www.ingramcontent.com/pod-product-compliance
Lightning Source LLC
Chambersburg PA
CBHW071954110526
44592CB00012B/1084